W9-BDZ-341

Religion and Society in Tension

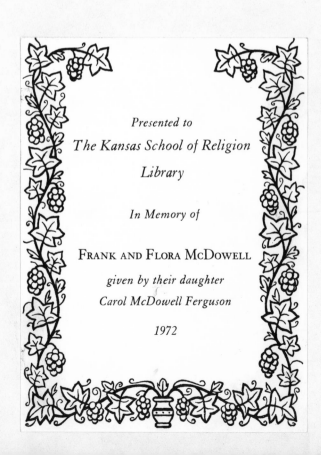

Presented to

The Kansas School of Religion

Library

In Memory of

FRANK AND FLORA MCDOWELL

given by their daughter
Carol McDowell Ferguson

1972

Department of Religious Studies
Moore Reading Room
University of Kansas

KANSAS SCHOOL OF RELIGION
University of Kansas
1300 Oread Avenue
LAWRENCE, KANSAS 66044

Religion and Society in Tension

CHARLES Y. GLOCK
University of California,
Berkeley

RODNEY STARK
University of California,
Berkeley

A publication from the Research Program in
the Sociology of Religion Survey Research
Center, University of California, Berkeley

BL60
.G562

Rand McNally & Company

Chicago / New York / San Francisco / London

RELIGION AND SOCIETY IN TENSION—32651

RAND McNALLY SOCIOLOGY SERIES
EDGAR F. BORGATTA, ADVISORY EDITOR

Alford, PARTY AND SOCIETY
Borgatta and Crowther, A WORKBOOK FOR THE STUDY OF SOCIAL INTERACTION PROCESSES
Christensen, ed., HANDBOOK OF MARRIAGE AND THE FAMILY
Demerath, SOCIAL CLASS IN AMERICAN PROTESTANTISM
Faris, ed., HANDBOOK OF MODERN SOCIOLOGY
Glock and Stark, RELIGION AND SOCIETY IN TENSION
Hadden and Borgatta, AMERICAN CITIES: THEIR SOCIAL CHARACTERISTICS
Kaplan, ed., SCIENCE AND SOCIETY
March, ed., HANDBOOK OF ORGANIZATIONS
Nye and Hoffman, THE EMPLOYED MOTHER IN AMERICA
Scott, VALUES AND ORGANIZATIONS: A STUDY OF FRATERNITIES AND SORORITIES
Warren, THE COMMUNITY IN AMERICA
Warren, ed., PERSPECTIVES ON THE AMERICAN COMMUNITY
Webb, Campbell, Schwartz, and Sechrest, UNOBTRUSIVE MEASURES

1. Religion and sociology
2. United States — Religious life and customs

Sixth Printing, 1973

Copyright © 1965 by Rand McNally & Company

All rights reserved

Printed in U.S.A. by Rand McNally & Company

Library of Congress Catalogue Card Number 65:25356

To

MICKEY AND KAREN

Contents

Introduction

In Judeo-Christian cultures religion is expected to be at odds with the world around it. While the religious life must perforce be lived in this world, it is not to be of it. Indeed, it is held to be the duty of priests and prophets to take those who become enmeshed in the trivial affairs of this world and turn them towards more eternal concerns. Thus, the church is seen to exist in a hostile and evil world, and to have a sacred mission to denounce and resist matters of the flesh, for all this shall pass away.

But, somehow, religion rarely — if ever — seems to act upon these principles. Despite a long line of prophets, saints, and reformers, who have condemned the worldliness of the church, the majority of religious leaders have been practical men who have gone about the business of managing the mundane interests of religion. Judged on purely theological grounds, this might be deemed a failure of the churches to keep the faith, but it seems entirely predictable when viewed from the perspective of social science. Whatever its claims to divine inspiration and authority, religion is also a human activity that takes place within human societies and hence must deal with the worldly problems and pressures inherent in social organization. Seen in these terms, it would be miraculous indeed if religions commonly maintained the kind of tension with society envisioned by their founders and occasional saints. However, if we examine religion as one of several major social institutions, it is quite accurate to say that religion is subject to tensions with regard to other aspects of society — as are all such institutions. It is with these kinds of tensions, as well as with the inability of religion to maintain its idealized tension, that this volume will be primarily concerned.

The study of religion from the point of view of social science was a major concern of scholars in the nineteenth century. The most seminal figures in the development of psychology, sociology, and anthropology are closely identified with the study of religion. Freud, Weber, Durkheim, William James, and even Marx, as well as the famous men of British anthropology, are all remembered for their major contributions to an understanding of the role of religion in social life. But for a variety of reasons, scholarly interest in religion all but vanished during the twentieth century. This state of affairs prompted Gordon W. Allport to write in 1950 that "the subject of religion seems to have gone into hiding," and "the persistence of religion in the modern world appears an embarrassment to the scholars of today."[1]

Since World War II, however, there has been a renewal of interest in religion among social scientists. In part, perhaps, this may have been due to research findings that religion does indeed still make a difference in people's attitudes and behavior. Particularly, survey studies of voting behavior seem to have rekindled interest in religion as a social variable. The widely hailed religious revival in America may also have aroused new scholarly attention to religion. In any event, during the past decade there has been increasing research activity into the social sources and consequences of religion. Indeed, two social science journals, devoted entirely to articles on religion, have been founded in America in the last few years. While the amount of attention given religion is still far less than that given such other institutional spheres as politics, the family, or economics, the differences are no longer quite so great. Still, we know a great deal less about such things as the basis of religious involvement than we do about why people join labor unions, elect particular political parties, or choose certain models of new cars.

This represents a crucial lack both for the social sciences and for society in general. Whether one feels religion basically has 'good' or 'bad' effects on the quality of the human experience, undeniably it has important and significant effects. To neglect the study of such a major influence in human affairs is to be negligent in the quest to build an adequate science of society. For this reason the Survey Research Center of the University of California, Berkeley, has encouraged and initiated a number of studies of religion. The present volume represents the third of these to be published by Rand McNally.

This book combines new material with revisions of previously published papers. In bringing them together, we have

1. Gordon W. Allport, *The Individual and His Religion* (New York: The Macmillan Co., 1960), p.l.

sought to build on a number of related and sustaining themes in an effort to achieve a degree of integration of the book not characteristic of a simple collection of essays. As an overview of what is to come, it seems useful to summarize these themes briefly.

The tasks we have assumed in Part I are to specify what it means to view religion from a social-scientific perspective and to clarify the conceptual problems of treating religion as a social phenomenon. Armed with the conceptual ideas advanced in Part I, we have sought in Part II to apply them to an analysis of religion in contemporary America.

In Part II, we are more concerned with description than with explanation; we have attempted to characterize religion in America both from the perspective of those who practice it and from the perspective of the institution—the parish church—around which it is primarily organized.

Having examined certain features of religion in our present society, we turn in Part III to more universal questions concerning the function of religion in human societies; particularly, the role of religion in social change. Finally, in Part IV, religion is examined in contrast with the humanist perspectives of the physical and social sciences.

In the preparation of the volume, we have been assisted by a number of persons whose contributions we acknowledge and for which we are deeply grateful. Gertrude Jaeger Selznick, Fredric Templeton, Samuel Klausner, Robert Mitchell, John F. Lofland, Yoshio Fukuyama, Walter Kloetzli, Stephen Steinberg, Neil Smelser and Robert Lee provided us with editorial advice and assistance on individual chapters. Benjamin Ringer and Philip Roos, who shared in the authorship of the original versions of Chapters 12 and 7 respectively, are owed a special thanks for allowing us to include their contributions. Roderic Frederickson and his staff in the Survey Research Center's data processing facility prepared most of the tabular materials which the book presents, and Wendy Shuken undertook the prodigous amount of work necessary to prepare the manuscript for the printer.

We are also grateful to the publications in which earlier versions of some of the chapters appeared, for permission to reprint them here, albeit in revised form.

"On the Study of Religious Commitment," reprinted from the *Review of Recent Research Bearing on Religious and*

Character Formation, published as a Research Supplement to The July-August, 1962 issue of *Religious Education,* by permission of the publisher, The Religious Education Association, New York, N.Y.

"A Taxonomy of Religious Experience," *Journal for the Scientific Study of Religion,* Vol. V, No. 1, Fall, 1965.

"The Religious Revival in America?" in Jane Zahn, ed., *Religion and the Face of America* (Berkeley: University Extension, University of California, 1959), pp. 25–42. Reprinted by permission.

"The New Denominationalism," originally published in *Review of Religious Research,* Fall, 1965. Copyright 1965 by the Religious Research Association, Inc.

"A Sociologist Looks at the Parish Church," afterword to Walter Kloetzli, *The City Church—Death or Renewal* (Philadelphia: The Muhlenberg Press, 1961), pp. 177–198.

With Philip Roos, "Parishioners' Views of How Ministers Spend Their Time," originally published in *Review of Religious Research,* Vol. II, No. 4, Spring, 1961, 170–175. Copyright 1961 by the Religious Research Association, Inc.

"Religion and the Integration of Society," originally published in *Review of Religious Research,* Vol. II, No. 2, Fall, 1960, 49–61. Copyright 1960 by the Religious Research Association, Inc.

"Class, Radicalism, and Religious Involvement in Great Britain," *American Sociological Review,* Vol. XXIX, No. 5, October, 1964, 698–706.

With Benjamin Ringer, "Church Policy and the Attitudes of Ministers and Parishioners on Social Issues," *American Sociological Review,* Vol. XXI, No. 2, April, 1956, 148–156.

"The Role of Deprivation in the Origin and Evolution of Religious Groups," from *Religion and Social Conflict,* edited by Robert Lee and Martin E. Marty, copyright 1964 by Oxford University Press, Inc., reprinted by permission.

"On the Incompatibility of Religion and Science," *Journal for the Scientific Study of Religion,* Vol. III, No. 1, Fall, 1963, 3–20.

PART I:

RELIGION AS A SOCIAL PHENOMENON

DURING the centuries when the study of man's religions was the exclusive province of theologians, or at least of scholars working within a theological point of view, the central concern was with belief. The study of religion was generally limited to recording — and often to condemning — the religious ideologies that flourished in various cultures. In the course of this work, a number of conceptual distinctions were developed for the purpose of classifying and organizing religions, perhaps the most important being the distinction between monotheistic and polytheistic religions.

With the advent of social science interest in religion, this concern with doctrine subsided, and scholars turned instead to exploring, the social functions of religious institutions. Questions such as why do religions exist in human societies, and what difference do they make, became the major issues. But in order to take up such questions, new ways of classifying and conceptualizing religion had to be developed. At the present time this task has only been begun, and the conceptual tools available for the study of religion from a social science perspective are rather primitive and unsatisfactory. For this reason the first part of this volume will be devoted to conceptual questions. In it we shall attempt to provide some general analytic distinctions which will provide a systematic basis for subsequent chapters concerning the social functions of religions.

Chapter 1

A Sociological Definition of Religion

THE necessary starting point for studying any phenomenon is to establish criteria by which it may be identified and distinguished from all other phenomena. This chapter takes up the difficult problem of determining just what sorts of things we mean by religion and attempts to provide systematic distinctions for isolating religion from other aspects of human societies.

The difficulties of finding an abstract, transhistorical, and cross-culturally applicable definition of religion have vexed scholars for generations. It is agreed that all societies, in all times, have religion. But even though in an unrigorous, intuitive way we understand that the word 'religion' describes such different events as ritual cannibalism and Quaker meetings, theorists have been hard put to define religion in any precise way without losing much of this descriptive power. As Georg Simmel commented near the turn of the century:

> Thus far, no one has been able to offer a definition which, without vagueness and yet with sufficient comprehensiveness, has told once for all what religion is in its essence, in that which is common alike to the religion of Christians and South Sea islanders, to Buddhism and Mexican idolatry. Thus far it has not been distinguished, on the one hand, from mere metaphysical speculation, nor, on the other, from the credulity which believes in 'ghosts'.[1]

---

1. Georg Simmel, "A Contribution to the Sociology of Religion," *American Journal of Sociology,* November, 1905, pp. 359–376.

Several years later Emile Durkheim came to grips with this problem of defining religion in a way that would encompass all the varieties of man's religious expression.[2] Pursuing the quest for a universal substrate, an irreducible element common to all religions, Durkheim proposed that all known religions of all societies ". . . presuppose a classification of all things . . . into two classes of opposed groups . . . *profane* and *sacred.*"[3] From this insightful dichotomy Durkheim constructed his now famous definition:

> *A religion is a unified system of beliefs and practices relative to sacred things, that is to say, things set apart and forbidden — beliefs and practices which unite into one single moral community called a Church, all those who adhere to them.*[4]

But if religion is concerned with sacred things, the question remains: What things in societies will be invested with sacredness, and why? Durkheim's original attempts to answer this question have been further refined by several recent writers, among them Talcott Parsons[5], J. Milton Yinger[6], Elizabeth K. Nottingham[7], and J. Paul Williams.[8] Their various formulations can be synthesized into the following generalization: *Religion, or what societies hold to be sacred, comprises an institutionalized system of symbols, beliefs, values, and practices focused on questions of ultimate meaning.* By 'institutionalized' is meant that religion is a stable property of groups to such a degree that it will be maintained even though the personnel of the group continues to change.

The crucial term in this formulation is, of course, 'ultimate meaning.' By this is meant those matters pertaining to the na-

---

2. Emile Durkheim, *Les formes élémentaires de la vie religieuse,* first published in Paris, 1912; translated by J. W. Swain, it was published as *The Elementary Forms of the Religious Life* (London: George Allen and Unwin Ltd., 1915).

3. *Ibid.,* p. 37 (italics in the original).

4. *Ibid.,* p. 47 (italics in the original).

5. Talcott Parsons, *The Social System* (Glencoe: The Free Press, 1951), Chapter VIII.

6. J. Milton Yinger, *Religion, Society and the Individual* (New York: The Macmillan Co., 1957), Chapter I, especially p. 9.

7. Elizabeth K. Nottingham, *Religion and Society* (New York: Random House, 1954), Chapter I.

8. J. Paul Williams, "The Nature of Religion, "*Journal for the Scientific Study of Religion,* II:1 (Fall, 1962), 3–14.

ture, meaning, and often, purpose, of reality—a rationale for existence and a view of the world. The late Clyde Kluckhohn referred to this as the "philosophy behind the way of life of each individual and every homogeneous group at any given point in their histories."[9] For example, a system of ultimate meaning would likely provide answers to questions about man's nature, purpose, origin, fate, and the like. The proposition being advanced is that things related to matters of ultimate meaning, or what Paul Tillich has called 'ultimate concern,'[10] will be regarded as sacred. In particular, things will be regarded as sacred as they provide, or symbolize, *solutions* to questions of ultimate meaning.

Religion, as we have defined it thus far, is a particular kind of *perspective* as that term has been introduced by Tamotsu Shibutani to indicate the frame of reference assumed by a person, or group, for the organization of experience:

> . . . A perspective is an ordered view of one's world—what is taken for granted about the attributes of various objects, events, and human nature.[11]

Shibutani notes that modern men are members of many 'worlds,' or perspectives, as a result of playing many roles in their daily rounds, and that the more differentiated and complex the society the greater the number of perspectives in which an individual may share. Most of these worlds are partial and fragmentary in the sense that they confine their interpretations to small segments of the actor's total experience. Thus, a single individual may be a plumber, a bridge player, a stamp collector, a father, and a sports fan, and the perspectives attached to these roles tend to be highly compatible. Persons find little difficulty in shifting from one to another because these perspectives do not inform actions other than those specific to them. Bridge rules in themselves imply nothing for plumbing, and vice versa.

While many perspectives are of this highly compatible na-

---

9. Clyde Kluckhohn, "Values and Value-Orientations in the Theory of Action: An Exploration in Definition and Classification," in Talcott Parsons and Edward Shils, eds., *Toward a General Theory of Action* (New York: Harper Torchbooks, 1962), p. 409.

10. Paul Tillich, *Systematic Theology* (Chicago: University of Chicago Press, 1956), I, 12.

11. Tamotsu Shibutani, "Reference Groups as Perspectives," *American Journal of Sociology,* LX (May, 1955), 569.

ture, as Shibutani pointed out, and can occur in virtually any combination, this is not true of all perspectives. Some perspectives do foster definitions that extend beyond a specific sphere of activity, and to the degree this is the case they become at least potentially incompatible. It is on this basis, for example, that social scientists predict that a man who inhabits the perspective of the college professor tends to reject the perspective of conservative Republicanism, because these perspectives overlap and conflict on the aspects of the world they define and interpret. Once perspectives reach the point of addressing reality in general, of becoming, in effect, all-embracing *Weltanschauungen*, then alternative perspectives of this same order can no longer be accommodated. The commitment to one perspective at this more general level virtually prohibits commitment to another.[12] Peter L. Berger makes this same observation in reference to what he calls "more fully elaborated meaning systems." He notes that

> . . . these systems can provide a total interpretation of reality, within which will be included an interpretation of the alternative systems and of the ways of passing from one system to another. Catholicism may have a theory of Communism, but Communism returns the compliment and will produce a theory of Catholicism. To the Catholic thinker the Communist lives in a dark world of materialist delusion about the real meaning of life. To the Communist his Catholic adversary is helplessly caught in the "false consciousness" of a bourgeois mentality.[13]

As Berger is aware, Communism and Catholicism constitute perspectives which inform men broadly about the general nature of reality, and which tend, therefore, to penetrate all the more fragmentary worlds in which their adherents participate — as golfers, lawyers, millworkers, etc. — and to organize and define the way they will perceive and relate to society in general.

It is in relation to these kinds of perspectives that we observe the phenomenon of *conversion,* which may well be defined as the process by which a person comes to adopt an all-pervading world view or changes from one such perspective to another.

---

12. Demonstrations of the mutually exclusive character of religious and scientific perspectives are presented in Chapters 14 and 15.

13. Peter L. Berger, *Invitation to Sociology: A Humanist Perspective* (Garden City: Anchor Books, Doubleday & Co., 1963), p. 51.

We do not seriously use this word to characterize changes from one fragmentary perspective to another, *e.g.*, from stamp collecting to flower gardening. Rather, the word conversion denotes a major discontinuity in behavior, a wrenching of the personality, associated with such descriptive phrases as "rebirth," "finding the light," "visitation of the Holy Spirit," and "attaining true class consciousness," all of which indicate that the convert has apparently experienced a drastic shift in the orientation of his valuation of reality.[14]

What is it about these broad perspectives that gives them this peculiar and dominating quality? The answer seems to be that each is organized around some statements concerning ultimate meaning, that is, each provides a set of general principles by which men understand and perceive their experience in general. Or, to return to Durkheim, holders of such perspectives constitute moral communities in that they share in "a unified system of beliefs and practices relative to sacred things."

In pursuing our definition of religion, we are ready now to connect this discussion of 'ultimate meaning' and 'broad perspectives' with still another set of relevant theoretical constructs: *values,* and *value orientations.* As used in the social sciences, these terms are associated with the work of Talcott Parsons, Clyde and Florence Kluckhohn, and, more recently, Neil J. Smelser. The term 'value' is defined by Smelser as: "The most general component of social action . . . Values state in general terms the desirable end states which act as a guide to human endeavor."[15]

Values, then, are statements about what 'ought to be.' They

---

14. The meaning of the term 'conversion' has been muddied by the inconsistent usage given it by Christian religious writers. Often they have used 'conversion' to refer to an arousal of concern among persons who already accept the essential truth of the ideological system. Yet, in keeping with the earliest Christian examples of conversion, such as that of St. Paul, they have used the word to describe changes from one such system to another. These seem very different kinds of events and ought to be indicated by separate terminologies. Furthermore, examination of actual conversions suggests that the change in perspective is not so swift nor so drastic as converts seem to think it is. Berger, *op. cit.*, suggests that a central feature of conversions is a *post hoc* reconstruction of one's biography in light of the newly adopted meaning system whereby new interpretations are read into acts which, at the time they occurred, were defined in a rather different way.

15. Neil J. Smelser, *Theory of Collective Behavior* (New York: The Free Press of Glencoe, 1963), p. 25.

are taken for granted, and, moreover, are seen as unchallengeable because they are self-evident.[16] For example, personal happiness is a value of American society, and while men may disagree hotly over how to best attain happiness, no one seriously suggests that men ought not be happy.

But, as will be considered in some detail in Chapter 9, values by themselves are virtually incoherent. That is, values can only meaningfully define desired ends as they are more or less systematically encompassed in some rationale — some conception of the nature of reality. If, for example, men hold righteousness to be a value, it is necessary to have some explanation of why it ought to be valued: Perhaps because an all-powerful God requires men to be righteous and rewards and punishes them on the basis of their conformity. Furthermore, such a value requires some specification of what constitutes righteousness, which again might be a set of statements about behavior pleasing or displeasing to God. Thus, some beliefs about the nature of the universe, its natural and, perhaps, supernatural properties are required to provide a context of meaning for values. Clyde Kluckhohn identified such rationales or contexts as a set of "existential premises" and recognized that they "are almost inextricably blended" with values "in the over-all picture of experience."[17] At any given moment, in any stable society, a number of values and existential premises, or beliefs about reality, are agreed upon.[18] The sum total of these shared beliefs and values — this overall world view — Kluckhohn called a "value-orientation." This combination of terms indicated the blending of values and a rationale or orientation into a general perspective on life. As Kluckhohn put it:

> . . . a *value orientation* may be defined as *a generalized and organized conception . . . of nature, of man's place in it, of*

---

16. Louis Wirth wrote: ". . . The most important thing, therefore, that we can know about a man is what he takes for granted, and the most elemental and important facts about society are those that are seldom debated and generally regarded as settled." See his preface to Karl Manneheim, *Ideology and Utopia,* translated by Louis Wirth and Edward Shils (New York: Harvest Books, 1959), pp. xxii–xxiii.

17. Kluckhohn, *op, cit.,* p. 411.

18. The question of what happens when members of a society no longer agree upon values will be considered in Chapters 9, 10, and 11.

man's relation to man, and of the desirable and nondesirable as they may relate to man-environment and interhuman relations.[19]

Value orientations have been further characterized by Florence Kluckhohn and Fred Strodtbeck as:

. . . complex but definitely patterned (rank ordered) principles . . . which give order and direction to the ever-flowing stream of human acts and thought as these relate to the solution of "common human" problems.[20]

Elsewhere, Florence Kluckhohn described these "common human" problems as basic questions of the meaning of life that "arise inevitably out of the human situation."[21]

Value orientations, then, can appropriately be identified with the *solutions* men adopt to questions of ultimate meaning as we have earlier used that term. As such they are invested with sacredness and are seen as unchallengeable. Thus, the concept of value orientation seems to be a satisfactory label for those special kinds of all-encompassing perspectives which stand in opposition to one another, each making an absolute claim upon the allegiance of all who partake of its vision of reality.

Henceforth in this chapter we shall use the term *value orientation* to identify those *over-arching and sacred systems of symbols, beliefs, values, and practices concerning ultimate meaning which men shape to interpret their world.*

It is not intended, however, to consider value orientation as a synonym for religion. Rather, we mean for value orientation to designate a more general phenomenon, of which religion, as it has been generally conceived, is the *most common, but not the only, manifestation.* To do this we must introduce additional elements into our definitional scheme to distinguish several varieties of value orientations.

Reconsidering the nature of this concept as we have developed it thus far, it is apparent that it applies to Communism as

19. Kluckhohn, *op. cit.*, p. 411 (italics in the original).
20. Florence Kluckhohn and Fred Strodtbeck, *Variations in Value Orientations* (Evanston: Row, Peterson, 1961), p. 4.
21. Florence Rockwood Kluckhohn, "Dominant and Variant Value Orientations," in Clyde Kluckhohn, Henry A. Murray, and David A. Schneider, eds., *Personality in Nature, Society, and Culture* (New York: Alfred A. Knopf, 1956), pp. 342–357.

readily as to Catholicism. Both constitute value orientations since they offer systematic statements concerning ultimate meaning which bind their members into a moral community. But classifying both of these institutions under a single rubric involves us in a current social science controversy. Given the functionalist proposition that religion is necessary to the maintenance of societies, the continuing existence of Soviet Russia has required that functional alternatives to religion be considered. For, clearly, Soviet Marxism is not religious in a traditional sense, yet Russian society maintains itself. Thus it has been argued that Marxism must either be functioning instead of religion or must somehow be a religion.[22]

However, this difficulty appears to evaporate within our conceptual scheme where traditional religions and Communism are similarly classified as value orientations. For if the functionalist proposition that religion is a universal and necessary feature of social systems is reassigned to value orientations, there remains neither need nor possibility of considering alternatives.[23] But such universal applicability of the term value orientation gives rise to an important terminological and analytic problem. Do we really want to lump together things traditionally thought of as religious and irreligious and argue that there are no relevant differences between them? Since the word 'religion' has a well-established common usage which denotes a narrower range of phenomena, it may be realistic as well as useful to restrict our interpretation along similar lines. This can be done by distinguishing *kinds* of value orientations, and locating traditional religion as one among these types.

We shall retain the universal applicability of the concept of value orientation (they are to be found in all societies) but we will divide these orientations into two discrete types, or clusters, which may be thought of as *perspective realms*. In one realm, all value orientations include some statement affirming the existence of a supernatural being, world, or force, and predicate their

---

22. For example, see the discussion by Charles Y. Glock, "The Sociology of Religion," in Robert K. Merton, Leonard Broom, and L. S. Cottrell, Jr., eds., *Sociology Today* (New York: Basic Books, 1959), pp. 153–177; as well as: Paul Tillich, *The Shaking of the Foundations* (New York: Charles Scribner's Sons, 1948); Reinhold Niebuhr, *Christianity and Power Politics* (New York: Charles Scribner's Sons, 1940); and Jacques Maritain, *True Humanism,* translated by M. R. Adamson (London: Geoffrey Bles: The Centenary Press, 1938).

23. This point is considered in Chapter 9.

ultimate solutions on this assumption. We shall call these *religious perspectives*. Value orientations in the second realm do not posit a supernatural, but limit their statements about ultimate meaning to the material world, although often to past or future versions of it. We may refer to this second type as *humanist perspectives*. Through this distinction we may separate the so-called secular or irreligious world views from the supernatural.[24] But it must be kept clear that they represent *alternative* forms of the *same* basic phenomenon.

Obviously there is a great deal of variation within each of these perspective realms. Images of the nature and meaning of the supernatural differ widely, as do humanist conceptions of the nature and meaning of the material world. However, this particular dichotomy seems to isolate the important similarity within each type and to recognize the crucial difference between them. Future research could fruitfully seek the important differences which likely inhere in each type, both for the future of the value orientation itself and for other aspects of society. For example, are humanist perspectives more likely to commit themselves to determinate statements about the empirical world and hence be more prone to disconfirmations? One supposes that predictions of a "Thousand Year Reich" would be considerably more fragile than those concerning "a thousand year Invisible Rule of Christ." In any event the subject seems to warrant serious study.

To summarize our conceptual discussion thus far:

1) Value orientations are those institutionalized systems of beliefs, values, symbols and practices that are concerned with the solution of questions of ultimate meaning. Such orientations are a universal feature of human societies and are mutually exclusive.

2) Value orientations may have a supernatural referent (religious perspectives), or they may not (humanist perspectives).

3) Both alternative forms are on the same level of abstrac-

---

24. Although this distinction bears certain similarities to the traditional this-world/other-world dichotomy, the two should *not* be equated. Such a distinction should remain a useful tool within the framework of our scheme for studying both religious and humanist perspectives. In the latter instance, it may be important to distinguish humanist outlooks which concentrate on 'this-world' (the present) from those which are 'other-worldly' — (preoccupied with a Utopian tomorrow — or yesterday).

tion and are functionally equivalent, although they may have somewhat different consequences for other societal institutions.

So far, our discussion has tended to concentrate on the ideological aspect of value-oriented perspectives and we have stressed how these constitute a set of statements concerning ultimate meaning. We should not forget, however, that value orientations do not exist as concrete entities, they are not 'things' which hover over societies. Rather, value orientations exist only as they are believed and acted upon by groups of men. The sociologist is little interested in ideologies in the abstract, but rather in ideologies as properties of groups of men.

There are a variety of ways in which value orientations may be incorporated or manifested in human societies. The crucial factors for classifying these variations in the relation of value orientations to social structure seem to be:

1) the degree to which they are the focus of formal organization;

2) the extent to which they are differentiated from, or fused with, other social institutions.[25]

It is recognized that both of these dimensions are likely to be continuous rather than dichotomous, but for heuristic purposes the variety of existing religious and humanist perspectives can be classified as more or less formally organized, and more or less differentiated from other social institutions. Juxtaposing the two, we may speak of four ways in which value orientations can be embodied in societies:

I. Formally organized and differentiated;

II. Not formally organized, but differentiated;

III. Formally organized, but not differentiated;

IV. Not formally organized, and not differentiated.

To more fully explicate the importance of these four types, it seems useful to consider some examples of each. While such 'cell-filling' in no way creates knowledge or theory, the process may nonetheless reveal similarities and differences among forms

---

25. It is, of course, evident that organization and differentiation tend to occur together. The more an institution concerned with values is differentiated from other institutions within a society, probably the more complex the society, and likely, the greater strain towards formal organization to increase the institution's power to maintain itself and reach its goals. However, as is apparent in subsequent discussion, organization and differentiation do not always occur together, and hence can be treated as distinct variables.

of religious and humanist perspectives in the real world that would not have been immediately apparent. Such 'surprises' may suggest where we should seek further specifying variables for characterizing these types or point out some interesting questions about processes in the evolution of value orientations.

I. FORMALLY ORGANIZED AND DIFFERENTIATED FROM ALL OTHER INSTITUTIONS

Religious Perspectives

This is a common type, characterized by religious institutions as we are familiar with them in Christendom. These are formally organized churches which are discrete institutional units within the society, that is, not merged with political, economic, or family institutions. This is not to imply, of course, that important interdependencies are absent between religious and other institutions in Western nations. Indeed, the basic assumption of a social system's approach to the study of such societies is that such institutions are functionally interrelated. However, religious institutions of this type perform distinct functions and enjoy relative autonomy *vis-à-vis* these other social institutions and vice versa. Even in medieval times, when the church was considerably more enmeshed in affairs of state, the division between sacred and secular authority was reasonably clear and there was relatively little overlap in personnel or duties between the two institutional spheres.[26]

Humanist Perspectives

As humanist perspectives go, this is also a common type. Social movements such as Communism and Nazism would be classified here unless, or until, they become fused with other social institutions such as the political or economic at which time they become Type III below. Also representing this type are explicitly humanist perspectives similar to churches, such as Ethical Culture, some forms of Unitarianism, and the like.

26. The degree to which social science tends to be culture-bound is apparent when we recognize that virtually all the existing work in the sociology of religion deals with religious perspectives classified in this cell of the typology. It should be pointed out, too, that the body of theory that has been built up, such concepts as church-sect, and the like, can be plugged into the present scheme to distinguish further distinctions and processes within various cells.

II. NOT FORMALLY ORGANIZED, BUT DIFFERENTIATED

Religious Perspectives

This seems to be a rather rare type, but is illustrated by the American occult milieu, which consists of occasional audiences for lectures, books, magazines. Although clearly differentiated from other social institutions, the world of the 'seekers' has no distinct boundaries or any real organizational features beyond the possession of a mailing list. This occult scene is more properly considered a public or loose-consensus collectivity rather than a group. The strain towards formal organization that one might expect to operate where there is differentiation is apparent in this setting where dozens of cults are generated, usually around charismatic leaders. Such cults, when they have formed, transform this type into type I above.

Humanist Perspectives

Like the occult milieu, there exists in contemporary America what might be called the free-thought milieu. This comprises an unorganized public which claims an explicit and separate identity as it attends to varieties of humanist speakers, books, and magazines such as *The American Atheist*. Amid this scene, too, a strain towards formal organization is manifest, and emergent groups such as the American Association for the Advancement of Atheism, the Truth Seekers, and several varieties of Realists and Humanists, transform this type into type I above.

III. FORMALLY ORGANIZED, BUT NOT DIFFERENTIATED

Religious Perspectives

This is a relatively common type, distinguished from examples of type I by religious institutions being fused with one or more other major social institutions. A relatively common form is the theocracy where political and religious functions are merged in a single institution, as in Tibet prior to its recent conquest by Red China, or in the Pilgrim colonies. Other forms, indicating the need for further specifying variables within this type, include the fusion of religious and economic institutions, as in some religious communal systems where they are often merged with political institutions as well (the Mormons of

Brigham Young's day). Also classed here are religions in primitive tribes where all major institutions tend to be merged in a relatively undifferentiated social structure.

Humanist Perspectives

This is perhaps a more common form of humanist perspective than type I. For some reason, organized humanist perspectives seem especially resistant to differentiation. Major instances of this type are Communism in Russia and other nations where it holds power and is merged with political and economic institutions. The Nazi Party in Germany from the early thirties to the mid-forties is another example, as is Confucianism during its classic period in the Chinese court. Also of this type are humanist communal groups such as Madalyn Murray's short-lived community for atheists in Kansas.

IV. NOT FORMALLY ORGANIZED, NOT DIFFERENTIATED

Religious Perspectives

For sheer incidence, this is overwhelmingly the most common form in which religious perspectives are embodied in social organization. Of this type are the vast number of folk and tribal religions which are not explicitly the focus of much formal organization and often sustain no full-time priestly roles, but are instead simply diffused through other institutions, particularly the family. Indeed, in some instances there may even exist temples and holy men, such as in Hinduism and Taoism; yet these features are auxiliary and subsidiary to the main embodiment of the religious perspective in the family.

Humanist Perspectives

This may also be the most common form of humanist perspective, where the value orientation is not the property of a formally organized group, but is instead diffused through other institutions. For example, the scientific humanism of American intellectuals and scholars (see Chapter 14) which is diffused through educational, political, and family institutions.

Having cross-tabulated our variables and considered some examples of each type, we must now take up the question of pluralism. In some recent societies, a number of value orientations—organized and unorganized, differentiated and undifferentiated—coexist. The problem thus posed for classification requires specification of several levels of analysis.

At the level of the society as a whole, *none* of these competing value orientations (many of them embodied in formal churches) operates as the value orientation upon which there is general consensus on ultimate meaning. The value orientation that informs and integrates such a system tends to draw heavily on nonreligious elements of the society and likely restricts its religious components to vague generalities held in common by most or all of the competing value orientations. Such overall value orientations are typically not the focus of formal organizations, nor are they differentiated from other social institutions. Instead, the value orientation of a pluralistic system such as the United States is diffused through other institutions such as the political, the educational, and the familial, and only to a small degree through the various religious organizations.

At a lower level of analysis, however, it is apparent that the value orientation of some groups of persons within such societies is embodied in formal organizations. That is, despite the fact that society as a whole is informed by an unorganized and diffuse value orientation, the basic world view of many Americans is provided by a formal church. This seems especially true for members of the more fundamentalist denominations and sects, as well as the cults (see Chapter 5). As is clear from the examples provided in the various cells in the typology, the world views of many American, some of whom constitute relatively isolated sub cultures, fit a number of the types we have presented. Thus, while the overall value orientation of American society which holds all these disparate elements into a single political entity would have to be classified as type IV, the religious and humanist perspectives of certain groups of Americans would be classified otherwise. Hence, there is a constant need to specify what level of analysis is intended in order to discuss the value orientations of complex, pluralistic societies.

Returning to the cells generated by typologizing, further examination gives rise to a variety of theoretically important questions, among them:

1) Under what conditions do various types emerge; how are they transformed into other types; what are the possible developmental routes for transformation of types, and what routes are

common? To some extent, these questions will be considered in Chapter 13.

2) What are the consequences of contact between various types? Which can coexist, and which conflict; and, as a result of contact, what kinds of changes take place in each and to what degree? These questions will be taken up in some detail in Chapters 10, 11, 14, and 15.

In conclusion, it is hoped that this chapter has made some contribution to clarifying the meaning of the term 'religion' from a social science perspective. In the chapters that follow, the term religion will be used in the way specified in this chapter — as one variety of value orientations, those institutionalized systems of beliefs, symbols, values, and practices that provide groups of men with solutions to their questions of ultimate meaning.

Chapter 2

On The Study of Religious Commitment

THE last chapter dealt with religion as an aspect of human groups. This chapter gives attention to religion as an aspect of individual behavior. In it, the question of personal commitment to religious institutions will be taken up and an effort made to clarify how such commitment may be classified and assessed. While primary attention will be with involvement in religious perspectives, particularly those that are the focus of formal organizations, the issues discussed and the scheme developed could also be adapted to studying involvement in unorganized religious perspectives as well as commitment to humanist perspectives.

What it means to be 'religious' is not the same to all men — either in modern complex societies or in even the most homogeneous primitive groups. Even within a single religious tradition, many variations can be found. This simple fact scarcely needs documentation. Evidence that people think, feel, and act differently when it comes to religion is all around us.

In the face of this great diversity, the student of the individual and his religion is faced with the formidable task of deciding how to conceptualize the phenomenon of religiousness and how to distinguish people in terms of their degrees of religious commitment. These are not, certainly, questions that have been entirely ignored by students of religion. There have been attempts to distinguish people religiously and to discover what leads people to be religious or not. But the efforts have been surprisingly few and, on careful examination, incomplete. All things considered, the task of constructing a conceptual framework for the systematic study of differential commitment to religion still lies ahead of us.

The present chapter is an effort to move closer to that goal. Taking past work into account, it considers the question of what is required for a comprehensive and operationally useful definition of religiousness, and suggests a research strategy for meeting these requirements. The intrinsic importance of religion in the life of man would be enough to justify the study of individual religiosity. But having a way to measure differential commitment to religion would do more than simply satisfy our curiosity. It is a prerequisite to moving on to the more compelling questions of what are the sources and the consequences of religious involvement—both for individuals and for societies.

THE DIMENSIONS OF RELIGIOSITY

A first and obvious requirement if religious commitment is to be comprehensively assessed is to establish the different ways in which individuals *can* be religious. With some few exceptions, past research has curiously avoided this fundamental question. Investigators have tended to focus upon one or another of the diverse manifestations of religiosity and to ignore all others. Thus, in one study, attention will be confined to studying religious belief, and, in another, to studying differences in religious practices. The particular aspect of religion being studied is rarely, if ever, placed within the broader context of its relations to other expressions of religiousness. Nor is the question raised of whether commitment manifested in one way has anything to do with its being expressed in other ways.

If we examine the religions of the world, it is evident that the details of religious expression are extremely varied; different religions expect quite different things of their adherents. Catholics and Protestants, for example, are expected to participate regularly in the Christian sacrament of Holy Communion. To the Moslem such a practice is alien. Similarly, the Moslem imperative to undertake a pilgrimage to Mecca during one's lifetime is alien to the Christian.

In the midst of the great variation in detail, there nevertheless exists among the world's religions considerable consensus as to the more general areas in which religiosity ought to be manifested. These general areas may be thought of as the core dimensions of religiosity. Five such dimensions can be distinguished; within one or another of these dimensions all of the many and diverse manifestations of religiosity prescribed by the different religions of the world can be ordered. We shall call these dimensions the *experiential,* the *ritualistic,* the *ideological,* the *intellectual,* and the *consequential.*[1]

The *experiential dimension* gives recognition to the fact that all religions have certain expectations, however imprecisely they may be stated, that the religious person will at one time or another achieve direct knowledge of ultimate reality or will experience religious emotion. Included here are all of those feelings, perceptions, and sensations which are experienced by an actor or defined by a religious group as involving some communication, however slight, with a divine essence, i.e., with God, with ultimate reality, with transcendental authority. The emotions deemed proper by different religions or actually experienced by different individuals may vary widely — from terror to exaltation, from humility to joyfulness, from peace of soul to a sense of passionate union with the universe or the divine. The emphasis placed on religious feeling as an essential element of religiosity may also vary widely; even within Christianity, groups differ widely in their evaluation of mysticism or in the importance they attach to the experience of conversion. Nevertheless every religion places some value on subjective religious experience as a sign of individual religiosity.

The *ideological dimension* is constituted, on the other hand, by expectations that the religious person will hold to certain beliefs. The content and scope of beliefs will vary not only between religions but often within the same religious tradition. However, every religion sets forth some set of beliefs to which its followers are expected to adhere.

The *ritualistic dimension* encompasses the specifically religious practices expected of religious adherents. It comprises such activities as worship, prayer, participation in special sacraments, fasting, and the like.

The *intellectual dimension* has to do with the expectation that the religious person will be informed and knowledgeable about the basic tenets of his faith and its sacred scriptures. The intellectual and the ideological dimensions are clearly related since knowledge of a belief is a necessary condition for its ac-

---

1. The intellectual dimension was suggested by Yoshio Fukuyama.

ceptance. However, belief need not follow from knowledge nor, for that matter, does all religious knowledge bear on belief.

The *consequential dimension*, the last of the five, is different in kind from the first four. It encompasses the secular effects of religious belief, practice, experience, and knowledge on the individual. Included under the consequential dimension are all those religious prescriptions which specify what people ought to do and the attitudes they ought to hold as a consequence of their religion. The notion of 'works,' in the theological meaning of the term, is connoted here. In the language of Christian belief, the consequential dimension deals with man's relation to man rather than with man's relation to God.

These dimensions, it is proposed, provide a frame of reference for studying religion and assessing religiosity. There is no single piece of research in the literature which has looked at all five dimensions simultaneously; with a few exceptions,[2] most research on the individual and his religion has taken a unilateral rather than a multidimensional approach. Aside from the early works of Hall, Leuba, Starbuck, and James, almost no attention has been given to the experiential dimension of religion.[3] There have been some denominationally sponsored studies of religious knowledge among Christians, but no major piece of research has focused primarily or even incidentally on this dimension. The indicators of religiosity most often used fall under the ritualistic and ideological dimensions.[4]

It is the nature of the consequential dimension of religiosity that it cannot be studied apart from the other dimensions. Attitudes and behavior in secular areas of life can be used as measures of religious commitment only where they are grounded in religious conviction—where they follow from religious belief, practice, experience, and knowledge. Studies of the conse-

---

2. For example, Joseph H. Fichter, *Dynamics of a City Church: Southern Parish* (Chicago: University of Chicago Press, 1951); Gerhard Lenski, *The Religious Factor* (Garden City: Doubleday & Co., 1961).

3. Stanley Hall, "The Moral and Religious Training of Children and Adolescents," *Pedagogical Seminary*, June, 1891; J. H. Leuba, *A Psychological Study of Religion* (New York: The Macmillan Co., 1912); E. D. Starbuck, *The Psychology of Religion* (New York: Charles Scribner's Sons, 1899); William James, *The Varieties of Religious Experience* (New York: Longmans, Green and Co., 1902).

4. For example, Louis Bultena, "Church Membership and Church Attendance in Madison, Wisconsin," *American Sociological Review*, XIV (June, 1949), 384–389; and Gerhard Lenski, "Social Correlates of Religious Interest," *American Sociological Review*, XXVIII (October, 1953), 533–544.

quences of differential commitment to religion have necessarily, therefore, followed the pattern of comparing the secular attitudes and behavior of churchgoers and non-churchgoers, believers and nonbelievers, in an effort to discover whether religion does, in fact, have its effects.[5]

Until there is research which measures religiosity in all of its manifestations, the question of the interrelatedness of the five dimensions cannot be wholly explored. It is scarcely plausible that the various manifestations of religiosity are entirely independent of each other. However, several recent studies strongly suggest that being religious on one dimension does not necessarily imply religiosity on other dimensions.[6] Fukuyama found, using a sample of Congregationalists, that those who scored high on ritual observance and biblical literacy tended to score low on religious belief and religious feeling, and vice versa.[7] Lenski, in his recent study, *The Religious Factor,* found a relatively low order of association between the four indicators of religiosity he used: ritual participation, doctrinal orthodoxy (religious belief), devotionalism (religious experience), and associationism (religious self-segregation).[8]

In this general connection, it has recently been suggested that some of the contradictory findings of past research on religion and social class may be the result of different investigators conceptualizing religiosity in different ways. Demerath, in a book on this topic, cites some studies which show no relation between social class and religiosity, some which report a positive relation between class and religion, others which show a negative relationship, and still others which show a nonlinear relationship between the two.[9] In his discussion, Demerath points out that the way religiosity is manifested varies by social class. Thus, findings can be expected to vary from study to study if the indicators of religiosity used also vary, sometimes measuring one dimension, sometimes another.

---

5. Lenski, *op. cit.,* and Samuel Stouffer, *Communism, Conformity, and Civil Liberties* (Garden City: Doubleday & Co., 1955).

6. These studies rely only on single indicators to place people within particular dimensions; hence a question may be raised as to the adequacy of those indicators to represent a dimension.

7. Yoshio Fukuyama, "The Major Dimensions of Church Membership," *Review of Religious Research* (Spring, 1961), pp. 154–161.

8. Lenski, *op. cit.*

9. N. J. Demerath III, *Social Class In American Protestantism* (Chicago: Rand McNally, 1965).

As will be considered in detail in Chapter 4, the controversy over whether America has been experiencing a religious revival or a decline in recent years seems to have stemmed from different observers defining religious commitment in different ways without recognizing that religiousness may be a multidimensional phenomenon, and that changes in one direction need not imply changes in others.

The mere identification of the different ways in which religious commitment may be expressed turns out to be useful in a number of respects. It provides a perspective for locating the gaps in past and present research. It clarifies some of the discrepancies in what has been observed and reported about religiosity. And it establishes, at least roughly, the requirements to be met if we are to study the phenomenon of religion comprehensively.

It does not, however, afford a prescription as to how to go about studying religious commitment. This is the task to which we now wish to turn. The premise which will inform our efforts is that insofar as the comprehension of religiosity in its whole is possible, this can only follow from an understanding of its parts. Consequently, principal attention will be given to considering how religiosity may be studied within each of its core dimensions. How it might be studied across dimensions will be briefly considered in conclusion. The orientation in the following pages is toward the study of religion in societies which are in the Judeo-Christian tradition. However, on occasion, some of the special problems that arise in the crosscultural study of religion will be mentioned.

It would ease the burden of analysis and research if each of the core dimensions delineated above could be assumed to be itself unilateral. Such an assumption would allow us to ignore the question of subdimensions and to move directly to discussing ways of distinguishing more religious people from less religious ones. Unfortunately, the matter is not so simple. Within every dimension it is necessary to make distinctions in kind as well as in degree.

RELIGIOUS BELIEF
(THE IDEOLOGICAL DIMENSION)

Religious belief may be studied in a number of ways. It may be approached from the perspective of the doctrines of institutionalized religion or from the point of view of a definition of religion which transcends traditional doctrine. In studying religious belief, one may inquire simply into what people believe. Or, one may go on to inquire into the saliency of belief, or going even farther, into the functions of belief for the individual. To understand belief, it will probably be necessary in the end to adopt all of these perspectives.

For the most part, past research has studied religious belief from the standpoint of traditional church doctrine and has asked simply, "How do people differ with respect to their acceptance of church doctrine."[10] A number of scales and indexes have been developed, some simple and some complex, whose purpose usually is to order people along a continuum ranging from traditional belief through liberal or modern belief to unbelief.[11] Almost always, these measures are conceived in unilateral terms and assume, implicitly at least, that the greater the number of beliefs that a subject holds, the stronger is his belief.

Such an approach, while useful for certain purposes, obviously avoids the problems of assessing the saliency and the function of religious beliefs for the individual. Before discussing the questions of saliency and function we should first like to consider the appropriateness of conceiving of religious belief, even traditional belief, in a unilateral way. The failure to make distinctions in kind within the general category of religious belief may obscure some fundamental differences in *types* of belief and in *types* of unbelief.

The belief structure of any particular religion may be divided into three parts. First of all, every religion has beliefs whose primary role is to warrant the existence of the divine and to define its character. Within Christianity, such *warranting beliefs* would be represented by belief in God, in Christ and his miracles, in the virgin birth, and so on. Those who accept these beliefs are, in effect, accepting the existence not only of God but of a personal God. To be distinguished from warranting beliefs are those which explain divine purpose and define man's role with regard to that purpose. Within Christianity, *purposive*

---

10. For example, Gordon Allport, J. M. Gillespie and J. Young, "The Religion of the Post War College Student," *The Journal of Psychology*, XXV, (1948), 3–33; Daniel Katz, F. H. Allport and Margaret B. Jenness, *Students' Attitudes* (Syracuse: Craftsman Press, 1931); Lincoln Barnett, "God and the American People," *Ladies' Home Journal*, LXV (September, 1948), 36–37.

11. Allport, *op. cit.*, Lenski, *op. cit.*, Murray G. Ross, *Religious Beliefs of Youth* (New York: Association Press, 1950).

beliefs would include belief in original sin, in the possibility of man's redemption, in a day of final judgment, in eternal salvation or damnation. Purposive beliefs give rise, in turn, to a third category of beliefs, namely, those which bear on the means by which the divine purpose is to be implemented. *Implementing beliefs* establish what is the proper conduct of man toward God and toward his fellow man for the realization of the divine purpose. Implementing beliefs thus provide the ground for the ethical strictures of religion.

Different religions give·different emphases to these three components of belief. Jainism, for example, stresses the implementing component as does Confucianism. Hinduism, on the other hand, places high value on the purposive element. These components are also given different emphases in Christianity. Lutheranism stresses the warranting and purposive components, the Society of Friends the implementing one.

The conclusion that emerges from these considerations is that in all probability degree of religiosity cannot be measured simply by the sheer number of beliefs that are assented to. Just as different religions stress different beliefs, so we can expect to find some individuals whose religious creeds encompass primarily implementing beliefs and others who place major emphasis on warranting or purposive beliefs. Future research will probably reveal the need to develop typologies of religious belief within which degree of religiosity can be measured rather than a single scale of religious commitment on which all individuals can be measured.

It seems equally inappropriate to conceive of nonbelievers as a single type, as most past studies have done. Perhaps in these studies there were too few atheists and agnostics to justify distinguishing between them. Yet, on the face of it, it would appear that a person who openly rejects religious belief is radically different from one who contends that the question of belief is beyond his ability to decide.

The question of saliency—how important the beliefs he holds are to the individual—is, of course, inexorably bound up with the problem of measuring the range and degree of religious conviction. There are many people who acknowledge holding a belief without its being important to them. Between 95 and 97 per cent of Americans acknowledge a belief in God, for example. It is possible, of course, to ask people directly to assess how important their beliefs are to them. But the saliency of belief is more appropriately studied in terms of the kind of religiosity individuals express on other dimensions. How active one is ritualistically, the kinds of religious experiences he has, how well informed he is religiously, and the extent to which he acts out his beliefs in practice are all measures of the saliency of belief.

These suggestions, while moving us toward a more sophisticated operational definition of religious belief, do not touch on the problem of discovering the functions of beliefs for individuals. Here, the objective is not to know what people believe or how salient their beliefs are to them, but to understand the role of religion in their psychological and social adjustment. To probe into the functions of religion is to attempt to answer the question, "Why are people religious?" in terms of the psychological and social benefits of religious commitment. It is a question which cannot be answered by asking people directly. They are likely either to find the question incomprehensible or to give an answer which is irrelevant to the concept of function, for example, "I believe in Christ because he died for my sins." The direct approach is faced with the fact that individuals are seldom consciously aware of the latent functions of their belief, though depth probing of a qualitative kind by a skilled interviewer could conceivably provide clues to them.

A functional approach to religious belief transcends particular religious traditions and focuses on the more generic functions of belief. Many hypotheses have been and will be proposed as to what the functions of religion are. In all likelihood, religious belief performs a variety of functions, depending on the belief itself and on the individuals who hold it.

One hypothesis offered in Chapter 1 is that all religions provide the individual with an interpretation of his existence. In a world whose purpose cannot be ascertained by reason, religion stands ready with an explanation, however partial it may be, to fill the vacuum. One significant aspect of belief in religious doctrine, therefore, may be that it resolves the problem of ultimate meaning for those to whom it is a concern.

Support for such an hypothesis would be evidence to the effect that believers are actually more deeply concerned than nonbelievers with the problem of meaning and that religious doctrine actually allays the 'metaphysical anxiety' of its adherents. Should it be found, as it may very well be, that religious belief is only one way of resolving the concern about meaning, the question would still remain as to whether religion is a more or less satisfactory way to do so than its functional alternatives.

It has also been suggested that religious beliefs help individuals to transcend many of the deprivations they experience, to meet their needs for being the object of someone else's concern, to overcome loneliness, and so on. Such meanings will clearly be latent to the believer. That they exist can be established only by methods that must rely for their cogency on the existence of an association between need and deprivation, and manifest expressions of belief.

Until now, we have analyzed belief largely within a framework which defines religion in traditional ways. However, religious belief may also be conceptualized in other ways. One alternative, implicit in what has just been said, is to conceptualize religion in terms of the individual's concern with discovering the purpose and meaning of life and of the beliefs he adopts to resolve that concern. Believers would then be represented by all those who have experienced this concern and have resolved it. Those who have the concern but who have not resolved it may be thought of as seekers. Nonbelievers would be those for whom the concern does not even exist.

Another alternative, as suggested in Chapter 1, might equate being religious with having a deep and ultimate commitment to a set of values. From this view, any deep and ultimate commitment is regarded as defining what is 'sacred' to the individual whether or not he also regards it as grounded in divine or supernatural authority. Whether or not a person subscribes to traditional religious doctrine becomes, then, essentially irrelevant to an assessment of his religiosity.

The possibility of alternative definitions of religious belief raises the question of how religion is to be defined and by whom. From the point of view of research, there are no true and false definitions of religion, but only more and less fruitful ones. The justification for any conceptualization does not depend on how widely it is accepted. Religionists, by and large, reject Durkheim's conceptualization of religion. In the last analysis, however, what counts is how well the conceptualization works in adding to our understanding of men and society.

RELIGIOUS PRACTICE
(THE RITUALISTIC DIMENSION)

In the case of religious belief, the main research interest has been in what people believe rather than in the meaning of belief for those who have it. A parallel situation obtains with regard to research on religious practice. Again, the primary focus has been on what people do rather than on the meaning of their activity to them. However, even within this framework, the effort has been neither systematic nor comprehensive.

Reliance is usually placed on church membership and frequency of church attendance as indicators of religiosity within the ritualistic dimension, and there exists a plethora of studies describing the social correlates of these indicators.[12] Participation in sacraments has been studied occasionally as has the recitation of prayers. Probably the closest approximation to an effort to be comprehensive is Joseph Fichter's study of the degree to which Roman Catholic parishioners in a New Orleans parish participate in the prescribed rituals of the church.[13] Fichter, however, did not study the interrelatedness of different forms of participation nor did he look at private religious practice in contradistinction to public practice.

Taking a fresh view of the problem, three possible approaches to studying the religious practices of individuals suggest themselves. First, one may give attention to distinguishing individuals simply with respect to the frequency with which they engage in ritualistic activity and to investigating the interrelatedness of various practices. A second approach is to study variations in the nature of a particular practice—prayer, for example. Third, there exists the possibility of studying the meaning of ritual acts for the individuals who engage in them.

The study of the frequency and the patterns of religious practice is perhaps the simplest of the three. It would require, to begin with, a specification of the variety of religious practices which exist. Since different religions have different practices, one would have to decide whether to focus on practices common to different traditions or to take account of differences as well. A study in the United States limited to Christians and Jews would encompass a considerable variety of practices—worship,

---

12. For example, Lenski, op. cit., Bultena, op. cit., Demerath, op. cit., Walter Goldschmidt, "Class Denominationalism in Rural California Churches," American Journal of Sociology, XLIX (January, 1944), 348.

13. Fichter, op. cit.

prayer, scripture reading, penance, obeying dietary laws, confession, tithing, and many more.

No study has yet been published on patterns of religious practice either within a particular religious group or within a total population. Aside from its descriptive interest, a study of this kind would provide an empirical basis for deciding whether religious practice can be conceived of in unilateral terms or, whether like religiosity itself, it must be conceived of in multi-dimensional terms. It would also provide a basis for deciding whether a distinction has to be made between being religiously active and being religiously involved.

The possibility for confusion between activity and involvement is perhaps best conveyed by an example. Two persons may be equally diligent about attending worship services every Sunday. They are equally active ritualistically on this measure. However, for one, this may be the only form of religious practice engaged in during a week. For the other, attendance at worship may be one of a wide variety of religious acts performed during the week. It is evident that to equate the two on the grounds of their equal participation in worship services is to obscure a major difference in their involvement in ritualistic activity. This illustrates the inherent weakness of relying on a single indicator to distinguish individuals on this, as well as other dimensions of religiosity. What combination of indicators might best be used to provide a reliable measure would be one of the questions which could be resolved by the research suggested above.

Studies of the frequency and the interrelatedness of religious practices need to be paralleled by studies which look at the phenomenon of religious practice more deeply. It is one thing to investigate variations in the frequency of prayer among different religions and among different people in the same religious group. It is quite another thing to investigate variations in the nature of the prayers themselves. We have remarkably little empirical knowledge of the occasions on which people pray or of the content of their prayers. Qualitative differences in the practice of praying may conceivably be of such a magnitude as to invalidate the use of the simple act of prayer as an indicator of religiosity.[14]

---

14. The same point can, of course, be made with reference to each kind of ritual activity. It cannot be assumed that even attendance at worship services connotes the same thing for different individuals.

Knowledge of the variations which exist in particular forms of religious practice is perhaps a first step to understanding their meaning for the individual. Prayers of praise, for example, suggest a meaning different from prayers of petition. Knowledge of the varying meanings with which individuals invest religious acts is, in turn, a first step toward explaining differential religious participation and experience.

RELIGIOUS FEELING
(THE EXPERIENTIAL DIMENSION)

There has been a tendency to associate religious feeling with the more extreme forms of religious expression—the conversion experience, talking in tongues, being visited by the Holy Spirit, and the like. In the little research done in the past on religious experience, it is precisely such expressions of religious feeling that have been focused on. That there are more subtle and less public feelings which accompany religious belief and practice has also to be recognized. Faith, trust, and communion connote these kinds of feelings.

The difficulties of studying the experiential dimension of religiosity, even in its extreme forms, are reflected in its research history. The flowering of interest in the subject occurred around the turn of the last century. As early as 1881, the psychologist Stanley Hall was engaged in empirically studying religious conversion, and two of his students, Leuba and Starbuck, carried on the tradition he had established.[15] At the time, their work enjoyed wide acclaim. With the appearance in 1902 of James' classic *Varieties of Religious Experience,* it might have been supposed that the psychological study of religion had truly come of age.[16] Yet, despite the seeming promise of this early work, the suggested leads were not followed up and, since James, there has been no major and memorable work on religious experience.

Finding a way to begin anew the study of the experiential component of religion is complicated, not only by the absence of a strong research tradition but also by the relative lack of everyday experience with the phenomenon which could provide the empirical raw material for developing concepts. Except where they are expressed in overt and extreme forms, the individual's

15. Hall, *op. cit.,* Leuba, *op. cit.,* Starbuck, *op. cit.*
16. James, *op. cit.*

feelings toward or sensitivity to the divine are not likely to be openly expressed in everyday life. The research strategy proposed below must be viewed, therefore, as tentative and in need of the kind of refinement which only experience with its use can provide.

To begin with, it seems self-evident that religious feelings may be expressed in more than one way. We would suggest a fourfold ordering around the notions of *concern, cognition, trust or faith,* and *fear.* Individuals, we suspect, differ in their concern or need to have a transcendentally based ideology. Where there is a *concern,* it may find expression in a wish to believe, a seeking after a purpose in life, and a sense of dissatisfaction with the world as it is. How concerned one is in this sense would be one component of his religiosity within the experiential dimension.

A second component would be the individual's capacity for *cognition* or awareness of the divine. Reverend J. Moran Weston has suggested the possibility of there being spiritual talent much as there is musical or artistic talent.[17] Insofar as he may be right, this is likely to be manifested in one's subjective experience of a divine presence, of a closeness to God, of being saved. The cognition may be intense, as in the case of conversion, or mild, as when an individual senses God in the beauties of nature. It may be manifested publicly—in a religious service—or privately—in isolation from others.

The third—*trust* or *faith*—bears on the individual's sense that his life is somehow in the hands of a divine power in which trust can be reposed. This component is not present in some religions though it has a primary place in Christianity. The problem of measuring faith is obviously a complex one. One can ask individuals directly concerning their sense of being watched over and cared for by the divine. Studying the matter indirectly-may be more fruitful, however. Freedom from worry, having a feeling of well being, and the like are possible indicators of the fruits of faith.[18]

Though there is an admixture of fear and trust in most religions, one is likely to predominate over the other. The *fear*

---

17. This suggestion was made to the authors by Rev. Dr. Weston.

18. They are also, of course, indicators of the function of religion for the individual and of its consequences. Given the interrelatedness of the different dimensions, it is impossible to examine each of them in a completely independent way, and it is inevitable that some indicators will have significance for assessing religiosity in more than one of its dimensions.

component, though present in Christianity, is not as strongly emphasized by it as by Islam, for example. As with faith, it can be studied directly by asking people whether they fear the divine and in what ways. Again, a more productive approach is to see whether and how fear is represented on other dimensions of religiosity—in beliefs about the nature of God, for example.

In Chapter 3 the question of subdimensions within the general experiential dimension of religious involvement will be considered in detail. It is recognized that the experiential dimension of religious commitment is inextricably bound up with the other dimensions and must be studied within this more general context. However, the chapter will perhaps demonstrate the need for additional systematic conceptualization of each of the general dimensions in order to grapple empirically with variations in human religious behavior.

RELIGIOUS KNOWLEDGE
(THE INTELLECTUAL DIMENSION)

The expectation that the religious person will be informed about his faith is common to all religions. There is considerable variation, however, in the kind of knowledge valued by different religions. Classical knowledge was esteemed by the Confucianists. Knowledge of Jewish history and of the law is highly regarded in Judaism. Within the most proselytizing of all religions—Christianity—communicating the Gospel is given great emphasis but being highly informed about the origin and history of the faith is not. Attitudes toward secular knowledge and higher criticism also vary in different religions. In some Christian sects, an effort is quite consciously made to limit exposure to secular knowledge and only literal interpretation of the 'facts' of the faith is tolerated.

This great variation within and between faiths as to what the religious person ought to know and what should be the quality of his knowledge makes it difficult to judge what kinds of knowledge ought to be considered as indicators of religious commitment. It may be that attributions of religiosity based on knowledge cannot be made without reference to the individual's orientation on the other dimensions of religiosity, particularly religious belief. It is certainly not inconceivable, and perhaps even likely, that the atheist will tend to be highly informed religiously. Yet, by definition, he is a nonbeliever. It becomes a matter of considerable research interest to learn the relationship between how much and what kinds of religious knowledge the individual possesses and his patterns of belief, practice, and experience.

In evolving ways to measure this component of religiosity, we are obliged to start without the benefit of past research. There may be a dissertation literature on this subject, and perhaps it has been given attention in unpublished denominational studies. The published literature, however, is almost wholly devoid of research on religious literacy.

We may begin by asking just what it is that we wish to measure. First of all, it would be of interest to learn simply how much people know about what. Thus, religious literacy tests could be constructed to include a wide range of questions on the origin and history of the religion in which a subject was reared as well as questions about other religions. A variety of types would undoubtedly emerge from the administration of such tests. There would, of course, be those who are religiously illiterate. Many would be found who are knowledgeable about their own faith and not about others. Knowledge about origins, at least in Christianity and Judaism, would probably be much greater than knowledge about subsequent history. As already suggested, it is unlikely that greater and broader knowledge will be uniformly associated with stronger religious feelings, more regular religious practice, and greater adherence to religious beliefs. On the contrary, those with limited knowledge about their own faith will probably be found to be more religious in these other ways than either those with no knowledge or those with great knowledge. It is also likely that people hold to many misconceptions about the origin and history of their religion, and that these misconceptions are associated with certain patterns of religious belief, practice, and feeling.

Attitudes toward knowledge are also likely to be relevant. How much time is spent in reading religious literature—one indicator of an interest in acquiring knowledge—would ordinarily be studied within the area of religious practice. Beyond this, however, it would be useful to discover the importance given to knowledge and the kind of knowledge considered appropriate. We have in mind here distinguishing between those who would consider it inappropriate to become informed about the critical literature on religion and those who are willing to expose themselves to all that has been said and thought. Open- and closed-mindedness in this respect could conceivably help to account for types of religious belief and unbelief.

Finally, the factor of religious knowledge could be further probed by inquiring into the degree of intellectual sophistication brought to the reading of scripture and other religious literature. This is measurable in terms of the degree to which there is, for example, an uncritical acceptance of scripture as literally true. Looking at religious knowledge from these different perspectives and relating what is learned to differential religious commitment on the other dimensions seems a necessary part of coming to understand the religious side of man. Its seemingly obvious importance makes the absence of research on what we have called the intellectual dimension of religiosity all the more surprising.

RELIGIOUS EFFECTS
(THE CONSEQUENTIAL DIMENSION)

The implications of religion for practical conduct are stated very explicitly in some religions and very abstractly in others. The more integrated a religion is into the social structure, the more likely it is that the everyday actions of man are defined by religious imperatives. In Hinduism, for example, how a man deports himself from the time that he arises in the morning until he goes to bed at night is defined by customs which have the support of religious authority. In the more highly institutionalized religions, which have an existence in large measure independent of the social structure, religiously inspired imperatives are less likely to inform the conduct of daily life in explicit ways. The religion sets general standards, which the individual is left to interpret for himself as he confronts the decisions of daily existence. Thus, in Christianity, man is exhorted to be 'a steward of God,' 'to exercise choice and initiative in his use of leisure time in keeping with the new life in Christ,' 'to manage economic wealth in terms of Christian responsibility and leadership,' 'to accept the political responsibilities of Christian citizenship on the basis of his citizenship in the Kingdom of God.' But how these general injunctions are to be interpreted in concrete circumstances is left for the individual to decide.

Despite these differences, there is agreement among religions that consequences follow, or should follow, from religious commitment. These consequences have to do both with what the individual can expect to receive as a result of being religious and with what he is expected to give. The rewards may be immediate or promised for the future. Immediate rewards would include such things as peace of mind, freedom from worry, a sense of well being, or even, in some religions, material success. Among future rewards would be included salvation, promises of eternal life, reincarnation in a higher social category, and the like. Expectations about what a person will do as a result of being religious include both avoiding certain kinds of conduct and actively engaging in others. As in the Ten Commandments, there are always both Thou Shalt and Thou Shalt Not injunctions.

As we have had occasion to point out before, research on religious effects cannot be done in isolation from research on other aspects of religiosity. How religious a person is on these other dimensions provides the warrant for asserting that a given act is, in fact, a religious effect. By definition, an act can be a religious effect only if it flows from religiosity.[19]

In this light, then, what research has been done on religious effects? On the reward side of our 'reward-responsibility' dichotomy, research on the actuality of future rewards is, of course, automatically excluded. Research into the saliency of such promised rewards is important and feasible, though it is most appropriately studied within the framework of religious beliefs. Research on the immediate rewards of religion has been relatively sparse.[20] For the most part, research on religious effects has focused on the 'responsibility' side of the dichotomy, on what the individual does or does not do as a consequence of his

---

19. It is possible, of course, to define religion only in terms of the degree to which its ethical principles are acted out in everyday life, leaving out all consideration of belief, ritual, feeling, and knowledge. While the utility of such a definition might be questioned, adopting it would provide, perhaps, the one condition under which consequences may be studied apart from the other dimensions of religiosity.

20. It is difficult to draw the line between the functions that religious belief serves for the individual, as discussed under the ideological dimension, and the idea that religion provides immediate rewards to the individual. For example, religion may function to give the individual peace of mind, or its psychological equivalent. At the same time, one of the promised rewards of religion may be peace of mind. Insofar as a distinction may be thought necessary, we may define as consequences of religion, those promised rewards of religion which are, in fact, produced. The functions of religious belief, on the other hand, would be the needs which religion serves which are not explicitly or implicitly stated in promised rewards.

religion.[21] A number of studies have examined the effect of religious adherence on individual attitudes and values. The work of Hartshorne and his associates, during the 1930s, on the effects of Christian education are relevant here.[22] They found no religious effect, though the indicators used to define religion were limited to attendance at worship services or at Sunday School. Joseph Fichter, in the final chapter of his book, *Southern Parish,* examines the degree to which parishioners judged to be highly religious in their ritualistic behavior subscribe to certain moral and ethical standards of the Roman Catholic Church.[23] His general conclusion is that adherence to the standards of the church is high only where they do not conflict with secular values. In his study, *Communism, Conformity, and Civil Liberties,*[24] Samuel Stouffer found that, contrary to his expectations, the religious are less civil libertarian in their attitudes than the nonreligious. In this instance, frequency of church attendance was the indicator used to judge religiosity.

The most ambitious attempt to study religious effects is Lenski's *The Religious Factor.*[25] Lenski adopts four indicators as measures of religiosity and relates each of them to series of questions having to do with respondents' political, economic, and family values. His conclusions show generally that religiosity is related to the values studied, though the nature of the

21. It is sometimes difficult to distinguish between consequences which follow from explicit expectations formulated in the implementing beliefs of a religion, consequences which follow from an expectation expressed in abstract terms in an implementing belief, e.g., 'The Christian should be a steward of God,' and consequences which follow from the associations which the individual forms in his religious practice, or from the feelings he experiences in his response to the divine. A finding that Roman Catholics do not practice artificial birth control would represent a clear consequence of the first kind. A finding that believers are more likely to engage actively in community affairs might represent a consequence of the second kind. A result showing that believers are more likely to vote Republican than nonbelievers might represent the third kind of consequence. In our discussion of past research, we shall not try to distinguish between the three types of consequences, though the reader may wish to make his own interpretation as to the category in which specific findings fall.

22. H. Hartshorne and J. B. Maller, *Studies in Service and Self Control* (New York: The Macmillan Co., 1929); H. Hartshorne and M. A. May, *Studies in Deceit* (New York: The Macmillan Co., 1928); H. Hartshorne and F. K. Shuttleworth, *Studies in the Nature of Character* (New York: The Macmillan Co., 1930).

23. Fichter, *op. cit.*

24. Stouffer, *op. cit.*

25. Lenski, *op. cit.*

relationship varies according to the indicator of religious commitment used.

These studies, even Lenski's, are less than comprehensive in the indicators used to measure the religious commitment of their subjects. And, because they are all cross-sectional studies done at one point in time, they do not allow warranted conclusions as to the causal direction of the associations they find. Though Stouffer concluded that church attendance leads people to be less civil libertarian, the opposite conclusion is just as plausible, namely, that being non-civil libertarian leads people to more church attendance.

Despite their limitations, these studies are suggestive of the possibilities for more systematic research on the consequences of religion. However, precedence ought probably be given to studying the nature of religiosity in its man-to-God dimensions. For until we have established more adequate grounds for distinguishing people on these dimensions, the study of consequences will necessarily be tentative and incomplete.

Nevertheless, the potentialities seem very great indeed. Religion in our society would not be so viable had it no consequences for the individual. We suspect that these consequences are more of the 'reward' than the 'responsibility' variety. Yet both possibilities warrant further study. It would obviously be of major significance to know how and in what ways religion contributes to mental health. It would also be important to know more about what it implies for morality, for altruistic behavior, for the decisions people make as they move through the life cycle.

CONCLUSIONS

We are still far from an adequate understanding of the individual and his religion. The burden for this must rest primarily on our failures, thus far, to comprehend the nature of religion. In our zeal to explore the correlates of religion and to understand its effects, we have somehow ignored the phenomenon itself. It may turn out that there is no greater depth to religion than the simple indicators which have been used to measure it. However, until the effort is made to comprehend religion in all of its manifestations, we can neither rest easy in this thought nor have confidence in our research.

What is required first is a slow process of beginning to build more adequate measures of religious involvement within and between dimensions. We cannot assume *a priori,* as previous research has tended to do, either that the dimensions are unilateral or that a single indicator will be sufficient to distinguish religious orientations within a dimension. Nor can we assume that religiosity expressed on one dimension automatically assures its being manifested on other dimensions as well. Recent research has already begun to suggest that different modes of religious expression may, in fact, be quite unrelated.[26] This lead needs to be followed up by examining, more systematically, the interplay between different aspects of religiousness.

It is quite conceivable that we shall end with not one but a set of operational definitions of religious involvement and that the correlates and effects of each may vary greatly. On reflection, it seems very unlikely indeed that so complex a phenomenon as religion can be wholly understood either in unidimensional terms or within a framework borrowed exclusively from the expectations of traditional religion. The possibilities of doing research using concepts of religion which are informed by sociological and psychological theory have not been explored. Yet there is, perhaps, as much promise in following up such leads as in continuing to rely too exclusively on more traditional conceptualizations of religion.

For the future, the real challenge probably lies in the cross-cultural study of religious commitment. However, until we have found a more adequate way to study commitment in our own culture, it would perhaps be unwise to plunge headlong into comparative research. The potentialities, though, seem exciting indeed.

---

26. Fukuyama, *op, cit.,* Lenski, *op. cit.*

Chapter 3

A Taxonomy of Religious Experience[1]

THE preceding chapter distinguished five general expectations that religious institutions universally make upon their adherents, and suggested how these expectations could serve as dimensions along which to classify persons according to their degree of commitment to religion. The present chapter focuses on one of these dimensions of religious commitment and attempts to specify criteria with which to organize and investigate religious experience.

The study of religious experience provides an example of those strange discontinuities which seem to beset the social sciences.[2] At the turn of the century it was a major concern of a number of eminent scholars, among them James Leuba,[3] Edwin

1. This chapter and Chapters 5 and 8 make use of data collected as part of a five-year research program on anti-Semitism being conducted by the Survey Research Center under a grant from the Anti-Defamation League of B'Nai B'rith. The authors are deeply grateful to the Anti-Defamation League for having made this research possible.
2. The scientific study of religion in general suffered a similar lapse. One of the authors has recently noted that after the golden era of Troeltsch, Weber, and Durkheim, the sociological study of religion virtually disappeared during the period between World Wars I and II. See Charles Y. Glock, "The Sociology of Religion," in Robert K. Merton, Leonard Broom, Leonard S. Cottrell, Jr., (eds.), *Sociology Today* (New York: Basic Books, 1959), pp. 153–177.
3. James H. Leuba, *The Psychology of Religious Mysticism* (New York: Harcourt, Brace, and Company, Inc., 1925).

Diller Starbuck,[4] and, of course, William James.[5] But the next generation of social scientists failed to pursue these promising beginnings and in subsequent decades virtually nothing of merit has been added to our understanding of religious experience.

If the quest is to be taken up once more, the initial task to be accomplished is conceptual. James' work was primarily descriptive, while the explanatory efforts of Leuba and Starbuck were addressed to rather narrowly restricted aspects of religious experience.[6] But the term 'religious experience' covers an exceedingly disparate array of events from the vaguest glimmerings of something sacred, to rapturous mystical unions with the divine, or even to revelations. Clearly, some basic elements must be systematically extracted from these diverse phenomena if theory and empirical investigation are to be carried much further.

The present chapter is intended as a beginning of this conceptual task. In it we shall attempt to develop some basic subtypes and ordering dimensions for organizing the variety of experiences to which men attach religious definitions.

The conceptual scheme has been informed by data from a sample of Protestant and Roman Catholic church members residing in the San Francisco Bay area. These data include both quantifiable and qualitative information on the religious experi-

---

4. Edwin Diller Starbuck, *The Psychology of Religion* (New York: Charles Scribner's Sons, 1899).

5. William James, *The Varieties of Religious Experience* (New York: Mentor Books, 1958); first published in 1902.

6. Although James gave a bit of attention to what class of things he meant to consider as religious experiences, he made little systematic attempt to classify these disparate psychological events. For the most part he accepted the categories which occur in the natural religious language: conversion, mysticism, and the like. His only original addition was to distinguish between religious experiences emanating from "sick" and "healthy souls." However, aside from these primitive "source" categories, his lectures were mainly devoted to a detailed recounting of individual reports of religious experiences. Leuba was only concerned with religious ecstasy, particularly "extravagant instances," and drew most of his material from case studies of the lives of saints. While the experiences of such dedicated religious adepts are a fruitful source of data, we must surely give attention to the more ordinary experiences of more ordinary persons. Starbuck's classic work, based on one of the earliest surveys ever conducted, dealt solely with conversion among American Protestants. While conversion is likely an important kind of religious experience, any general treatment must take into account a much broader array of phenomena. The only other significant writings on religious experience are the autobiographical and biographical accounts of mystics. While Leuba and James demonstrated that these materials contain valuable data, they can hardly be expected to yield a sophisticated conceptual scheme.

ences of respondents. Where appropriate, these data will be introduced both to indicate the relative frequency of different forms of religious experience and to illustrate how people perceive such experiences.[7]

Following many previous writers, we suggest that the essential element characterizing religious experience, and distinguishing it from all other human experience, is *some sense of contact with a supernatural agency.*[8] Or, as it was put in the preceding chapter, religious experiences are

---

7. The study is based on a random sample of the church member population of four metropolitan counties in Northern California. The data were collected through use of a self-administered mail questionnaire. Three thousand persons, or 72 per cent of the Protestants, and 53 per cent of the Catholics, in the original sample responded. A study of nonrespondents revealed that bias in returns was negligible. Details of sampling procedures and data collection methods will appear in a volume on religion and anti-Semitism by the authors scheduled for Spring publication 1966. Although this research was supported by a grant from the Anti-Defamation League of B'nai B'rith, the sponsor is in no way responsible for the views expressed in this chapter.

Just prior to answering a series of structured items on various religious experiences, respondents were asked:

> So far, we have asked about your religious activities, your religious knowledge, and your religious beliefs. The next series of questions has to do with your religious experiences, that is, with what feelings you may have had which you would think of as religious.
> 42. To begin, would you describe briefly any experience which you have had in your life which at the time you thought of as a distinctly religious experience.

The material reported in this chapter is from written responses to this open-ended question. Several structured items also included in the questionnaire, will be reported as they are used.

8. James, *op. cit.,* for example, defined religion as:

> the feelings, acts, and experiences of individual men in their solitude, so far as they apprehend themselves to stand in relation to whatever they may consider divine. (p. 42. Italics in the original.)

He then characterized religious experience specifically in terms of contact:

> It is as if there were in the human consciousness a *sense of reality, a feeling of objective presence, a perception* of what we may call 'something there,' more deep and more general than any of the special and particular 'senses' by which the current psychology supposes existent realities to be originally revealed. (p. 61. Italics in the original.)

Similarly, Leuba, *op. cit.,* defined "mystical" as:

> . . . any experience taken by the experiencer to be a contact . . . or union of the self with a larger-than-self, be it called the World-Spirit, God, the Absolute, or otherwise. (p. 1.)

Strickland also took this position:

> For the distinctive thing about religious experience is the attitudes and relations to power or personality conceived to be divine.

Francis L. Strickland, *The Psychology of Religious Experience* (New York and Cincinnati: The Abingdon Press, 1924), p. 66.

. . . all of those feelings, perceptions, and sensations which are experienced by an actor or defined by a religious group or a society as involving some communication, however slight, with a divine essence, i.e., with God, with ultimate reality, with transcendental authority.

It ought to be made clear that various events or feelings are only religious experiences if a person *defines* them as such. Obviously, many of the events we shall be discussing are most often *not* given religious definitions by persons these days. We are not, then, concerned with such events in themselves, but only when someone attaches to them some sense of contact with the supernatural. This does not mean, of course, that certain kinds of events aren't more likely than others to elicit religious definitions, but that is another question beyond the domain of our present concern with classification and description.

As we define the term, all religious experiences, from the dimmest to the most frenzied, constitute occasions defined by those experiencing them as an encounter between themselves and some supernatural consciousness.[9] For analytic purposes we shall treat these as inter-'personal' encounters, and, as we shall attempt to show in some detail later, an important dimension along which these encounters can be ordered is the sense of intimacy between the two 'persons' involved. By conceiving of the divinity and the individual undergoing the religious experience as a pair of actors involved in a social encounter, we may specify some general configurations of relations between them which can be ordered in terms of social distance. To anticipate our discussion we may sketch four such possible configurations of inter-actor relations:

---

9. By limiting our definition of religious experiences to only those occasions when men have some sense of contact with divinity, we isolate a relatively homogeneous collection of behavior, but we also exclude a great deal which might be designated as religious experience. (See discussion of the experential dimension in Chapter 2.) However, if we let the term 'religious experience' stand for all emotional states, feelings, sentiments, etc., which men link to religion, its rituals, practices, beliefs, and institutions, or even their love of their faith in general, we include too much for any meaningful conceptualization. These subjective states which fall outside our definition are clearly important to investigations of religion broadly conceived, but it seems likely that they may be most usefully treated in connection with the specific aspects of religion to which they are linked.

1) The human actor simply notes (feels, senses, etc.) the existence or presence of the divine actor;
2) Mutual presence is acknowledged, the divine actor is perceived as noting the presence of the human actor;
3) The awareness of mutual presence is replaced by an affective relationship akin to love or friendship;
4) The human actor perceives himself as a confidant of or a fellow participant in action with the divine actor.

As in normal human affairs, encounters of the former types are more frequent than those of the latter—one has many more acquaintances than friends. Similarly, any more intimate relationship has likely passed through less intimate previous states. We shall attempt to show shortly that this order coincides with the frequency which various kinds of religious encounters are distributed within a general population, as well as with the frequency of different kinds of divine encounters in the career of a single individual.

While the majority of religious experiences seem to consist, at the sensory level, of feelings or other emotional states, these may also be accompanied by visual and auditory phenomena usually referred to as *visions* and *voices*. We shall give specific attention to the way these visions and voices may be wedded to our conceptual scheme, but for the sake of clarity these matters will be postponed. Having made these brief preliminary statements, we may now consider whether these simple inter-actor configurations are adequate to organize and classify the remarkably varied phenomenon of religious experience.

I.   THE CONFIRMING EXPERIENCE

The most general kind of religious experience, the one most frequently reported by individuals in America,[10] will be called the *confirming experience*. We use the word confirming to indicate that such experiences provide a sudden feeling, knowing, or intuition that the beliefs one holds are true, that one's *Weltanschauung* provides an accurate interpretation of the ultimate meaning of reality. What is meant here is not simply the conviction that one's beliefs are true, but rather a sudden intensifica-

---

10. The Gallup organization reported in April, 1962, that 20 per cent of a national sample of Americans reported that they had had a religious experience during their lifetime. The greatest proportion of these fit the confirming type.

tion of this conviction—a special occasion of certainty induced by an experience of the presence of sacred influence.[11] We may distinguish confirming experiences into two subtypes on the basis of the specificity of the perception of divine presence.

The first of these subtypes we may call a *generalized sense of sacredness.* Here we mean to classify diffuse, ill-defined, emotional experiences of reverence, awe, or solemnity which lie on the borderline between the sacred and profane. These are the least spectacular occurrences which people will label as religious experiences. Typically these are instances of special ritual or emotional significance which are accompanied by a mild quickening of faith and a sense of surrounding holiness. Often such experiences are associated with sacramental acts such as communion or baptism, or with other special church occasions:

> I took the 4:30 a.m. time at our church for World Day of Prayer. I was about to step up to the altar, and it was as if I was walking on Holy Ground. I had to back up and walk around it. That Hour of Prayer was one of the most wonderful and meaningful I have ever experienced.[12]

Another common association of general senses of sacredness is with major life-cycle milestones, for example, a great sense of sacredness invested in such moments as marriage ceremonies or the death of loved ones. All in all, while these religious encounters clearly have deep meaning and impact for those who experience them, they are very general and unspecified feelings; indeed, they are described primarily in terms of an emotional state. For example:

> A very deep sense of peace and well-being, a kind of warm surge of assurance that all is well within and without.[13]

Beyond these borderline phenomena, however, lies a more focused confirming experience.

This more focused subtype of confirming experiences will be referred to as a *specific awareness of the presence of divinity,*

---

11. Strickland, *op. cit.,* p. 268, says in this connection that, "The feelings of certainty which come to me at times when I seek the presence of God are stronger than the feelings of certainty which come as a result of my rational reflection upon the nature of God and the grounds in reason for his existence."

12. Respondent #0117, Methodist, female, age 47. (Grammar and spelling in this and other quotations have been left unedited.)

13. Respondent #0146, Nazarene, male, age 25.

akin to what James called the "something there" experience.[14] The characteristic feature of these experiences is the perception that divinity in a specific sense (e.g., God, Jesus, a creator) is present in a special way (close at hand, in the room) as opposed to a general sense that the divine exists and is present everywhere. However, to mark these events off from those to be included in later types, we must emphasize that the present divinity *is not* perceived as specifically acknowledging the presence of the individual. For example:

> Once when I entered a darkened church alone I suddenly knew I had come at a moment when God was in that church. Not just the way I have felt before that God is everywhere but that in a very personal meaning of God he was there then. I stood very quietly and felt this presence until it was suddenly gone and I knew God had gone somewhere else.[15]

Such feelings seem commonly to occur in response to what strikes the individual as empirical confirmation of the validity of his religious perspective. For example, the wonders of nature commonly elicit confirming experiences among Christians, often during a visit to the forest or countryside by an urbanite unaccustomed to these sights. As a twenty-six-year-old, male Presbyterian wrote, "Sometimes when I'm alone out in the wide open places, I feel Him close!"[16] Others reported a sense of God's close presence when awed by an especially nice sunset, or other phenomena which indicated to them that the world is indeed complex and testified to God's handiwork.

The sagging stockmarket in 1962 touched off a rash of confirming experiences among members of a West Coast millenarian cult whose members think the Kingdom is at hand and will be preceded by a collapse of temporal powers.[17] As stock prices fell, members reported an increasing number of encounters with agents of the spirit world.

Whatever their origins, confirming experiences are relatively common among members of American churches. Forty-five per cent of the Protestants in our San Francisco sample responded they were "sure" they had experienced "a feeling that [they] were somehow in the presence of God." Forty-four per cent of

14. See footnote 1.

15. Respondent #2358, Lutheran, female, age 35.

16. Respondent #0121.

17. A brief account of field work done with this group will be reported in John Lofland and Rodney Stark, "To Become a World Saver: A Theory of Conversion to a Deviant Perspective," *American Sociological Review*, December, 1965.

the Roman Catholics were also sure. As would be expected, among the Protestants, these experiences were much more common among the fundamentalist groups than among mainline bodies. Differences ranged from 25 per cent of the Congregationalists to 80 per cent of the Southern Baptists.

These perceptions of divine presence, as we shall discuss more fully later, may immediately lead to more complex religious experiences. However, since confirming experiences are statistically rather more common than the further types we shall consider, many people who go this far go no further.

II. THE RESPONSIVE EXPERIENCE

The next most common type of religious experience may be called the *responsive*. Where the confirming experience indicates only an awareness of the existence or presence of divinity, the responsive refers to occurrences when a person feels this awareness is mutual, that the divine has also taken specific notice of the individual's existence.

> During church one Sunday I had a most wonderful feeling that God was there before me and acknowledged especially me.[18]

These responsive experiences may be further subdivided into the three basic modes by which the divine may be interpreted as taking notice of an individual: *salvational*, *miraculous*, and *sanctioning* experiences.

The *salvational* subtype denotes states during which persons feel that the divine has chosen to count them among his own, to remark their existence by sealing their election into eternal reward. It is in this category that the vast body of literature on Christian 'conversion' (at least in the 'twice born' sense) belongs.[19] Belief in a judging God who rewards or punishes eter-

---

18. Respondent #0120, Methodist, female, age 21.
19. The word 'conversion,' long used in this connection, is probably not an especially apt choice. What is usually meant is an arousal of concern among persons who already accept the essential truth of the ideological system. Yet, as indicated in Chapter 1, the term should probably be reserved for instances when a person changes from one ideological system to another, e.g., for Catholics who become Communists, and the like. Two excellent studies which treat conversion in the sense of awakening interest are: L. Wyatt Lang, *A Study of Conversion* (London: George Allen & Unwin, Ltd., 1931), and Alfred Clair Underwood, *Conversion: Christian and Non-Christian* (New York: The Macmillan Co., 1925).

nally gives special salience to this particular kind of religious experience and leads to expectations concerning salvation, which probably accounts for this experience being so widespread. Thirty-six per cent of the Protestants in our sample, and 26 per cent of the Roman Catholics, said they were "sure" they had experienced "a sense of being saved in Christ." Denominational differences among Protestants varied from 9 percent of the Congregationalists to 93 per cent of the Southern Baptists. These differences reflect the degree to which salvational experiences are encouraged by liberal and fundamentalist churches in America. Such activity is at best unseemly among the liberal denominations, while it is highly esteemed by their more conservative brethren. Indeed, many fundamentalist Christian bodies explicitly require such an experience as a necessary qualification for full membership in the group. For example, the Nazarenes and the Assemblies of God count only 'bornagain Christians' who have experienced 'salvation through the Holy Ghost' as formal members of the church.

Thus it is no surprise that these church bodies have developed well-organized and institutionalized mechanisms to generate and channel predispositions for salvational experiences. And their 'saved' members have a well-developed rhetoric concerning how one best seeks this experience, which reveals that it may take a long time to build up sufficient group pressure on an individual to get him 'saved.' For, typically, such an experience is a consequence of building up a sense of sin and guilt which is triggered by the pleading and urging of preacher, congregation, and often close friends, during prayer meetings specifically intended for 'saving souls.'[20]

> At the age of 11, as a result of home environment, Bible study, and religious services (preaching, Sunday School, etc.,) I came to feel a heavy sense of guilt. I went forward in a revival service, prayed a prayer of repentance, confessed my wrongdoings to my

---

20. Strickland, *op. cit.*, wrote of conversions in "testimony meetings" as passing through three stages,

". . . (1) The period of dissatisfaction, depression, and even sorrow, commonly called conviction. This leads to (2) the crisis, which is followed by (3) the coming of reassurance, peace, joy." p. 112.

Perhaps the best analysis of the conversion process is provided by a nineteenth century handbook written to tell young aspiring evangelists how to stage a revival campaign, see: James Watson, *Helps to the Promotion of Revivals* (New York: Carlton and Porter, 1856).

parents, etc., and accepted Christ as my Saviour and Lord. I felt
a great release and peace which has remained constant except for
brief intervals when I have slipped and yielded to willful desires.[21]

Indeed, this engrossment with sin as the dynamic of salvation
led Starbuck to define *conversion* as *"a process of struggling
away from sin, rather than of striving toward righteousness."*[22]
And one of Starbuck's respondents frankly admitted that failure
to build up guilty tension lay at the root of his inability, for
several years, to gain a salvational experience. "The chief trouble was I did not feel myself so great a sinner as I thought I
ought."[23] On these grounds, Leon Salzman argues that conversions are likely to be "regressive" and "psychopathological,"
typically occurring "during attempts to solve pressing and serious problems in living, or to deal with extreme, disintegrating
conflicts. . . It is a pseudo-solution and is likely to occur in
neurotic, prepsychotic, or psychotic persons."[24] Given this
preoccupation with guilt, and its role in salvational experiences,
it is no wonder that the common theme in accounts of such
experiences is cleansing and purification.

> When I got saved . . . the burden of guilt and sin was lifted, the
> peace of God flooded my soul.[25]

> When Christ came into my heart and took the load of sin and guilt
> away.[26]

Despite this rhetoric of cleansing, Philip Rieff argues that
revivalism and salvational experiences are considerably more
successful in creating anxiety than in eventually discharging it.[27]
It must be emphasized that while we have drawn heavily on
traditional Christian salvational experiences for illustrations, we
do not mean to limit the salvational type to this narrow range of
events. Rather, we mean to classify here all occasions when
individuals sense that the divine has turned his attention to

21. Respondent #0527, Nazarene, male, age 62.
22. Starbuck, *op. cit.*, p. 64, italics in the original.
23. *Ibid.*, p. 87.
24. Leon Salzman, "The Psychology of Religious and Ideological Conversion," *Psychiatry*, XVI (1953), 177–179.
25. Respondent #0006, Assemblies of God, female, age 26.
26. Respondent #0137, Nazarene, female, age 50.
27. Philip Rieff, "The Evangelist Strategy," in Zahn, *op. cit.,* especially p. 21.

them, acknowledged special interest in them, and extended some verification of their special status in his eyes. For example, this Methodist female felt herself acknowledged as properly faithful without seeing the experience in terms of a fundamentalist doctrine of being 'saved':

> . . . I dreamed that I was in an amphitheatre on top of a lonely mountain staring at a rude cross. It seemed as if it were Good Friday. Christ suddenly appeared before me and said that if I believed enough I would find one of my thumbs missing. I remember staring at my hand and seeing the thumb gone. I knew my faith in Him was strong. I awoke thrilled.[28]

The *miraculous* subtype of responsive experiences is less a thing of the spirit than of the flesh. It denotes those instances when an individual feels that the divine has taken note of him during a period of crisis and difficulty and actively intervened in the processes of the physical world on his behalf. A common incident is the healing miracle:

> Facing a serious operation, I felt a definite uplifting of my faith and a *direct* physical result—(decreased blood pressure, reduced pulse rate, complete calmness with *no* medication whatsoever) after a very emotionally disturbed two weeks. This happened during the last 24 hours and I *know* was the direct [result] of my own searching prayers and the intercessory prayers of my friends. It came to me at the *exact* moment they had gathered together to pray for me.[29]

> We were praying for a child who was deathly sick and even as we looked the fever left.[30]

> One night I awoke gasping for breath—I thought I was dying and felt like I was—Just about to give up—I saw a vision of Jesus at the foot of my bed—the complete figure—He stretched out His hand and said, "No—not yet—Be not afraid." At that moment I felt a *peace* and *joy* come over me—such as I have never experienced in my life. This happened seven years ago.[31]

A second common variety of miraculous experiences involves escapes or rescues from danger:

---

28. Respondent #0040, Methodist, female, age 33.
29. Respondent #0002, Methodist, female, age 38.
30. Respondent #0489, Lutheran, female, age 56.
31. Respondent #0933, Baptist, female, age 51.

> When sixteen years old I was present at an oil well site when some-one set the natural gas on fire. Before the explosion, an inner voice warned me to leave — I "argued" and remained — others died from burns, I was among those unharmed and it burst upon me that my life had been given back to me to serve. . .[32]

> Faced imminent death in a mid-air collision during WWII and felt complete assurance of salvation.[33]

A number of respondents cited unexpected survival of auto accidents as instances of miraculous intervention by God.

Another common event attributed to divine intervention was a good turn in economic affairs:

> On two occasions I prayed for guidance as to how to make some extra money without having to leave my family for full time em-ployment. Both times jobs have been offered to me "out of the blue" without making application and from people I didn't know.[34]

Many other respondents reported getting jobs, finding lost letters, getting new appliances, etc., as a direct result of divine action in their behalf.

The prototype of the miraculous, however, is probably the healing or life-sparing intervention and thus it could be called a 'foxhole' variety of religious encounter. Like the salvational, it is based on emotional strains — typically fear — but, unlike salva-tion, it does not commonly occur in specially prepared social situations. Lacking the reinforcement such situations provide, the miraculous is probably much less likely than the salvational to have long-lasting consequences for religious commitment.[35] For although some men do turn forever to a deep religious involvement in gratitude for an apparent response to their emergency prayers (as did Luther after he survived the thun-

---

32. Respondent #0560, Disciple of Christ, male, age 48.
33. Respondent #0107, Baptist, male, age 41.
34. Respondent #0752, Congregational, female, age 47.
35. Many salvational experiences, of course, are not permanent either. For example, Respondent #0101, a Nazarene female, age 37, wrote:
> I know a few years ago when I knelt at a altar God saved me. But Im not saved today. But if God would have me I meen to be again.

Studies of the aftereffects of large-scale evangelism campaigns, such as those conducted by Dwight L. Moody, Billy Sunday, and Billy Graham, indicate that salvations occurring among persons *already* anchored into a religious commu-nity — active church members — seem to endure; but those produced among the unchurched, who are, after all, the main targets of such campaigns, seem very transient. This emphasizes the importance of social bases for maintaining religious commitment over personal, psychological bases.
See: William G. McLoughlin, Jr., *Modern Revivalism* (New York: The Ronald Press Co., 1959). See also Chapter 6 of this book.

derstorm), they perhaps more commonly behave like the scared soldier in Hemingway's vignette who promised to tell the world about Jesus if he lived through the shelling, but who never told anybody.

The miraculous has been characterized as perceptions of divine intervention in the material world to the advantage of the individual. However, the divine may be felt to intervene in negative ways, that is, to interfere in temporal affairs to punish or deflect the individual from his goals. We shall call this genre of divine response the *sanctioning* experience.

Persons who undergo sanctioning experiences often report in retrospect that it was all for their own good, that while God sent them apparent misfortune this prevented them from subsequent unanticipated harm.

> I know God sent me reverses in business which caused me to miss out on the chance to become wealthy. Now I realize that while I was succeeding I was losing sight of my responsibilities to others (my family most of all) as well as of true Christianity. Now I thank God that in His wisdom He punished me for my sins and saved me from myself.[36]

In the above quotation it is apparent how similar sanctioning and miraculous subtypes of responsive experiences are. The element being extracted for separate classification under sanctioning is the aspect of punishment as opposed to the unmitigated and direct good implied in the miraculous types.

Some persons report a less indirect linkage between sanctioning experiences and a valued outcome: God simply made them aware of his displeasure towards them for certain acts or attitudes and they ceased their 'sinning,' thus becoming happier directly.

> I have felt God's wrath when I slid into sin and right away I straightened up and felt so much better for it.[37]

III. THE ECSTATIC EXPERIENCE

The third general type of religious experience shall be designated the *ecstatic*. This involves all the components of the two less intimate types—an awareness of the divine and a sense that the awareness is returned—and in addition denotes a deepening of this sense of mutual awareness into an affective personal relationship. If we may say that confirming experiences are like

---

36. Respondent #2701, Methodist, male, age 43.
37. Respondent #1305, Lutheran, male, age 31.

knowing of God's presence, and the responsive are like being introduced to God, then the ecstatic are comparable to the intimacy of friendship, or, perhaps, even courtship. Indeed, a heavily sexual motif runs through the ecstatic writing of Catholic monastics, past and present, and similar reports of physical sensations and exhilaration dominate Protestant and non-Christian ecstasies as well.[38]

The dominance of this sexual theme led Leuba to argue rather convincingly that sexual frustration and preoccupation were major psychological sources of the religious ecstasies of the Grand Mystics of the Middle Ages.[39] Observation of religious ecstasy among rather more ordinary people in recent times reaffirms this impression of a close linkage between religious ecstasy and sexual arousal.[40]

---

38. The ecstatic writing of cloistered nuns is especially sexual. For example, Mechthild of Magdeburg recounted her love affair with Christ and advised "all virgins to follow the most charming of all, the eighteen-year-old Jesus," so He might embrace them. In her *Dialogue Between Love and the Soul,* she wrote, "Tell my Beloved that His chamber is prepared, and that I am sick with love for Him. . . . Then He took the soul into His divine arms, and placing His fatherly hand on her bosom, He looked into her face and kissed her well." It was not uncommon for many ecstatically adept nuns to determine that they had been embraced by Christ and had conceived by Him. Some of these nuns even sustained false pregnancies as a result of such convictions. It is interesting to note that these sexual religious ecstasies were lent support by the consecration ceremonies of nuns during the Middle Ages, some of which are continued today in certain orders. The young candidate was given a gold wedding ring and called a bride of Christ. One ceremonial response was "I love Christ whose bed I have entered." And later in the ceremony they were urged to "forget there all the world, and there entirely out of the body; there in glowing love embrace your beloved [Savior] who is come down from heaven into your breast's bower, and hold Him fast until He shall have granted whatsoever you wish for." (See: G. Rattray Taylor, *Sex in History* [New York: Ballantine Books, 1954], especially Book One.) But this sexuality of religious ecstasy is not limited to nuns or even females. For example, read the intensely sexual and violent poem of the modern Catholic monk, Brother Antoninus, "The Song The Body Dreamed In The Spirit's Mad Behest," *The Atlantic Monthly,* August, 1962, p. 115.

39. Leuba, *op. cit.*

40. Observation of two female members of the West Coast cult, previously referred to, undergoing a religious ecstasy during a long prayer session gave the distinct impression that they achieved orgasm during what they defined as an entirely spiritual encounter. Weston La Barre reports that women members of a Southern snake-handling cult seem to exhibit decidedly sexual responses during ecstatic services. *They Shall Take Up Serpents* (Minneapolis: University of Minnesota Press, 1962). H. L. Mencken provides a portrait of sexuality in religious ecstasy in his graphic, if irreverent, account of a mountain camp meeting near Dayton, Tennessee, during the days of the Scopes 'Monkey Trial.' See: "The Hills of Zion," in Alistair Cooke, editor, *The Vintage Mencken* (New York: Vintage Books, 1956), pp. 153 – 161.

In any event, the prototype of this kind of religious encounter is a physical and psychological upheaval of intense proportions, similar to orgasm, intoxication, seizures — an overpowering of the senses by divine 'touch.' Into this category we may classify such occurrences as 'visitations of the Holy Spirit,' often expressed by jumping, shaking, screaming, and '. . . [speaking] in other tongues as the Spirit gave utterance.'[41] Frequently, physical sensations associated with ecstatic experiences are likened to electrical current:

> The healing power of Jesus Christ was like a tremendous bolt of electricity passing through.[42]

> . . . I felt as if a wave started at my crown and continued down through my body, out through my feet. I truly felt as if God had passed his hand over me. I felt as if I had been reborn. It was a miracle! I went back to sleep without a care or concern in the World.[43]

These physical sensations are perhaps the most common feature of the ecstatic experiences reported by cloistered nuns. It may be noted that similar sensations of being touched by electric current, X-rays, or radar, are common features of the delusional systems of psychotics.

The character of these sensations is even more clearly described in the following account written by a middle-aged male member of the Assemblies of God. After a series of vivid dreams and visions of Christ, he underwent the following experience:

> . . . A month later at a mass meeting (evangelical and a healing campaign) I went forward and as I approached the platform the Power of God enter my body with tremendious feeling as electricity. I stood still just waiting. One of the evangelist helper said you better go forward the evangelist is waiting to pray for you. As I walked forward the Holy Spirit released His Power. But after the evangelist anointed and said, "In Jesus name it is done" and he released his hand from contact on my forhead the Power of God, He, The Holy Spirit, came back into my body and with great power and took possession. I laid down easily on the floor and within seconds I was stiff and couldn't move. The Holy Spirit

---

41. Respondent #0004.
42. Respondent #0465, Episcopalian, female, age 45.
43. Respondent #1422, Presbyterian, female, age 39.

had *complete control* over my body and I was on my back for 5½ hours before I was again able of my own strength and will to get up. All morning and next day I felt the power vitalizing me with great energy. When it wore off I was left weak in my own natural body. I was weak in the natural because this was the third day of fasting.[44]

It becomes clear from these examples that the distinction between ecstatic experiences and responsive experiences of the salvational variety is somewhat difficult to draw. Clearly, there is a sense of intimacy and relatedness between the human and divine actors during encounters marked by the divine designation of the person as of special interest and worth—chosen for divine approval. But such intimacy, which is likely to be a once-in-a-lifetime encounter, falls short of what we mean to call ecstasy. *Ecstasy* denotes a sense of union and distinct involvement between the actors. Seeing how ideal examples of the salvational and ecstatic can be distinguished from one another is not difficult—to a sense of being marked and chosen is contrasted a sense of being engulfed by divine love usually accompanied by extraordinary sensory manifestations and psychic states akin to loss of consciousness or seizures. The difficulty lies in deciding the status of borderline encounters—the extremely intense salvation or the relatively mild ecstasy. Here, for now, we can only suggest focusing on the emphasis given to being chosen as against being embraced, and also note that salvational experiences may lead directly into ecstatic experiences during a single divine encounter.

IV. THE REVELATIONAL EXPERIENCE

The fourth, and least common, type of religious experience is the *revelational*. Here the divine has not only taken the person to his bosom, but into his confidence. The recipient is given a message concerning divine wishes or intentions. Upon occasion, the divine may give such messages through signs or symbols,

---

44. Respondent #2896, Assemblies of God, male, age 45. The circumstances preceding this experience and accompanying it seem worth emphasizing. The respondent clearly was greatly concerned about reaching the divine, as evidenced by earlier elaborate dreams and visions which he pondered a good deal. The experience took place in a situation designed to produce great emotional response to religion—a revival meeting—the respondent well understood the rhetoric concerning these experiences and came seeking and expecting one, and as a guarantee, almost, he had not eaten for several days.

and some men have even claimed the divinity sent them written messages, but, typically, revelations are spoken. This raises the issue, which we have postponed until now, of visions and voices as characteristics of religious experiences.

Visions — occurrences which persons define as visually beholding the divinity — may accompany any or all of the types of religious experiences we have discussed, although they are probably more common during the more intimate varieties. However, even confirming experiences can take the form of a vision — the divinity is seen, but does not acknowledge the presence of the viewer:

> One Sunday in Church I visualized Christ on the Cross. This was a very moving experience I can not explain.[45]

Voices, on the other hand, by definition cannot be part of a confirming experience since if the divine speaks to you he acknowledges your presence. Furthermore, in a general sense any time the divine speaks one might say he has given the auditor a message. Yet, we make the revelational category a messy one indeed if we include all experiences accompanied by a voice. The criteria for classifying voice-accompanied religious encounters can be taken from the content of what was said. If the voice simply acknowledged the person's existence, summoned him to salvation, urged him to be comforted, or gave directions on how to solve problems or escape trouble, and the like, then we may classify it as part of a responsive experience. If the voice speaks primarily of love, blessing, or affection, then it is likely to be part of an ecstatic experience. However, if the voice imparts *confidential information about the future, divine nature or plans,* then we must consider it to be revelational.

Even having excluded a variety of divine messages from consideration as revelations, we are still faced with an extraordinarily heterogeneous genre of religious experience. For the revelational, as now constituted, applies equally to persons receiving divine instructions to grow a beard and to those presented with new theologies. For this reason, we shall introduce three further distinguishing characteristics which, if treated dichotomously, would generate an eight-fold typology of revela-

---

45. Respondent #141, Methodist, male, age 30.

tionary experiences.[46] In this chapter, we shall not attempt to consider systematically the cells of the typology, but shall limit discussion to the variables and sketch some of the more interesting combinations.

Perhaps the most crucial distinction to be drawn is that between revelations which are *orthodox* and those which are *heterodox*. By *orthodox* revelations we refer to divine messages which are consonant with existing interpretations of divine nature, will, and desires, and which, at most, simply elaborate on what is already accepted as true. This is best illustrated by saintly and papal revelations. It seems likely that most revelations are orthodox, since cultural innovation is a relatively uncommon human activity. However, the possibility of heterodox revelations makes this type of religious experience fraught with disruptive potential for existing religious institutions (and those secular institutions which are sanctioned by prevailing theology), for the information imparted by the divinity may contradict and challenge prevailing theological 'truths.' As James S. Coleman has noted:

> . . . one consequence of the 'communication with God' is that every man who so indulges is in communication with a different 'person' outside society; a person he has in part shaped with his own thoughts. That is, whenever a mystic or a monk or a devout believer engages in meditation and interpretation of the scripture, he can create a new creed. This possibility poses a constant threat of cleavage within a religious group.[47]

We need only think of Jesus Christ for a classic example of the devastating role that revelations may play in the career of religious institutions. This threatening characteristic of revelations has led religious institutions in nearly all times and places to develop strict controls on revelationary activity, and often to ban it entirely. Foremost among these controls in Western society have been means for distinguishing 'true' from 'false' revelations. The standard employed has been orthodoxy, the argument being that, since no true revelations could be hetero-

---

46. As is evident in the discussion, however, these variables tend to be continua rather than simple dichotomies.

47. James S. Coleman, "Social Cleavage and Social Change," *Journal of Social Issues*, XII (1956), pp. 49–50. Leuba also wrote of this disruptive potential of revelations, *op. cit.*, p. 406.

dox, *heterodox revelations* are self-impeaching and false by definition. As the New Testament author of *I John* put it:

> But do not trust any and every spirit, my friends; test the spirits, to see whether they are from God, for among those who have gone into the world there are many prophets falsely inspired. This is how we may recognize the Spirit of God: every spirit which acknowledges that Jesus Christ has come in the flesh is from God, and every spirit which does not thus acknowledge is not from God.
>
> (4:1–3; The New English Bible)

Subsequently, the criteria for judging the authenticity of spirits were considerably elaborated as Christian orthodoxy took on greater detail; nevertheless the logic remained the same.

This distinction between 'good' and 'evil' spirits is closely related to notions of black and white magic, and in the Catholic tradition is complemented by the practices of canonization and anathematization. But despite these controls and the many other mechanisms which have been employed to preclude or channel revelationary activity,[48] men continue to return from their encounters with divinity with new and heretical versions of 'eternal truth.' Even the contemporary American scene, for all its

---

48. Among these are attempts to bring closure to revelations by declaring that "the age of revelations is past," or that "the Word is complete." Another technique has been through role differentiation—limiting divine access to incumbents of speical roles over which the institution has maximum control. For example, the Roman Catholic Church tends to hold that asceticism is necessary for revelationary experiences and thus to limit such activity to those within the Church hierarchy, especially those in cloisters, where the institution's control of the practitioners is extensive. This kind of restriction may also take the form of only limiting who may interpret revelations, while allowing revelationary activity to be carried on generally. Thus, all Pentecostals are encouraged to 'speak in tongues,' but only a select few, clergymen usually, are recognized as having the gift for translating the 'tongues' into English. Institutions may also attempt to cöopt new revelations, that is, turn them to their own purposes and thus rob the revelations of potential divisiveness. The proliferation of Catholic orders has had this function and kept many potential heresies and religious revolutionaries within the Church. Max Weber has pointed out the differences in the degree to which prophecy was allowed in several ancient societies and has related this to the political structure. Weber's distinction deals with the *methods* by which the prophet acted on the basis of his message and is not directly relevant to the message receiving experience itself. In the present study, we are more concerned with what Weber called *ethical* prophecy since it typically derived from a revelationary experience of the prophet. *Exemplary* prophecy, when it did not involve revelation, falls outside our consideration. See Reinhard Bendix, *Max Weber, An Intellectual Portrait* (Garden City: Anchor Books, 1962), pp. 247–248.

secularization, abounds in messiahs, prophets, and messengers bearing new revelations and often acknowledging new gods.[49] Hence, the distinction between orthodox and heterodox revelations remains of both historical and current use for classifying and investigating religious experience.

A further division in revelationary experiences may be made between what might be called *enlightenment* and *commission*. By *enlightenment*, we mean to indicate that aspect of divine communiqués which provides information concerning ultimate truths, and by *commission*, instructions to take particular actions to further divine designs. That is to say, the divine may be perceived as simply offering information, or he may also commission the recipient to play a divinely inspired role in human affairs. For example, many Catholic saints felt themselves recipients of extensive insights into proper doctrine, without being called upon to go forth and do much of anything about it. Others were given divine missions such as organizing crusades to free the Holy Land or agitating for moral reforms. While these two varieties of revelations are analytically distinct, it should be noted that they frequently occur together and, indeed, commissions are perhaps most commonly combined with enlightenment, although the reverse is true to a slighter degree.

Enlightenment itself proves amenable to subdivision into what we shall call the *prophetic* and the *theological* types. The *prophetic* designates enlightenment concerning future events and states in the empirical world, while the *theological* refers to enlightenment on eternal verities (e.g., the nature of divine will and character) of a timeless, other-worldly kind. Either variety of enlightenment may or may not be combined with a commission, and we may look to the prophets of the Old Testament for classic instances of revelations which commissioned men to act on the basis of their foreknowledge of impending events. Typically, it would seem, prophesy foretells calamity, often the imminent destruction of society or even of the material world.

---

49. The resurgence of scholarly interest in religion has yet to produce a sophisticated analysis of the cult. However, there has recently been a spate of journalist treatments of America's 'kook milieu,' including several useful summaries, among them: Charles S. Braden, *These Also Believe* (New York: The Macmillan Co., 1949); Richard R. Mathison, *Faiths, Cults, and Sects of America* (Indianapolis and New York: The Bobbs-Merrill Co., Inc., 1960); and Marcus Bach, *Strange Sects and Curious Cults* (New York: Dodd, Mead & Co., 1961).

Such revealed prophetic visions remain potent social forces in the modern world, and are especially common among groups whose old world view has corroded under the impact of contact with a technically more advanced and complex culture.[50]

The third distinction which we shall note concerns the scope of the revelation's application. Perhaps most frequently, revelations have significance or application only for the recipient or for some of his personal associates.[51] For example, many prophetic revelations foretell the nearing death of loved ones or provide other personal foresights. Commissions too may only concern the personal behavior of the recipient. However, on some occasions the message has relevance for all mankind, or for at least significant numbers of men, such as in the case of new theologies, eschatological prophesies, or commissions to launch social reforms. We shall speak of the former, those with only individual relevance, as *personal revelations,* and of the latter as *general revelations.*

In future research it should prove worthwhile to consider each of the possible combinations of these three variables and to discuss empirical examples of each, seeking to discover differences in the causes and consequences of these types of revelationary experiences.[52]

Having elaborated the specific subtypes in our taxonomy,

50. An extensive literature exists on the religious innovations of groups experiencing rapid social change, especially primitives. The Cargo Cults of the Southern Pacific Islanders in recent years, the Ghost Shirt Dances of the Plains Indians, and the current rash of prophets and messiahs in Korea and Japan are particularly good examples of this phenomenon.

51. The Seventh Day Adventist leader, Mother White, constantly went into trances and received instructions from heaven about minor daily activities (for example, what style bloomers she ought to wear), especially when her associates were reluctant to consent to her wishes. See: Ronald M. Deutsch, *The Nuts Among the Berries* (New York: Ballantine Books, 1961), especially Chapters V and VI. Another famous American female religious leader, Mrs. Mary Baker G. Eddy, was similarly fortunate in obtaining constant divine support for her wishes. See: Edwin Franden Dakin, *Mrs. Eddy* (New York: Charles Scribner's Sons, 1929).

52. Two examples of such 'cell filling': The experience commonly referred to by Christians as 'The Call,' often required of men who desire to enter the clergy, would be classified in this scheme as a revelation that was (1) personal; (2) orthodox: (3) a commission. The revelation of Mrs. Kreech, reported by Festinger, *et al.,* that the world would be destroyed while a small group of initiates would be rescued the night before by a flying saucer, would be classified as (1) general; (2) heterodox; (3) prophetic; and (4) a commission. See: Leon Festinger, Henry W. Riecken, and Stanley Schachter, *When Prophecy Fails* (Minneapolis: University of Minnesota Press, 1956).

we must consider criteria of order. The presentation of the types was governed by an order of analytic complexity—simple to elaborate—and it was also suggested that they represent discrete stages through which persons pass in developing greater intimacy in their contacts with divinity.[53] This is not to suggest that the less complex and less intimate types are *always* experienced by persons prior to more complex and intimate contacts, but most often this is probably the course of passage. It is also probably true that several stages may be passed through during one spiritual encounter, the incident beginning with a simpler state and passing shortly into the next more complex type. However, it is *not* suggested that having attained a more complex type marks the end of less complex experiences. On the contrary, indications seem to be that the more intimate contacts one has, the more often the less intimate contacts are experienced too. For example, nuns who have had ecstatic experiences report voluminously on daily or even hourly confirming experiences. Some of the West Coast millenarians had confirming and responsive experiences as often as several times a day, commonly had ecstatic experiences once a week or oftener, and had revelationary experiences fortnightly. This suggests that not only does this ordering of types of religious experience indicate their frequency within a population, but also their frequency for individuals who manifest all four types.

Besides being ordered on the basis of increased intimacy and decreased frequency, this succession of the types reflects the degree to which they are encouraged or discouraged by religious institutions as well as by secular norms. While confirming experiences are strongly encouraged by most churches, responsive experiences are encouraged by fewer churches, ecstatic experiences are encouraged by even fewer, and, as we have noted,

---

53. This order refers to the four major types only, and we are not presently prepared to suggest ordering among the subtypes within a major category. Yet, it should be noted that within each type runs a dimension of intensity. For example, the salvational experience may be a very mild affair: One has only a very vague sense that the divine is beckoning and choosing him, or, at the other extreme, the salvational experience may involve a vision of the divine countenance and hearing the divine voice seal one's salvation.

Similarly, there are clearly degrees of ecstasy, from a sense of being touched and adored by the divine to the extraordinarily intimate and lengthy encounters of the Grand Mystics—some of whom thought they had entered into sexual union with the divine. Revelations, too, may vary from the trivial to grand unveilings of eternal truths.

revelational experiences are discouraged or even opposed by the vast majority of religious institutions. Secular society values religious experiences in the same order, and the public definition of these types ranges from 'saints' to 'nuts.' It has been truly said that many who were canonized during the Middle Ages would be in asylums today.[54]

Before concluding this taxonomic exercise, one further matter must be considered. Thus far we have discussed only experiences that constitute encounters with 'good' divinity; however, the voluminous reports of Satanic encounters—including such famous incidents as the Inccubi attacks on the nuns of Loudon[55] or Martin Luther's violent engagements with a variety of devils[56] —suggest that, historically, 'evil' and 'good' supernatural forces have been about equally common.[57] Simply to keep these two kinds of contacts separate we may speak of *divine* and *diabolic* religious experience. Because there seem to be reasonable grounds to assert that diabolic contacts have played nearly as important a role as the divine in Western religious life, any attempt to provide a classificatory scheme for religious experiences should address both kinds of supernatural contacts.

Since the same elements are involved in diabolic contacts as in the divine—encounters of increasing intimacy with what is

---

54. This has been nicely demonstrated by public and ecclesiastical responses to the small grass roots movement of 'speaking in tongues,' or glossolalia, which has recently appeared in liberal Protestant churches in America, especially on the Pacific Coast. The movement has been most concentrated in the Episcopal Church (although many actual participants come from many other main-line denominations) with a major center of activity in Portland, Oregon, and a second in Corte Medera, California. In May of 1963, the glossolalia movement became a nine-day wonder in the San Francisco press when the Episcopal Bishop of California, James A. Pike, condemned the practice in a much publicized pastoral letter. Bishop Pike's letter, interestingly enough, combined both religious and secular sanctions against the practice— he pointed both to dangers of heresy and to psychological dangers inherent in this form of group religious ecstasy. The public seemed generally amused by accounts of grown men mouthing gibberish and attributing it to the Holy Spirit, and references to 'the gift of tongues' were incorporated into jokes and wisecracks current at the time.

55. See: Aldous Huxley, *The Devils of Loudon* (New York: Harpers, 1952); also, Taylor, *op. cit.*

56. This important aspect of Luther's life and character, largely ignored in the vast literature about this great Protestant, is treated sensitively by Erik H. Erikson, in his *Young Man Luther* (New York: W. W. Norton and Co., 1962).

57. For an excellent summary see: Jules Michelet, *Satanism and Witchcraft: A Study of Medieval Superstition,* translated by A. R. Allinson (New York: The Citadel Press, 1960).

defined as a supernatural consciousness—it is possible to directly adapt the types we have just presented to the 'evil' experiences. Because, as will be seen, this adaptation is relatively uncomplicated, and because the general remarks made about divine experiences also apply to the diabolic, we shall only briefly sketch the taxonomy of diabolic experiences.

I. THE CONFIRMING EXPERIENCE

The *confirming* experience, it will be recalled, includes a generalized sense of sacredness; correspondingly, the vaguest and most ill-defined diabolic experiences can be described as a *generalized sense of evil.* Here we mean to classify such events as persons experiencing the presence of evil*ness* or sinful*ness.* The more focused confirming experiences with the diabolic, like those with the divine, are classified as *a specific awareness of the special presence of an evil supernatural being or force.*

II. THE RESPONSIVE EXPERIENCE

The *responsive,* of course, refers to encounters during which the supernatural actor acknowledges the presence of the individual. This acknowledgement may take three forms:

The *temptational* designates those occasions when the individual feels the evil being has specifically chosen to beckon him to sin and evil and to draw him from divine grace, which, of course, is the diabolic counterpart of the *salvational* experience. Many of our respondents reported such diabolic encounters:

> Being tempted to steal something. I felt that the devil was tempting me.[58]
> . . . being tempted by the Devil . . .[59]

Our data indicate that among Protestants temptational experiences are nearly as common as salvational experiences, and considerably more common among Catholics. Thirty-two per cent of the Protestants were "sure" they had experienced "a feeling of being tempted by the Devil," while 36 per cent of the Catholics were "sure." Again variation among Protestant groups was great: from 11 per cent of the Congregationalists to 76 per cent of the Southern Baptists.

---

58. Respondent #0448, Gospel Lighthouse, female, age 21.
59. Respondent #0491, Baptist, male, age 16.

The *damnational* corresponds to the *miraculous*. Here the evil supernatural forces are seen as intervening in worldly affairs to reward 'sin' and thwart 'righteousness.' The folk-saying, "the Devil helps his own," captures the essence of the experience. The damnational experience differs from the temptational primarily by being an unexpected intervention in time of trouble or need rather than an offer of inducements to act.

The *accursed* is the diabolic counterpart of the *sanctioning*, and refers to instances when the evil being is perceived as intervening in the material world to bring misfortune to individuals who have rejected sinfulness. Among the West Coast cultists, who defined the world in precise terms of a struggle between evil and divine supernatural forces, all failure and misfortune were explicitly explained as 'satanic influences,' directed towards them because they were God's elect. These people fell down because Satan pushed them, lost jobs because Satan acted on the manager's judgments, and when their water pipes burst, that was Satan plaguing them too.

III. THE TERRORIZING EXPERIENCE

The *Ecstatic* experience has its counterpart in the *terrorizing* experience. The latter refers to highly emotional encounters with diabolic agencies during which the individual feels horrified and terrified by a specific sense of being intimately assaulted by an evil being. As in the case of divine ecstasy, the best examples are to be drawn from the Grand Mystics of the monastic Middle Ages, especially the Inccubi and Succubi attacks, which Martin Luther described as the propensity of devils to come in the night and lie under men and on top of women.[60] The West Coast cultists frequently experienced loathsome 'Satanic attacks' in the night which left them terrified and shaken.

IV. THE POSSESSIONAL EXPERIENCE

While the *revelational* indicates messages from the divine being, and perhaps coparticipation in action with that being, the *possessional* refers to similar relations with the diabolic. Here we may classify perceptions of being given Satanic messages and confidences, and in the ultimate instances, feeling oneself taken over as an agent of Satan and lending assistance to him.

---

60. Erikson, *op. cit.*, p. 60.

While possessional experiences may seem outlandish in these relatively unbedeviled days, they are historically common, and, indeed may still be found. After all, many of the wretches burned during the witch hunts of the Middle Ages actually believed themselves to be in league with the devil. The West Coast cultists frequently explained away their own behavior, such as fits of temper or violations of religious prohibitions, in terms of having been taken over by Satan, and hence not personally responsible for these acts. They also frequently identified outsiders — including, eventually, the sociologists who observed them — as conscious agents of Satan.

SUMMARY

In summary, an attempt has been made to show that religious experiences, both diabolic and divine, can be analytically broken down into four general types and several further subtypes, on the basis of the configuration of relationships between the divine and human actor during any spiritual encounter. Moreover, we have argued that these four general types may be similarly ordered on the basis of complexity, intimacy of the inter-actor relationship, frequency, both in their distribution within populations and frequency of occurrence for individuals, and variation in the degree to which they are encouraged or discouraged by both religious and secular norms. Furthermore, we have suggested that this order represents a developmental model and that persons pass from the less complex to the more complex during the career of their religious encounters. A complete summary of the scheme is presented in Table 3.1.

Finally, perhaps a word or two should be said on the utility of and criteria for assessing conceptual schemes such as this in scientific inquiry. Any phenomenon or cluster of phenomena can be classified or characterized in a great many different ways. Aside from clarity, there is no compelling intrinsic reason why any particular way ought to be preferred. Yet, any conceptualization of a phenomenon, any attempt to say that it *is*, requires some assumptions that certain aspects of this thing are its essence while other things about it are trivial or irrelevant. When we ask irrelevant to what or to whom, we come to the underlying character of all scientific definitions or conceptualization. For the answer is: irrelevant to the tasks of predicting the occurrence of this phenomenon and other phenomena to

TABLE 3-1
A Taxonomy of Religious Experience

	DIVINE	DIABOLIC

MOST FREQUENT / MOST ENCOURAGED	I. *Confirming:*
	1. Generalized sense of sacredness
	2. Specific awareness of divine presence
	
	II. *Responsive:* awareness of divine presence *and* a corresponding sense that the divine is aware of you
	1. Salvational: being acknowledged special or chosen by divinity
	2. Miraculous: helpful divine intervention in one's worldly affairs
	3. Sanctioning: divine intervention to punish or prevent wrongdoing.
	
	III. *Ecstatic:* intimate and affective contact with divinity
	
	IV. *Revelational:* becoming a confidant and/or agent of the divine
	1. Orthodox-Heterodox
	2. Enlightenment and/or Commission
	  a. theological
	  b. prophetic
	3. Personal-General
		I. *Confirming*
		1. Generalized sense of evil
		2. Specific awareness of diabolic presence
		
		II. *Responsive:* awareness of evil presence *and* a corresponding sense that the evil being is aware of you.
		1. Temptational: being singled out to sin, evil, etc.
		2. Damnational: diabolic intervention to reward evil
		3. Accursed: diabolic intervention in worldly affairs bringing misfortune
		
		III. *Terrorizing:* intimate and loathsome contact with diabolic
		
		IV. *Possessional:* becoming a confidant and/or agent of the diabolic
		1. Orthodox-Heterodox
		2. Enlightenment and/or Commission
		  a. theological
		  b. prophetic
		3. Personal-General

LEAST FREQUENT / LEAST ENCOURAGED		

which we think it is related. Scientific concepts are essentially utilitarian as is the scientific definition of truth itself. For example. when Newton formulated his mechanics, he defined bodies as having certain basic properties such as mass, but quite ignored the fact that such bodies also have the property of color. Basic properties, from Newton's point of view, were those which would allow him to make accurate predictions about future states in a system of bodies. For this purpose, as it turned out, color was indeed irrelevant. The test of scientific concepts, then, comes from their usefulness in making predictions about various events. It is on the basis of how well they suit such tasks that we speak of them as true. Indeed, from the scientific perspective one does not even ask whether they are 'real,' for there is no other acceptable sense in which such concepts are believed to exist. No man can point, for instance, to a 'market' as economists use that term. The notion of the market is simply an abstract construct which allows for the summary of certain primary features of economic behavior in a fashion that facilitates accurate predictions about future states of affairs.

While the taxonomy we have elaborated in this chapter seems appropriate for classifying the reports written by respondents, any final judgment of its worth can only come when its utility is demonstrated in empirical investigations of man's religious experiences. If it is to be useful, the assumption that these types of religious experience represent a *developing sequence* of felt encounters between men and the supernatural must be verified by finding empirically that the data scale in this manner. If this proves to be the case, then the various theoretical considerations we have presented will give us some clearer understanding of why the data do scale, and ought to point out some beginnings for predicting the occurrence of religious experiences. To a limited extent, these tasks will be undertaken in Chapter 8.

PART II

RELIGION IN CONTEMPORARY AMERICA

THUS far, we have considered broad conceptual questions of how religion is to be conceived of from a social-science perspective. Within this general framework, we shall now turn to more concrete issues. Specifically, we shall be concerned with the character and status of religion in modern America.

Chapter 4

The Religious Revival in America?

THIS chapter employs the dimensions of religious involvement developed in Chapter 2 as a basis for assessing and clarifying issues and evidence in the debate over whether or not there was a revival in American religiousness following World War II.

Recent assessments of the state of religion in America appear curiously inconsistent. Some observers, a preponderance of them perhaps, perceive a major postwar revival in American religion.[1] Others, while agreeing that interest in religion has heightened in recent years, argue that the increase does not represent a revival so much as the continuation of a long-term upward trend in the religiosity of Americans.[2] Still others contend to the contrary, that the long-term trend is towards the increasing secularization of American life.[3] And, most recently, the idea has been expressed that the remarkable quality of American religion over the last century and more has been its stability; there has been a propensity neither towards greater religiousness nor towards greater secularization.[4]

---

1. Will Herberg, *Protestant, Catholic, and Jew* (Garden City, N.Y.: Doubleday & Co., 1955), pp. 59–84.

2. Michael Argyle, *Religious Behaviour* (London: Routledge and Kegan Paul, 1958).

3. William H. Whyte, Jr., *The Organization Man* (New York: Simon and Schuster, 1956).

4. Seymour Martin Lipset, "Religion in America: What Religious Revival?" *Columbia University Forum*, II:2 (Winter, 1959).

Not all of these assessments can be correct—or can they? The purpose of the present chapter is to cast a critical eye on the attempts being made to assess the state of religion in America and hopefully, in the process, to afford some new perspectives for studying religion's place in American life.

These disagreements over whether or not a revival has in fact occurred and concerning the nature of the long-term trend in American religiosity may simply be a result of some observers being mistaken and others being correct. This would appear to be a plausible conclusion, given the overtly contradictory assessments which have been made. On reflection, however, disagreement may stem from other factors. Religion is not necessarily the same thing to all men; perhaps, therefore, the source of the disagreement is that different observers are defining religion in different ways. Some may equate it with belief, others with practice, and still others with experience. If it should turn out that there has been an increase in one, a decline in the second, and no change in the third, much of the disagreement would be explained if not resolved.

A further possibility is that the observers agree on definitions but still disagree on what has happened because they adopt different criteria or indicators in making their assessments. Some may base their judgment on how many people go to church and others on how many so-called blue laws are still on the statute books. But even agreement here would not assure consensus, for there is still the evidence to consider, and different observers may turn to different evidence of the same indicator or interpret the same evidence in different ways. To sort out the pieces, some effort to order definitions, indicators, and evidence seems an obvious prerequisite.

RELIGIOUSNESS: DEFINITIONS, INDICATORS, AND EVIDENCE[5]

As pointed out in Chapter 2, religion, religiousness, and religiosity are of a *genre* of words which appear almost to defy definition, at least in a way to which everyone will agree. One is

---

5. In writing this section of the chapter, the authors benefited greatly from what they have learned about concept and index construction from Professor Paul F. Lazarsfeld of Columbia University. For a brief account of the principles involved, see Paul F. Lazarsfeld, "Evidence and Inference in Social Research," *Daedalus*, LXXXVII:4 (1958), 88–130.

tempted to suggest that there are as many definitions as there are people offering them. Yet, if we carefully examine the imagery which the words stimulate, it is not that people disagree on definitions so much as that they use these words, which are multidimensional in meaning, in an unidimensional way. They tend to equate religion with belief *or* with practice *or* with experience without recognizing consciously that the other dimensions exist. While it may not be possible to secure agreement on the importance of the dimensions, it is possible to specify what they are and, in so doing, to make manifest the different frames of reference with in which the religiousness of an entity—whether it be a person, a religious group or some larger collective such as a nation or a society—may be observed and assessed.

For present purposes, it seems helpful to think of religiousness as a concept which is divisible into five dimensions: dimensions which in Chapter 2 we called the experiential, the ritualistic, the ideological, the intellectual, and the consequential.

These dimensions, it was earlier proposed, are the principal frames of reference which may be adopted in assessing religiousness. The dimensions are interrelated rather than independent of one another and an assessment made within one dimension often implies an assessment in another. The dimensions are nevertheless a useful heuristic device for examining religious behavior.

It is not always possible to tell from the observation or assessment itself what dimension the observer has in mind. For example, we cannot tell the observer's frame of reference from his simple observation that "America is in the midst of a religious revival." He may be thinking along a single dimension or using some combination of the dimensions we have identified. Any attempt to be scientific about assessing the religious state of an individual or collective of some kind obviously requires that the observer make clear the dimension(s) that he is talking about. Any discussion of the religious revival, for example, requires that the discussants clarify whether they perceive the revival as occurring on one, several, or all of the five dimensions.

A further requirement is that the criteria or indicators of religiousness within a dimension also be cited. Indicators are simply the means used to locate objects within a dimension, i.e., to order them according to some degree of religiousness. The specification of the indicators constitutes, in effect, the observer's defining what he means by 'religious' within a given dimension.

Two types of indicators may be distinguished: indicators of degree and indicators of kind. The notion of a religious revival implies a distinction in *degree,* namely, that America is more religious today than in the immediate past. Distinctions in *kind* may also be made within any dimension, though these are less relevant to a discussion of the so-called revival than are distinctions in degree. The statement that Pentecostalists adhere to a fundamentalist theology (belief), whereas Congregationalists subscribe to a liberal theology (belief), represents a distinction in kind made within the ideological dimension.

In our everyday conversation, we constantly use indicators to make distinctions within concepts. Some of the indicators which we use—feet and inches to represent height, pounds and ounces to represent weight, and miles per hour to represent speed—have the quality of being accepted virtually universally, at least in our society. Indicators of other concepts, on the other hand, are not universally agreed upon; in some instances, they may almost be private to an individual.

Friendliness, for example, is a concept for which the indicators are neither precise nor widely agreed upon. It would be much easier to obtain consensus on how tall a person is than on how friendly he is. Actually, it is one of the functions of science—physical and social—to systematize the process of developing indicators and to develop a means—in the form of measuring instruments—for applying indicators. The measuring stick, the scale, and the speedometer are good examples of instruments developed to allow the uniform application of indicators for such concepts as height, weight, and speed. Intelligence tests, while less highly developed, constitute another example of the end point in the process we are attempting to describe. Such tests were developed by first specifying the dimensions of the concept of intelligence and then going on to construct indicators to distinguish individuals within dimensions. Finally, measuring instruments (tests) were evolved to allow the indicators to be uniformly applied by different observers.

In the development of indicators of religion, we are at a stage much closer to where we stand with respect to developing indicators of friendliness than that of developing indicators of height. The problem has not been approached in a scientific way. Yet, underlying any observation about the religiousness of an entity are indicators which the observer implicitly, if not explicitly, has in mind. This is true of those with scholarly interests in religion as well as those who comment on religion in the course of ordinary conversation.

However, the relative absence of precise indicators to make religious distinctions is, in some measure, a function of the lack of available evidence and the difficulty of obtaining it. That we can think of more indicators within the ritualistic dimension, for example, than within other dimensions results from the fact that ritual behavior and religious practice are more likely to be visible and conspicuous and therefore readily measurable.

Despite these problems, the dimensions of religious commitment developed in Chapter 2 provide a framework for examining the claims and counterclaims concerning the state of religion in America. In such an examination, we shall want to consider the frame(s) of reference which different observers adopt in making their assessments, the indicators of religiousness which they use to make distinctions within dimensions, and the kind of evidence to which they turn in applying their indicators. To do so will probably not enable us to reach conclusions upon which everyone will agree. In the last analysis, conclusions in this area will always vary depending upon individual commitments to different conceptions of religion. But we can hope to clarify the current confusion and perhaps establish some new perspectives for assessing religiousness in the future.

THE RELIGIOUSNESS OF AMERICANS:
PAST AND PRESENT

The current controversy about religion in America revolves about several issues rather than a single one. First, has there or has there not been a postwar increase in the religiousness of Americans? Second, does the postwar increase, if such there has been, represent a revival of religious interest, or is it rather the accelerated continuation of a long-term upward trend in the religiosity of Americans? Third, and in a sense countervailing both of these questions, has there or has there not been an increasing secularization in American life? Let us first consider the proposition that there has been a substantial postwar increase in religiosity, leaving aside, for the moment, whether this is more appropriately labeled a revival or an acceleration of a long-term upward trend.

Judging from the indicators of religiousness adopted and the evidence cited, the supporters of this propostion give greatest weight to the ritualistic dimension of religion. Some of their indicators touch on the ideological and experiential dimensions but none on the consequential dimension. The principal ritual indicators used are the proportion of Americans who are church members, the proportion who attend church on any given Sunday, the investment in church buildings, and contributions to religious institutions. On the belief dimension, indicators are almost exclusively limited to the proportion of Americans who hold to certain religious beliefs, most especially a belief in God. A further indicator, also classifiable as indicating belief, is constituted by the degree to which religion and religious institutions are subjected to criticism in the mass media and among intellectual elites. Indicators such as the amount of interest expressed in religious books and music and in commodities having a religious motif, are somewhat more difficult to classify, but we shall place them in the experiential dimension on the assumption that they represent spiritual concern in some undefinable way.

The claim is made that on each of these indicators, America has become increasingly more religious over the last few decades. Perhaps the most frequently cited evidence to this effect is statistical information on the proportion of Americans who belong to the nation's churches. Such information, compiled regularly by the Bureau of Research and Survey of the National Council of Churches in the U.S.A., is reported annually in the *Yearbook of American Churches*. Church membership as a percentage of the population for the period 1940 to 1962 is reported to have been as follows.[6]

The following indicates church membership as a percentage of total United States population:

1940 . . . . .49%
1950 . . . . .57%
1955 . . . . .60.9%
1956 . . . . .62%
1957 . . . . .61%

6. Benson Y. Landis, ed., *Yearbook of American Churches for 1964*, National Council of Churches of Christ in the U.S.A., 1964.

1958 . . . . .63%
1959 . . . . .63.6%
1960 . . . . .63.6%
1961 . . . . .63.4%
1962 . . . . .63.4%

Ignoring for the moment questions regarding the reliability of these statistics on church membership, the data indicate a long-term trend of growth from 1940 into the late fifties. However,since 1958 there has been no increase. Data on attendance at church on a typical Sunday does not show as consistent nor as great an increase in religious participation as the statistics on church membership, but they do confirm the leveling-off of any upward trend by the late 1950s. The data are the results of national polls conducted at irregular intervals by the American Institute of Public Opinion (Gallup poll) since 1939.[7] The percentage of adults who had attended church during the week preceding the interview is indicated below:

February, 1939 . . . . .41%
November, 1940 . . . . .37%
May, 1942 . . . . .36%
May, 1947 . . . . .45%
April, 1950 . . . . .39%
July, 1954 . . . . .46%
December, 1955 . . . . .49%
April, 1957 . . . . .51%
December, 1957 . . . . .47%
Annual Audit, 1959 . . . . .47%
Annual Audit, 1960 . . . . .47%
Annual Audit, 1961 . . . . .47%
Annual Audit, 1962 . . . . .46%
Annual Audit, 1963 . . . . .46%
Annual Audit, 1964 . . . . .45%

As can be readily seen in these statistics, the proportion of Americans attending church increased from 1950 through 1957, but then the upward trend ended and subsequently seems to be slowly falling. Thus, statistics on membership and church attendance indicate a moderate postwar increase in religious participa-

7. Reported in Landis, *op. cit.,*p. 283.

tion did occur. If this is to be called a revival, then it must also be acknowledged that the revival ended around 1957.

Reflecting the measurable increases in church membership and attendance are the increases in investments in church buildings and in per capita donations to congregational expenses and benevolences. In 1946, $76,000,000 was invested in church construction; by 1953 the figure had risen to $474,000,000.[8] Donations to eighteen Protestant denominations, computed as per capita contributions as a proportion of per capita income, declined between 1940 and 1943 but have increased almost steadily thereafter through 1952, the date of the last available statistics.[9]

The evidence on the proportion of Americans who identify themselves with a religious denomination and who express a belief in God suggests an increase on these indicators though comparable data over the last decade and a half is not available. However, the fact that in March, 1957, 96.4 percent of the American population fourteen years and over identified themselves with a religious denomination[10] and that a number of recent polls have shown that over 95 per cent believe in God[11] is taken as corroborating the trend data available on other indicators in the sense that earlier figures could scarcely have been any higher.

When it comes to such indicators as the amount of criticism of religion which exists and the degree to which religious subjects occupy attention in the mass media and popular arts, the evidence, while partly impressionistic, shows an increasingly favorable attitude towards religion over the last two decades.[12]

All of this evidence is by now well known and to elaborate further can only be repetitive. Does it justify the claim that there was a major postwar increase in religiousness in America? The claim may be questioned at several levels. First, the definition of religiousness which is implied in the indicators used omits any consideration of the consequential dimension, that is, the degree

---

8. Anonymous, "Construction of Religious Buildings," *Information Service,* National Council of the Churches of Christ in the U.S.A., May 8, 1954.

9. Argyle, *op. cit.,* p. 30.

10. Landis, *Yearbook for American Churches for 1959,* National Council of Churches of Christ in the U.S.A., 1958, p. 302.

11. Figures quoted in Herberg, *op. cit.,* p. 59. In Chapter 5 a reassessment is made of this seeming consensus on belief in God.

12. See Herberg, *op, cit.,* for a summation of this evidence, pp. 59–84.

to which religion increasingly or decreasingly has an effect on the way people act in daily life.

There is no authoritative way to decide whether or not the omission is a serious one. What contribution each of the dimensions makes or should make to the total concept—religion—is still a matter of judgment rather than fact. That the omission has been made, however, does reflect on the comprehensiveness of the claim.

More serious than this omission, however, is the inadequacy of the indicators to represent religiousness on any one or a combination of dimensions. Here, again, the point might be made that one must decide for himself how satisfactory the indicators are. Yet, to accept the indicators used as adequate representations of the concept is to ignore most of the issues which have maintained religion as a central feature of human life throughout time. On the other hand, there is also the possibility that there is little more to contemporary religion than what the indicators measure.

Leaving such issues for the reader to decide for himself, what about the evidence—how satisfactory is it? None of it actually is completely reliable although it is impossible to judge just exactly how reliable it is. The statistics on church membership are perhaps most suspect, judging from a perceptive critique of church statistics by W. H. Hudson.[13]

Hudson makes two crucial points. One, he notes that many of the denominations submitting the reports from which the over-all figures are compiled invariably report their membership in round numbers and report increases from year to year in round numbers. On logical grounds Hudson questions, for example, that the membership of the Church of Christ actually increased from 1,500,000 to 1,600,000 between 1955 and 1956 as the *Yearbook* reports. His second point is perhaps even more damaging. He indicates that the statistics make no provision for taking account of denominations which furnish membership reports for the first time in any given year. He cites the case of the Christ Unity Science Church which reports a membership of 682,172 in the 1952 *Yearbook*, the first year in which figures for this denomination ever appeared.[14] He claims that much of

13. W. H. Hudson, "Are Churches Really Booming?" *Christian Century*, LXXVII:51 (December 21, 1955), 1494–1496.

14. It is of incidental interest that this denomination does not appear in the *Yearbook* for 1959.

the increase from year to year can be accounted for by new denominations submitting membership reports for the first time.

Hudson is also concerned about the source of the so-called increase. He discovers, by looking at the statistics for the same denominations over time, that the largest increases are reported for the more fundamentalist denominations. The old line Protestant churches show no greater increase in membership from 1940 to 1952 than might have been expected given the general increase in population.

While casting considerable doubt on the reliability of the statistics, Hudson does not attempt to correct them in any systematic way. In general, he indicates that the method of compilation and reporting contributes to inflation rather than deflation.

To his observations may be added the additional one that congregations are notably lax in maintaining accuate reports on membership. Individuals are often retained on church rolls long after they have discontinued membership whether because of loss of interest or because of mobility. Given the high degree of mobility in the last decade and a half, there seems no doubt that some of the reported increase in church membership is a consequence of some indeterminate proportion of persons being counted more than once. In the sample of San Francisco area churches, referred to in Chapter 3, 14 per cent of the persons carried on the church rolls (both Protestant and Roman Catholic) should not have been, either because they had become members of another denomination, had moved away, or because they had died.

The Gallup poll data reporting an increase in church attendance, taken at face value, would appear less subject to criticism on reliability grounds. The method used to collect the data at different points in time was consistent, and logically, therefore, the changes observed would appear to be reliable. The data on contributions and on investments in church buildings is, in part at least, a reflection of the general prosperity but there seems no doubt about the increases reported. About contributions, however, Seymour Lipset makes the point that the per capita contributions in 1952 were lower than they were at the height of the depression.[15] The impressions, and the limited statistics underlying them, of increased interest in ideas and commodities with religious content cover so many aspects of popular culture, and

15. *Op. cit.*

the trend is so consistently upward, that one is convinced intuitively of their general reliability; however, the data have not been collected in such a way as to allow confirmation.

The evidence, then, while perhaps exaggerating the growth, appears reliable enough to justify a conclusion that, within the limitations of the indicators used, some postwar growth in religiousness has occurred.

The growth has been explained as a result both of the state of anxiety created by the 'cold war'[16] and of the need for third generation Americans to use religion to obtain some sense of identity to replace their rejection and subsequent loss of ethnic identity.[17] There is no evidence on which to check such interpretations or to offer alternative ones. However, as a further hypothesis, we would suggest that the increase may be, in part, the result of a self-fulfilling prophecy.

The earliest reports of the increase were based on the statistics of church membership issued by the National Council of Churches. These were given rather wide publicity in the late 1940s without any question being raised as to their reliability. It is conceivable that the publicity may have generated a commercial interest in producing and promoting religious literature, songs and plays with a religious motif, and commodities having religious connotations. The sudden flooding of the market with this material may have contributed to the impression that "religion was again in style," so to speak. This is how fads are generally created and there is some reason to suspect, given the current belief that the religious resurgence has reached its peak, that it may also have been no more than a fad.

Whether the increase represents a revival or an acceleration of religious interest has become an issue primarily because of a dispute over the accuracy of the historical statistics on church membership. These are also reported in the *Yearbook* with, however, the *caveat* that ". . . the figures in the table for 1920 and prior years are not on the same basis as those for 1930 and following years."[18] The statistics of church membership as percentage of population are:

---

16. Reinhold Niebuhr, "Is There a Revival of Religion?" *The New York Times Magazine,* November 10, 1950.

17. Herberg, *op. cit.*

18. Landis, 1964, *op. cit.*

1850	.16%
1860	.23%
1870	.18%
1880	.20%
1890	.22%
1900	.36%
1910	.43%
1920	.43%
1930	.47%
1940	.49%
1950	.57%
1955	.60.9%
1956	.62%
1957	.61%
1958	.63%
1959	.63.4%
1960	.63.6%
1961	.63.6%
1962	.63.4%

Taken at face value, the figures appear to show that the long-term trend in America has indeed been towards increased religious affiliation, thus supporting the contention that the current increase is more appropriately labeled an acceleration of a long-term trend than a revival. Will Herberg, for example, holds this view, though arguing for its support on slightly different grounds. Noting that 95 per cent of the American people in the 1950s regard themselves as belonging to some religious community, he comments:

"Such information as that which this survey provides is unfortunately not available for earlier times, and so direct comparison is impossible. But it seems safe to assume that these figures, reflecting the situation in the early 1950's, represent an all-time high in religious identification. Through the nineteenth century and well into the twentieth, America knew the militant secularist, the atheist or 'free-thinker' as a familiar figure in cultural life, along with considerably larger numbers of 'agnostics' who would have nothing to do with the churches and refused to identify themselves religiously. These still exist, of course, but their ranks are dwindling and they are becoming more and more inconspicuous, taking the American people as a whole. . . . The pervasiveness of religious identification may safely be put down as a significant feature of the America that has emerged in the past quarter of a century."[19]

Herberg's interpretation that the demise of the village atheist and the socially prominent militant secularist is evidence of an increase in religiousness, seems misconstrued. It is indisputable that great heretics in the tradition of Col. Robert G. Ingersoll no longer pack auditoriums and have little impact anywhere in America these days. But it is apparent too, that the targets of such nineteenth century skepticism have also largely vanished from American life. Such skepticism was primarily concerned with attacking fundamentalist Christian teachings about the material world — literal interpretations of the creation story, Noah and the Ark, and the other most magical and miraculous of fundamentalist teachings. Thus, the nineteenth century heretics responded to a direct collision between the developing physical and natural sciences and traditional Christian doctrines.

If it is granted that such attacks fail to gather any appreciable notice today, it must also be granted that such fundamentalist beliefs also fail to gather much militant support in the mainstream of theological thought. The attacks have ceased to have importance, not because a return of religiousness has caused them to be rejected, but because the battle has long since been won; most people now accept the truth of the basic charges of the nineteenth century heretics, and the church has accommodated itself to the findings of science. In mainstream American thought, both religious and secular, these issues have become irrelevant.

Perhaps the most poignant evidence that the demise of militant, anti-fundamentalist heresy signals religious change rather than religious revival is Mark Twain's *Letters from the Earth*. This volume attacking the fundamentalist Christianity of his day has recently been published, despite the fact that Twain himself felt it would be hundreds of years before publication would be possible. Rather than causing a storm of controversy and outrage, the book created little interest at all. It seemed merely quaint, for no one now takes the objects of Twain's attack seriously. This can hardly serve as evidence of a religious revival.

---

19. Herberg, *op. cit.*, pp. 59–60.

However, the claim that recent increases represent an acceleration of a general upward trend rests primarily on grounds of religious affiliation and identification. Lipset argues against the claim both by attacking the reliability of the statistics on religious affiliation and by pointing to other indications that there has been no long-term religious trend in any one direction.[20] Since Lipset agrees basically that a postwar increase in religiosity occurred and disagrees that this represents the continuation of a long-term trend, his article "Religion in America: What Religious Revival?" seems to be peculiarly titled. However, it is probably intended to reflect his proposition that religious affiliation and observance in America is better characterized by its stability than by its undulations over the last century and a half.

In support thereof, Lipset first of all points out that, from the time of de Tocqueville in 1830, foreign observers have been struck consistently by the evidence of great religiosity which they have found in America. He cites early estimates that, in 1832, well over 90 per cent of the population were church members. He questions the reliability of the historical statistics on the grounds that the definition of a church member has gradually grown more inclusive and, citing Argyle, he notes that when this is taken into account church membership is found to decline between 1906 and 1940 rather than to have sharply increased as the *Yearbook* figures indicate. He also presents evidence that the ratio of clergymen to the total population has been strikingly constant between 1850 and 1950.

Lipset also refers to more recent data showing that *per capita* contributions to churches were higher in the 1920s than in the 1950s, that the religious activity of business executives declined sharply between 1925 and 1950, and that among college students the proportion believing in God also declined between World War I and 1952. As we have already indicated, he does acknowledge that the trend since 1940 has been towards increased religiosity, citing about the same evidence as we have presented before. He disagrees, however, that the increase is a substantial one.

Lipset's adroit questioning of the historical statistical evidence on church affiliation and identification casts reasonable

---

20. Lipset, *op. cit.*

doubt on the claim of a long-term upward trend. However, his counter-evidence to support his contention of stability is also not entirely convincing. There simply are no reliable historical statistics on church membership and it is extremely doubtful that accurate statistics can be produced through manipulating the unreliable ones. Lipset's statistics on the stability of the ratio of clergy to the total population, as he himself points out, do not take into account the possibility that the contemporary clergyman may be serving larger congregations than his historical counterpart. What he has to say about shifts in contributions and in religious activity in the twentieth century do not wholly reflect stability nor can they reasonably be extended to represent the long-term situation back through the nineteenth century. To these observations must be added the further one that Lipset deals almost exclusively with the ritual dimension of religion. He gives some slight attention to the ideological, but none to the experiential and consequential dimensions.

This exploration into the long-term evidence on the religiousness of Americans does not lead us to any firm conclusions even within the limited perspectives of the observations discussed. Perhaps the confusion may be dissipated as we now go on to examine the alternative proposition that the long-term trend in America has been toward the increasing secularization of religion.

The spokesmen for this view are not all of one mind in the sense that they adopt the same frame of reference in making their observations. In general, however, they are more prone to emphasize the ideological or consequential dimensions than the experiential or ritual ones. And, where they adopt the same frame of reference as those who perceive a religious revival, they are likely to disagree with the 'revivalists' on the acceptability of given indicators.

Perhaps the most important attribute of those who perceive secularization to be going on is their commitment to a particular view of what religion means. Those who perceive the belief dimension as paramount, for example, are likely themselves to be committed to a set of beliefs. If these are transcendental beliefs, indications of a watering down of belief—the trend toward ecumenicity, for example, or the increasing propensity to see all religions as equally good—are cited as evidence of secularization.

It is not uncommon for ideological commitment to include secular beliefs which are accepted as sacred—the belief in the free enterprise system, for example. For those who have such a commitment, indications of an increasing trend toward a welfare state would be offered as *prima facie* evidence of secularization.

In some instances, those committed to a notion of secularization emphasize the consequential rather than the belief dimension. Their ideological commitment may be to a religion which has ethical consequences for those who experience, believe, and practice it. They want a religion which will intrude itself into all phases of life and make its weight felt in national affairs. Indications that religion is playing less and less of a role in family life, in education, in social welfare, and in economic life would be cited as evidence of secularization. At the same time, indications of increases in religious belief, practice, and experience would be rejected as meaningless without concomitant indications of increased religiosity on the consequential dimension.

Actually, there is nothing in the literature that would constitute a serious and systematic defense of the secularization hypothesis. Its advocates are likely to be clergymen, church administrators, theologians, or journalists, and where they have been social scientists they have tended to be oriented to qualitative rather than quantitative observation. The evidence which they cite tends to be neither systematic nor thoroughly documented. Their view of religion, as the examples indicate, is likely to be a circumscribed one, though in a different way from the views of the 'revivalists.'

In his paper, Lipset parallels his argument that there has been no long-term increase in religious affiliation and observance with the additional one that American religion is not becoming increasingly secularized. He does not deal systematically with all advocates of the secularization hypothesis but rather focuses his attention on those who see the process as manifest in the decline of transcendental belief. He acknowledges that the evidence is limited but argues that the secularization advocates ignore two things: One, the fact that evangelical religions are growing much faster than the traditional ones; and two, the possibility that "the secularized religion which these observers see as distinctively modern may have been characteristic of American believers in the past." In support of this possibility, he nctes that the same nineteenth-century foreign observers who were impressed by the religiosity of Americans also commented on its lack of depth and the unusual willingness of Americans to accept all religions as equally valid.

One may question whether the strength of transcendental belief constitutes a sufficient basis for testing the secularization hypothesis. But, even accepting it as such, some doubt may be cast on Lipset's implication that the two points he makes prove that secularization has not occurred.

The denominationalism which typified the nineteenth century is being slowly replaced by the ecumenicity of the twentieth. An interptetation of the shift is far too complex to be attempted in short compass. Yet, that church mergers are increasing suggests that their clergy and laity are willing to compromise somewhat on their beliefs in pursuit of other values and ends perceived as more important. However, it also appears to be the case, as Lipset points out, that the evangelical churches are gaining in strength.

One possibility has been ignored by all the participants in this dispute: that both kinds of theological changes may be occurring simultaneously—that, while the more evangelical and fundamentalist churches may be gaining new converts from certain sectors of the American public, the major denominations may be undergoing a transformation of their theology towards an increasingly less orthodox and more secularized faith. In the next chapter, the first available systematic data on the religious theology of rank-and-file members of the major American denominations will be presented in order to assess the basis for these claims that American religion is becoming secularized.

COMMENTARY

A general conclusion to be drawn from all that has been said is that none of the work done to assess the state of religion in America currently or historically meets even the minimum standards of scientific inquiry. Investigators and commentators have not given adequate attention to conceptualizing religion or religiousness in a comprehensive way. Consequently, they have been considerably less than thorough in their selection of indicators of religiousness. And, in applying the indicators they have selected, they have too often relied upon evidence of dubious quality. As a result, their work, does not provide a satisfactory basis for assessing either the state or the meaning of religion in America.

What can be concluded, at least tentatively, is that there was a postwar growth in religious affiliation and observance, but that these trends have now leveled off or even begun to turn downwards. These shifts were accompanied by an increase of interest in ideas and commodities having a religious content. However, it is not possible, given the evidence, to decide just how great the increase was, or to predict whether it could be confirmed using a more comprehensive set of indicators, or to understand the significance and meaning of the particular changes which have been observed. Furthermore, we cannot say authoritatively whether the increase constituted a revival or merely a brief acceleration of an historical trend towards increased church membership and religious interest.

Nevertheless, there are some indications that the qualitative character of American religion has been changing in at least two respects. One, there appears to be a decline in doctrinal rigidity. Americans seem more inclined to interpret scripture in the light of history and to accept the validity of faiths other than their own. Two, it seems that the church as an institution is playing a proportionately smaller role today than in the past in some of the aspects of American culture with which it has been traditionally identified—in education, for example, in family life, and in social welfare. However, even these trends cannot be accepted as demonstrated. The evidence of a revival in the strength of evangelical religion, as Lipset points out, casts some doubt on the notion of a decline in transcendental belief. And, there are some areas of our culture—politics, for example—where it is presently impossible to say whether the influence of religion has declined, increased, or remained the same.

It is problematical whether consensus can ever be achieved on the state and meaning of religion in America or, for that matter, anywhere else. Ideological commitments to different conceptions of what it means to be religious cannot be resolved scientifically. However, while ultimate resolutions may not be possible and the horizons may not be limitless, the challenge remains and it is doubtful that man will be satisfied with the limited understanding he has achieved.

Chapter 5

The New Denominationalism

IN the preceding chapter the evidence for a contemporary religious revival was systematically evaluated. Much of the confusion was shown to have resulted from indiscriminate use of different meanings of the term 'religiousness.' In part, the definitional problem reflects the absence of consensus, even among members of the same religious group, about what it means to be a religious person. This is demonstrated in the findings of the present chapter which asks: What are the religious beliefs of church-going Americans?

Whether or not there has been a religious revival, everyone seems to agree that American religion has been changing. In particular, churchmen, journalists, and scholars seem convinced that, despite the continuing existence of several hundred separately constituted Christian bodies in this country, a homogenization of theological viewpoints has made traditional denominationalism something of an anchronism; that American pluralism is more apparent than real.

This judgment, that the primary feature of American religion today is no longer its diversity but its unity of outlook, has received strong support from the recent series of denominational mergers and has fostered rising hopes for a general ecumenicalism.

It was a belief in such a doctrinal consensus that prompted Will Herberg to speak of the "common religion" of America in his now famous book.[1] While Herberg was sensitive to lingering diversities within Protestantism, he saw these differences as primarily organizational and ethnic, rather than doctrinal, and far outweighed by a consensus on fundamentals. Furthermore, in Herberg's judgment, this convergence of religious perspectives has marked an erosion of many traditional differences among what he thought to be the three major remaining divisions in American religion: Protestantism, Catholicism, and Judaism.[2]

A similar perception of religious consensus, particularly *within* Protestantism, recently led Robert Lee[3] to suggest that a "common core Protestantism" has developed because of the demise of the old "social sources of denominationalism" postulated by Niebuhr in his classic study.[4] Lee argues that changes associated with the development of an urban, mobile, national society are operating to break down old parochial religious boundaries; hence, it can be called the social sources of ecumenicalism.

The belief that there has been a unification of American religious perspectives has been ratified by a number of secular social scientists. Particularly the historic creedal schisms among Protestants have been declared to have little contemporary importance. Indeed, in searching for religious 'effects' on modern social behavior, no major investigator has differentiated among the Protestant bodies, but all have instead contrasted Protestants, Catholics, and Jews. The word denomination does not even appear in the index of the most widely acclaimed em-

---

1. *Protestant-Catholic-Jew* (New York: Doubleday & Co., Anchor Books, 1960).

2. As others have pointed out, Herberg neglected a most important 'religious' group in contemporary America, the secularists who stand outside religious perspectives. The prominence of this group, especially among scholars and intellectuals (see Chapter 14), and the degree to which this body of thought influences and shapes our present ethical, moral, and cultural conceptions, makes this exclusion a major omission in any attempt to apprehend the current state of religion. In our judgment, Herberg omitted secularists from his discussion primarily because the way in which he conceived of religion was too narrow to deal with persons who reject the supernatural traditions of Judeo-Christian theology. Thus, he would have faced the ambiguities of speaking of a religion of irreligiousness or of characterizing this group on the basis of its disbeliefs rather than in terms of what it does believe.

3. Robert Lee, *The Social Sources of Church Unity* (New York: Abingdon Press, 1960).

4. H. Richard Niebuhr, *The Social Sources of Denominationalism* (New York: Henry Holt, 1929).

pirical study of the effects of contemporary religion, Gerhard Lenski's *The Religious Factor*.[5] From reading Lenski's study, one might easily conclude that Protestants differ among themselves only on race and social class.[6] In taking the essential unity of Protestantism for granted, Lenski is merely concurring in a standard social science practice; it is the rare study which even records religious affiliation in greater detail than Protestant, Catholic, Jew, Other, or None.[7]

While there seems to be virtual unanimity that this convergence in American religion has taken place, there has been spirited disagreement over whether it is a blessing or a curse. Some churchmen feel this change portends a loss of religious concern and authenticity.[8] Their disapproval has been echoed by some social scientists who see this blending of theological traditions as another invidious symptom of the moral corrosion produced by mass society and the 'O.K. World' of suburban complacency.[9] In the main, these critics fear that religion has merely become what William Lee Miller has called a "moralized version of Americanism,"[10] and has thus lost its capacity to inform and shape men and society meaningfully.

Others, both churchmen and secular scholars, have hailed these changes. By sloughing off its divisive doctrines they see religion as regaining its lost relevance and forging a new faith in

---

5. (Garden City: Doubleday & Co., 1961).

6. For a recent review article reappraising Lenski's methodology, especially his decision to disregard differences among Protestant denominations (he did have data on specific denominational affiliation), see: Earl Babbie, "The Religious Factor — Looking Forward," *The Review of Religious Research*, (Fall, 1965).

7. For this reason, when social scientists these days speak of the effect of religion on such things as voting, civil libertarianism, and the like, they are typically referring only to Protestant-Catholic-Jewish comparisons, not to variations in religious commitment within any of these general categories.

8. For example, Martin E. Marty, *The New Shape of Religion* (N.Y.: Harper and Bros., 1959).

9. Dennison Nash and Peter L. Berger, "The Child, the Family, and the 'Religious Revival' in Suburbia," *Journal for the Scientific Study of Religion*, II–I (Fall, 1962), 85–93; Peter L. Berger, *The Noise of Solemn Assemblies* (Garden City: Doubleday & Co., 1961); and William H. Whyte, Jr., *The Organization Man* (Garden City: Doubleday & Co., 1956), especially Part VII.

10. William Lee Miller, "American Religion and American Political Attitudes," in James Ward Smith and A. Leland Jamison, eds., *Religious Perspectives in American Culture* (Princeton: Princeton University Press, 1961), pp. 81–118.

which men can unite in a common quest to enoble the human spirit.[11]

It is not our intention to enter this debate over the virtue of a homogenization of religious perspectives. Rather, we mean to raise a considerably more basic question: *Have such changes really taken place?* Is this portrait of a unified religious outlook in contemporary America, and especially of a 'common core Protestantism,' a good likeness?

The notion that American religion is characterized by doctrinal consensus rests on two main premises: First, that the old disputes separating the various faiths (such as adult versus infant baptism), particularly within Protestantism, have lost their force and relevance; that few persons believe in, or care about, the theological idiosyncracies that once rent Christianity. Second, that the demise of these historic creedal bases for conflict leaves Americans in general agreement, sharing the essential core of Christian (and Judaic) teachings. That is, Americans stripped of their secondary disagreements, are now in consensus on such bedrocks of faith as the existence of an all-powerful, personal God, the moral authority of the Ten Commandments, and the New Testament promise of salvation.

In the main, these two premises have been based on impressionistic judgments because systematic evidence has been extremely scanty. However, so important and sweeping an assertion about American religion seems to warrant more careful examination and firmer evidence. In this chapter, we shall draw upon empirical data from an extensive survey[12] of Christian church members to see to what extent American religion really is homogeneous. To do this we shall sketch theological profiles of the various denominations and see whether they do generally coincide. In assessing these data, several additional questions raised in the last chapter will also be considered: To what extent has American religious belief been secularized in recent years? and, To what degree are hopes for future unification of the denominations realistic?

11. See J. Paul Williams, *What Americans Believe and How They Worship* (New York: Harpers, 1952), pp. 71, 78, 368, 374; and H. M. Kallen, "Democracy's True Religion," *Saturday Review of Literature,* XXXIV (July 28, 1951), 6–7.

12. The data are from the same study, conducted by the authors, on which Chapter 3 is based. For further details of sampling, see footnote 7 in Chapter 3.

SUPERNATURALISM

We shall begin our examination of the religious perspectives of the American denominations by assessing belief in Christian traditions concerning supernatural beings, worlds, and forces. Subsequently we shall turn to beliefs in various aspects, intentions of, and obligations to, this supernatural realm.

Commentators on the current American scene are unanimous in thinking that all but a mere handful of Americans believe in God. Findings from national polls support this assumption; repeated Gallup surveys have found that 96 to 97 per cent of all American adults respond "yes" when asked, "Do you, personally, believe in God?" Although a few observers have been somewhat uncomfortable about the seeming lack of sophistication of such an either-or probe, and have wondered how many different images of God were subsumed within this gross summary, most have been content to accept these findings as a ratification of American virtue and the unchanging character of our religious faith, especially when contrasted with the much lower levels of belief in God disclosed by similar polling in European nations.

Given this virtual unanimity among the general public, it might seem pointless to examine belief in God among *members* of Christian churches. What could possibly be found but universal acceptance. Yet, it seems possible that there might be significant differences in the *images* of God held by different persons as well as in the *degree* they are certain about their belief. Looking at the data shown in Table 5–1, it is strikingly apparent that even in a sample of only church members, there are indeed important contrasts both in conceptions of God and in conviction. Furthermore, these variations sharply distinguish the denominations from one another.

In selecting the statement about God that came closest to their own views, only 41 per cent of the Congregationalists indicated unquestioning faith in a personal divinity. This proportion rises to 60 per cent of the Methodists, 63 per cent of the Episcopalians reaches about the three-quarter mark among the denominations in the center of the table, and is virtually the unanimous response of Southern Baptists and members of the fundamentalist sects. Overall, 71 per cent of the Protestants endorsed this traditionally orthodox position as compared with 81 per cent of the Roman Catholics.

"Which of the following statements comes closest to what you believe about God?"	Congregationalists	Methodists	Episcopalians	Disciples of Christ	Presbyterians	American Lutherans[c]	American Baptists	Missouri Lutherans	Southern Baptists	Sects[d]	Total Protestants	Catholics
"I know God really exists and I have no doubts about it."	41%	60%	63%	76%	75%	73%	78%	81%	99%	96%	71%	81%
"While I have doubts, I feel that I do believe in God."	34	22	19	20	16	19	18	17	1	2	17	13
"I find myself believing in God some of the time, but not at other times."	4	4	2	0	1	2	0	0	0	0	2	1
"I don't believe in a personal God, but I do believe in a higher power of some kind."	16	11	12	0	7	6	2	1	0	1	7	3
"I don't know whether there is a God and I don't believe there is any way to find out."	2	2	2	0	1	*	0	1	0	0	1	1
"I don't believe in God."	1	*	*	0	0	*	0	0	0	0	*	0
No answer	2	*	1	4	*	*	2	0	0	1	1	1
PERCENT[a] =	100	99	99	100	100	100	100	100	100	100	99	100
Number of respondents[b] =	(151)	(415)	(416)	(50)	(495)	(208)	(141)	(116)	(79)	(255)	(2326)	(545)

* Less than ½ of 1 per cent
a Some columns fail to sum to 100% due to rounding error
b The number of respondents shown for each denomination in this table is the same for all other tables in this chapter.
c A combination of members of The Lutheran Church in America and the American Lutheran Church.
d Included are: The Assemblies of God, The Church of God, The Church of Christ, The Church of the Nazarene, The Foursquare Gospel Church, and one independent Tabernacle

Looking at the second line of the table, we see that the greatest proportion of persons who rejected the first statement did not do so because they held a different image of God, but because they differed in their certainty. While they conceived of a personal divinity, they admitted having doubts about his existence. Denominational differences here too are marked: from 34 per cent of the Congregationalists to one per cent of the Southern Baptists.

The third possible response, line three in the table, is simply a more "doubtful" version of the second and did not draw much support. However, the fourth response category is especially interesting, for it marks a different conception of God, rather than differences in the certainty of faith. Again, contrasts are striking: 16 per cent of the Congregationalists, 11 per cent of the Methodists, 12 per cent of the Episcopalians, down to none of the Southern Baptists thought not of a personal God, but simply of some kind of 'higher power.' Overall, 7 per cent of the Protestants held this deist conception of God, while 3 per cent of the Roman Catholics did so.

To complete the findings, it should be noted that 2 per cent of the Congregationalists, Episcopalians, and Methodists took an agnostic position (line 5), and 1 per cent of the Congregationalists candidly said they did not believe in God.

Looking at the overall figures, if responses to the first four categories are added together, the totals would indicate that 98 per cent of both Protestants and Roman Catholics believe to some extent in what they think of as God, which is a very close match for the usual Gallup results. What the data reveal, however, is how much variation in the strength of belief and the kind of God believed in is suppressed by a simplistic inquiry.

Gallup studies also report that Americans are virtually unanimous in believing Jesus Christ to be the Divine Son of God. But in light of our findings about belief in God, we can expect this faith too needs to be qualified by degree of certainty as well as differences in the images of Christ.

Table 5–2 shows that indeed there are important contrasts in belief in the divinity of this central figure of Christianity. The pattern of denominational differences across the first line of the table is virtually identical to the pattern of belief in God. Differences range from 40 per cent of the Congregationalists who have no doubts that "Jesus is the Divine Son of God," to 99 per

TABLE 5-2

Belief in the Divinity of Jesus

"Which of the following statements comes closest to what you believe about Jesus?"	Congregationalists	Methodists	Episcopalians	Disciples of Christ	Presbyterians	American Lutherans	American Baptists	Missouri Lutherans	Southern Baptists	Sects	Total Protestants	Catholics
"Jesus is the Divine Son of God and I have no doubts about it."	40%	54%	59%	74%	72%	74%	76%	93%	99%	97%	69%	86%
"While I have some doubts, I feel basically that Jesus is Divine."	28	22	25	14	19	18	16	5	0	2	17	8
"I feel that Jesus was a great man and very holy, but I don't feel Him to be the Son of God any more than all of us are children of God."	19	14	8	6	5	5	4	0	0	*	7	3
"I think Jesus was only a man, although an extraordinary one."	9	6	5	2	2	3	2	1	1	*	4	1
"Frankly, I'm not entirely sure there was such a person as Jesus."	1	1	1	0	1	*	0	0	0	0	1	0
Other and no answer	3	3	2	4	1	0	2	1	0	1	2	2

cent of the Southern Baptists. The total Protestant figure is 69 per cent in contrast to 86 per cent among Roman Catholics.

Variations in the degree to which Christian church members ratify faith in an orthodox conception of Christ come into even sharper focus when we examine some specific details of Christology. As shown in Table 5–3, only 57 per cent of all Protestants responded "completely true" when asked to evaluate the statement, "Jesus was born of a virgin," while 81 per cent of the Roman Catholics did so. But even more startling differences can be observed among the Protestant bodies: From 21 per cent of the Congregationalists, the proportion rises to 99 per cent of the Southern Baptists.

The dispersion among Protestants is even slightly increased when we examine the second item in the table which reports the proportions who thought it "completely true" that "Jesus walked on water." Firm believers in this miracle commonly credited to Christ form a small minority in the large, liberal denominations, constitute half of Protestants in general, make up 71 per cent of the Roman Catholics, and 99 per cent of the Southern Baptists.

Like the question of the existence of God, that of the Saviour-hood of Christ produces mixed reactions among American Christians. Vast differences also exist among Protestants in the proportions who accept the promise of the Second Coming, while differences between Protestants in general and Roman Catholics are trivial. Fifty-eight per cent of the Congregationalists felt Christ will "definitely" or "probably" *not* return to earth as compared with 2 per cent of the Southern Baptists. Correspondingly, only 13 per cent of the Congregationalists, and 21 per cent of the Methodists thought Jesus will "definitely" return as compared with 75 per cent of the Missouri Synod Lutherans and 94 per cent of the Southern Baptists. Overall, less than half of both Protestants and Roman Catholics thought the Second Coming was definite, and less than 60 per cent even thought such an event probable. Clearly, Protestants cannot join together in affirming that old evangelistic slogan, "Christ Crucified, Risen, Coming Again." Indeed, such certainty is held only by a minority of Christian church members.

The extreme contrasts among the various denominations we have seen thus far are matched by widely different views on the authenticity of Biblical accounts of miracles. In Table 5–4 the

TABLE 5-3

Additional Beliefs About Jesus

	Congregationalists	Methodists	Episcopalians	Disciples of Christ	Presbyterians	American Lutherans	American Baptists	Missouri Lutherans	Southern Baptists	Sects	Total Protestants	Catholics
"Jesus was born of a virgin." Percentage who said, "Completely true."	21	34	39	62	57	66	69	92	99	96	57	81
"Jesus walked on water." Percentage who said "Completely true."	19	26	30	62	51	58	62	83	99	94	50	71
"Do you believe Jesus will actually return to the earth some day?" Percentage who answered:												
"Definitely."	13	21	24	36	43	54	57	75	94	89	44	47
"Probably."	8	12	13	10	11	12	11	8	4	2	10	10
"Possibly."	28	25	29	26	23	18	17	6	0	1	20	16
"Probably not."	23	22	17	12	12	6	6	4	1	2	13	11
"Definitely not."	25	17	11	6	8	7	5	1	1	3	10	12
No answer	3	3	6	10	3	3	4	6	0	3	4	4

TABLE 5-4
Miracles

"The Bible tells of many miracles, some credited to Christ and some to other prophets and apostles. Generally speaking, which of the following statements comes closest to what you believe about Biblical miracles?"

Percentage who answered:	Congregationalists	Methodists	Episcopalians	Disciples of Christ	Presbyterians	American Lutherans	American Baptists	Missouri Lutherans	Southern Baptists	Sects	Total Protestants	Catholics
"Miracles actually happened just as the Bible says they did."	28	37	41	62	58	69	62	89	92	92	57	74
"Miracles happened but can be explained by natural causes."	32	31	22	16	20	14	16	4	0	3	19	9
"Doubt or do not accept miracles."	32	24	27	14	14	13	9	5	3	5	17	9

proportions responding they believe the "miracles actually happened just as the Bible says they did," vary from 28 per cent of the Congregationalists and 37 per cent of the Methodists, 69 per cent of the American Lutheran bodies, 89 per cent of the Missouri Lutherans, to 92 per cent of the Southern Baptists. Seventy-four per cent of the Roman Catholics ratified miracles in contrast to 57 per cent of all Protestants.

Two more central Christian tenets will complete our exploration of American religious beliefs about deity: belief in life after death and belief in the existence of the Devil.

Again we see the marked differences in the proportions holding these beliefs across denominations from left to right in Table 5–5. While only 36 per cent of the Congregationalists are certain there is a life beyond death, 97 per cent of the Southern Baptists consider this a certainty. Greater variation occurs among Protestants on the existence of the Devil, with the proportions who are certain the Devil exists ranging from only 6 per cent of the Congregationalists and 13 per cent of the Episcopalians up to 92 per cent of the Southern Baptists. Overall, 38 per cent of the Protestants and 66 per cent of the Roman Catholics felt certain about the Devil's existence.

CONCEPTS OF SIN

Turning to the concept of sin, a new pattern of denominational schism is revealed in Table 5–6. Acceptance of man as sinful by nature (item 1) increases as one moves across the table from left to right. However, in comparision with the great differences we have seen on conceptions of the supernatural, the proportions accepting this image of man is relatively evenly spread across the Protestant groups. When we examine acceptance of the doctrine of original sin (item 2) some most interesting contrasts emerge. At different points on the left-right (liberal to conservative) spectrum, those denominations in a liturgical, or High Church tradition are readily distinguishable by their acceptance of original sin. That is, churches that have traditionally emphasized the importance of formal ritual, such as communion, absolution, and the like, and which have given greater liturgical emphasis to original sin (which is not amenable to personal efforts to redeem, but can only be absolved through the church), show up at all points of the left-right continuum. Among the very liberal bodies, the Episcopalians stand out from

TABLE 5-5
Life Beyond Death and Belief in the Devil

	Congregationalists	Methodists	Episcopalians	Disciples of Christ	Presbyterians	American Lutherans	American Baptists	Missouri Lutherans	Southern Baptists	Sects	Total Protestants	Catholics
"There is a life beyond death." Percentage who answered:												
"Completely true."	36	49	53	64	69	70	72	84	97	94	65	75
"Probably true."	40	35	31	32	21	23	19	10	3	4	24	16
"Probably not or definitely not true."	21	13	13	0	7	5	7	4	0	2	9	5
"The Devil actually exists." Percentage who answered:												
"Completely true."	6	13	17	18	31	49	49	77	92	90	38	66
"Probably true."	13	15	16	34	17	20	17	9	5	5	15	14
"Probably not or definitely not true."	78	66	60	38	48	26	29	10	1	5	43	14

TABLE 5-6
Sin

	Congregationalists	Methodists	Episcopalians	Disciples of Christ	Presbyterians	American Lutherans	American Baptists	Missouri Lutherans	Southern Baptists	Sects	Total Protestants	Catholics
"Man can not help doing evil." Percentage who answered:												
"Completely true"	21	22	30	24	35	52	36	63	62	37	34	22
"Probably true"	36	36	34	36	35	30	28	20	14	15	31	29
"Probably not or definitely not true"	39	38	31	38	25	15	27	13	22	42	30	43
"A child is born into the world already guilty of sin." Percentage who answered:												
"Completely true"	2	7	18	6	21	49	23	86	43	47	26	68
"Probably true"	2	4	7	2	7	12	9	4	3	3	6	10
"Probably not or definitely not true"	94	87	71	90	68	37	65	9	55	46	65	19

the other less liturgical denominations, 18 per cent saying "completely true," as compared with 7 per cent of the Methodists and 6 per cent of the Disciples of Christ. In the center of the table, the American Lutherans, traditionally liturgical, stand out sharply from the less ritualistic Presbyterians and American Baptists. On the far right, the Missouri Lutherans differ considerably from the Southern Baptists and the various sects. Overall, the generally more liturgical Roman Catholics contrast greatly with the Protestants, 68 per cent versus 26 per cent. (The more liturgical denominations are set in boldface for easy comparison.)

It is clear that there is a general relationship between belief in original sin and theological conservatism underlying these data, so that Lutherans are much more likely to hold this view than the Episcopalians, yet the marks of the formal doctrine show up all across the table. The majority of Episcopalians seemingly have reliquished much of their orthodoxy, but those who retain it tend to differ from those who have retained orthodox Methodism on the question of original sin. Thus, on the left of the table, vestiges of old doctrinal differences on original sin may still be detected, while on the right these differences retain much of their traditional force. Turning to further comparisons of the denominations, we shall discover other examples of these differences between the more and less liturgical bodies.

So far we have examined denominational variations on belief in some of the central figures and concepts of Christianity. We shall now turn our attention to Christianity's central concern and promise: salvation. The questions about salvation are separated into two general classes: first, those beliefs, ritual observances, and works which might be judged necessary requirements for salvation; second, those improper beliefs, ritual violations and acts which might be considered as resulting in certain forfeiture of the possibility of salvation.

REQUIREMENTS FOR SALVATION

Faith

While Christians have long battled over the question of whether faith *and* works are required for salvation, there has been virtual unanimity that faith is absolutely required. The central tenet of this required faith is belief in Jesus Christ as the divine son of God who died to redeem men from their sins. While some Christian traditions hold that more than faith in Christ is required for salvation, all agree that there is no salvation outside of Christ.

However, since we have seen earlier that members of American denominations are far from unanimous in crediting Jesus with divinity, it is hardly surprising to find them disagreeing markedly over whether belief in Christ is absolutely necessary for salvation.

Turning to the data in Table 5 – 7, we see that holding faith in Christ as "absolutely necessary" is the point of view of a minority among the more liberal denominations. Among the conservative and fundamentalist groups, however, there is virtual consensus about the necessity of faith in Christ for salvation. Overall, 65 per cent of the Protestants and 51 per cent of the Roman Catholics gave this answer. Recalling the findings on belief in life after death, it seems likely that among all Protestant groups, persons who accept the promise of an eternal salvation beyond the grave are also likely to feel that this eternal reward is contingent upon belief in Christ as saviour. However, since denominations differ widely in the degree to which they still accept this literal interpretation of New Testament promises, they also differ widely in the degree to which they see faith in Christ as a means to such salvation.

Looking at the second item in Table 5–7, we see that all denominational groups are less likely to feel that one must hold "the Bible to be God's truth" in order to be saved. Overall, the pattern follows the now familiar increases from left to right, with one notable exception. Though the Southern Baptists have been most unanimous in their assertion of traditional Christian positions, we may see here that they are not importantly different from the center denominations in seeing Bible literalism as required for salvation. As we will see in further data, this probably reflects the great emphasis placed on faith in Christ by Southern Baptists, and, consequently, they seem less inclined to see other aspects of Christian teaching as crucial for attaining grace.

Ritual Acts

On the basis of our earlier findings concerning original sin, we may anticipate that denominations with ritualistic orientations will stand out from the rest in giving importance to ritual

TABLE 5-7
Requirements For Salvation: Faith

	Congregationalists	Methodists	Episcopalians	Disciples of Christ	Presbyterians	American Lutherans	American Baptists	Missouri Lutherans	Southern Baptists	Sects	Total Protestants	Catholics
"Belief in Jesus Christ as Saviour." Percentcge who said "Absolutely necessary."	38	45	47	78	66	77	78	97	97	96	65	51
"Holding the Bible to be God's truth." Percentage who said "Absolutely necessary."	23	39	32	58	52	64	58	80	61	89	52	38

acts as requirements of salvation. This expectation is convincingly borne out by the data in Table 5–8. Looking at the first item in the table, "Holy Baptism," we see the Episcopalians are markedly different from the neighboring Congregationalists and Methodists; in the center of the table the American Lutherans stand out in sharp relief from the Presbyterians and the American Baptists, and on the right, the Missouri Lutherans differ enormously from the Southern Baptists and Fundamentalist sects. Overall, the generally less ritualistic Protestants differ greatly from the Roman Catholics (35 per cent to 65 per cent). A similar pattern can be observed in the proportions who believed that "regular participation in Christian sacraments, for example, Holy Communion," is "absolutely necessary" to gain salvation. However, fewer persons in all denominations saw this ritual requiremennt as crucial than did so on baptism. Ritualistic orientations can also be detected on the proportions who thought membership in a Christian church was necessary to salvation, although this view was held by only a small minority of members of any group.

The fourth item in the table not only examines requirements for salvation, but also seeks to assess the remnants of the denominational chauvinism and parochialism which once typified Christian schisms. The data clearly indicate that, whether through pluralistic experience or general loss of fervor, the days when bitter Christian factions each saw themselves as having a monopoly on religious authenticity and legitimacy have passed. While Roman Catholics are still frequently accused of believing theirs to be the single possible road to savlation, only about a quarter (28 per cent) felt that it was "absolutely necessary" to be a member of their particular faith in order to be saved. While they are still more prone to this view than Protestants, only 11 per cent of whom took this position, the overwhelming majority of Catholics rejected the belief that only Catholics could be saved. Among Protestants, the proportions giving this response increased among the Lutherans, the Baptists, and the sect members, but here too, only a small minority agreed.

Turning to more personal ritual requirements for salvation, we may see that Christians generally feel that prayer is absolutely necessary for redemption. Again looking at the left hand side of the table, we may note that among the Congregational-

TABLE 5-8

Requirements for Salvation: Ritual Acts

	Congregationalists	Methodists	Episcopalians	Disciples of Christ	Presbyterians	American Lutherans	American Baptists	Missouri Lutherans	Southern Baptists	Sects	Total Protestants	Catholics
"Holy Baptism" Percentage who said, "Absolutely necessary."	11	19	39	32	28	58	25	78	19	46	35	65
"Regular participation in Christian sacraments, for example, Holy Communion." Percentage who said, "Absolutely necessary."	7	10	27	22	17	36	15	55	10	31	22	39
"Membership in a Christian Church." Percentage who said, "Absolutely necessary."	7	8	17	22	13	21	13	33	14	24	16	23
"Being a member of your particular religious faith." Percentage who said, "Absolutely necessary."	3	6	7	8	8	14	12	16	16	25	11	28
"Prayer." Percentage who said, "Absolutely necessary."	39	48	44	62	52	67	55	67	57	87	55	54

ists, Methodists, and Episcopalians, fewer than half view prayer as absolutely necessary. This probably reflects their lower concern for, and acceptance of, the promise of salvation in general. The denominations in the center of the table show a major concern with prayer. However, proportions do not increase as we move to the more conservative and Fundamentalist groups. Again, this probably reflects the overwhelming emphasis that these groups place on faith in Christ.

Works

Having become accustomed, in previous tables, to seeing increases from left to right in the proportions holding any act of faith or ritual as necessary for salvation, it may come as something of a surprise to see these trends reverse in Table 5 – 9. Nevertheless, examining the first item in the table, "Doing good for others," it is obvious that a much higher proportion of persons in the denominations on the left than in those on the right consider this absolutely necessary for salvation. Whether or not members of the more conservative groups basically admire 'good deeds,' they are not inclined to give them any special relevance for salvation. These findings are even more striking when we consider that the absolute proportions of persons in churches on the left who think doing good for others is required for salvation is higher than the proportions of members of these same groups thinking faith in Christ is absolutely necessary. Indeed, *fewer* persons in the liberal churches were certain of the existence of life beyond death than thought doing good was absolutely necessary for salvation. To explain this seemingly inconsistent behavior, we may suggest that these responses on 'doing good' by persons who essentially rejected the traditional notion of salvation, represent their desire to ratify the ethical components of their religious outlook regardless of the context of their response. Indeed, given their lack of commitment to orthodox theology, ethics are likely the central component of their religious perspective.

This relatively larger support for good works among churches on the left is duplicated on the second item in the table, "Loving thy neighbor." However, the decline in proportions saying "absolutely necessary" is only moderate from left to right, and in general one might say that American denominations pretty much agree on this issue.

TABLE 5-9
Requirements for Salvation: Works

	Congregationalists	Methodists	Episcopalians	Disciples of Christ	Presbyterians	American Lutherans	American Baptists	Missouri Lutherans	Southern Baptists	Sects	Total Protestants	Catholics
"Doing good for others" Percentage who said, "Absolutely necessary."	58	57	54	64	48	47	45	38	29	61	52	57
"Loving thy neighbor" Percentage who said, "Absolutely necessary."	59	57	60	76	55	51	52	51	41	74	58	65
"Tithing" Percentage who said, "Absolutely necessary."	6	7	9	12	10	13	16	7	18	48	14	10

Turning from these two more personal forms of works to the more formal and institutionally oriented matter of tithing, it is clear that Christians in general are not inclined to connect this act with salvation. Only 14 per cent of the Protestants and 10 per cent of the Roman Catholics thought tithing absolutely necessary for salvation. Among the Protestant groups the proportions giving this response increase slightly from the left groups to those on the right. But only among members of the sects does any sizeable portion take this position.

In summary, these data have shown marked contrasts among Christian denominations in their conceptions of what is required for salvation.

BARRIERS TO SALVATION

Improper Faith

We have seen that Christians in general place great emphasis on faith in Christ as essential for salvation, although the denominations differ greatly on this question. We shall now attempt to assess the degree to which this position is translated into judgments about the kinds of religious faith which would automatically preclude the possibility of salvation. Looking at the data in Table 5–10, the same patterns among denominations found on requiring faith in Jesus for salvation are to be seen in rejecting the possibility of salvation for non-Christians. However, the extension of the positive requirement to the negative sanction is far from complete. Many in all denominations who held faith in Christ as absolutely necessary for salvation were unwilling to agree that persons outside the Christian faith could not be saved. For example, only 14 per cent of the Protestants and 4 per cent of the Roman Catholics said that "being completely ignorant of Jesus, as might be the case for people living in other countries," would definitely prevent salvation. Among Protestants, the proportion taking this position varied from a mere handful of Congregationalists, Methodists, Episcopalians and Disciples of Christ to 36 per cent of the Missouri Lutherans, and 41 per cent of the Southern Baptists. However, an additional and sizeable group of Christians were somewhat inclined to accept this view. Twenty-five per cent of the Protestants and 24 per cent of the Roman Catholics thought ignorance of Jesus

TABLE 5-10

Barriers to Salvation: Improper Faith

	Congregationalists	Methodists	Episcopalians	Disciples of Christ	Presbyterians	American Lutherans	American Baptists	Missouri Lutherans	Southern Baptists	Sects	Total Protestants	Catholics
"Being completely ignorant of Jesus as might be the case for people living in other countries."												
Percentage who said it would definitely prevent salvation.	3	7	3	8	11	15	17	36	41	32	14	4
Percentage who said it would possibly prevent salvation.	13	23	16	38	24	29	31	28	39	46	25	24
"Being of the Jewish Religion."												
Percentage who said it would definitely prevent salvation.	1	3	3	8	7	16	7	31	25	23	10	1
Percentage who said it would possibly prevent salvation.	6	9	10	18	12	16	25	23	28	33	15	11
"Being of the Hindu religion."												
Percentage who said it would definitely prevent salvation.	1	5	4	10	14	20	14	40	32	37	15	2
Percentage who said it would possibly prevent salvation.	12	11	12	28	15	22	25	16	27	31	17	13

would "possibly prevent" salvation. Again, differences among Protestants varied greatly from the left denominations to the fundamentalist groups on the right.

Moving to the next item, 10 per cent of the Protestants and 1 per cent of the Roman Catholics thought it impossible for a Jew to be saved. Again, there were great contrasts among Protestant groups. One per cent of the Congregationalists and 3 per cent of the Methodists and Episcopalians took this position, while 31 per cent of the Missouri Lutherans and 25 per cent of the Southern Baptists saw no hope for Jews to be saved. Again, a sizeable group thought it "possible" that a Jew could not be saved, and taken together, more than half of the members of the more fundamentalist groups at least doubted the possibility of a Jew's gaining salvation. These proportions increased when the question of salvation for a Hindu was raised. Forty per cent of the Missouri Lutherans and 32 per cent of the Southern Baptists felt that followers of the Hindu faith would definitely be prevented from gaining salvation, and 15 per cent of Protestants overall took this position as compared with 2 per cent of Roman Catholics.

In summary, a substantial minority of American Christians consider persons in non-Christian religions as beyond the hope of salvation.

Violations of Proper Ritual

The data in Table 5 — 11 show that American Christians attach little relevance for salvation to violations of the sabbath and "taking the name of the Lord in vain." Though we might expect fundamentalists to attach most importance to keeping the sabbath — and indeed they do — surprisingly, 19 per cent of the Roman Catholics also see this as definitely preventing salvation. All Christian groups are more likely to think cursing could definitely prevent salvation than they were to invest sabbath violation with such consequences. As might be expected, the more conservative groups were slightly more inclined to connect cursing with obstacles to salvation. However, Missouri Synod Lutherans differed sharply from all other groups on this question, and 41 per cent thought salvation would be denied to those taking the name of the Lord in vain. Roughly a quarter of both the Protestants and Catholics shared in this judgment.

TABLE 5-11
Barriers to Salvation: Violations of Proper Ritual

	Congregationalists	Methodists	Episcopalians	Disciples of Christ	Presbyterians	American Lutherans	American Baptists	Missouri Lutherans	Southern Baptists	Sects	Total Protestants	Catholics
"Breaking the Sabbath" Percentage who said it would definitely prevent salvation.	2	4	5	4	6	5	4	5	15	26	8	19
"Taking the name of the Lord in vain." Percentage who said it would definitely prevent salvation.	13	19	17	26	20	26	21	41	27	64	26	28

Improper Acts

Drinking is no longer regarded as a certain road to damnation by American Christians. Eight per cent of Protestants and 2 per cent of Roman Catholics said drinking would definitely prevent salvation. Only among the Baptists and the followers of fundamentalist sects did more than a handful attach temperance to their scheme of salvation, as seen in Table 5 – 12.

Virtually no Protestants (2 per cent) thought the practice of artificial birth control would prevent salvation, but perhaps even more interesting and surprising, *less than a quarter of the Catholics held this view.* Whether or not Catholics approve of birth control, more than three quarters of them are unwilling to agree it carries the supreme penalty of damnation.

The last two items in the table seem especially interesting and repeat the denominational pattern seen in evaluation of good works as relevant to salvation. On virtually all other items exploring possible barriers to salvation, the conservative and fundamentalist bodies have shown the greatest propensity to see them as preventing salavtion. However, on questions of racial discrimination and anti-Semitism, the fundamentalists are the *least* likely of all religious groups to see them as relevant to salvation. Thus, while 27 per cent of the Southern Baptists thought cursing would definitely prevent salvation, only 10 per cent of them viewed anti-Semites as disqualified from entrance into God's Kingdom, and only 16 per cent saw racial discrimination as a definite barrier. On the other hand, while only 13 per cent of the Congregationalists thought that taking the name of the Lord in vain would definitely prevent salvation, 27 per cent gave this response on racial discrimination and 23 per cent on anti-Semitism. Perhaps an even more suggestive contrast appears when we consider that about half of the members of all denominations thought it absolutely necessary to "Love thy neighbor" in order to be saved.

To sum up this section on salvation, we have seen that Christian denominations in America differ greatly in their beliefs about what a man must do in order to be saved. While most denominations give primary importance to faith, the liberal Protestant groups are inclined to favor good works. Protestant groups in a ritualistic tradition and the Roman Catholics place greater emphasis on the sacraments and other ritual acts than do those from low church traditions.

TABLE 5-12
Barriers to Salvation: Improper Acts

	Congregationalists	Methodists	Episcopalians	Disciples of Christ	Presbyterians	American Lutherans	American Baptists	Missouri Lutherans	Southern Baptists	Sects	Total Protestants	Catholics
"Drinking liquor." Per cent who said it would definitely prevent salvation.	2	4	2	0	2	2	9	1	15	35	8	2
"Practicing artificial birth control." Per cent who said it would definitely prevent salvation.	0	0	2	2	1	3	1	2	5	4	2	23
"Discriminating against other races." Per cent who said it would definitely prevent salvation.	27	25	27	34	22	20	17	22	16	29	25	24
"Being anti-Semitic." Per cent who said it would definitely prevent salvation.	23	23	26	30	20	15	13	22	10	26	21	20

CERTAINTY AND CONCERN ABOUT THE MEANING
AND PURPOSE OF LIFE

Chapter 1 defined religion as one kind of system of symbols, beliefs, values, and practices pertaining to solutions to questions of ultimate meaning. We would now like to explore, in a general way, the degree to which Christians feel that their religious perspective does satisfactorily interpret and give meaning to their lives. Beyond this, we shall also inquire how they came by their point of view, if indeed they have one. How many embraced their religious outlook after a period of questioning and seeking truth; how many have simply grown up with their religion?

To investigate these modes of religious commitment, respondents were asked: "How sure are you that you have found the answers to the meaning and purpose of life?" For convenience in explication we shall affix a descriptive label to each of the response categories to this item. The complete item and findings appear in Table 5–13.

The conformists are those persons who are "quite certain" they know the meaning and purpose of life, and report they "pretty much grew up knowing these things." Such individuals seemingly have never had occasion to question seriously the religious perspective they were taught in childhood, and have been content to conform to this early training. The conformist pattern is markedly related to denomination; about a quarter of the members of more liberal denominations are this type, as compared with more than 40 per cent of the Missouri Lutherans and Southern Baptists, up to virtually half of the Roman Catholics (49 per cent). Overall, conformists make up the slightly most common type among Protestants, 31 per cent reporting this pattern.

The converted are "quite certain" they know the answers now, but were once "pretty uncertain." While it is likely these respondents were also raised in a religious tradition, at some time in their lives they seriously doubted or perhaps even rejected this training. Thus, they have come to their present state of certainty after reflection and doubt, and can be considered converts in the sense of having changed their religious outlook, at least from a previous position of uncertainty. The converted type is much more common among the fundamentalists and proselytizing groups, such as the Southern Baptists where they

114 RELIGION IN CONTEMPORARY AMERICA

TABLE 5-13
Certainty and Concern about Belief

"How sure are you that you have found the answers to the meaning and purpose of life?"	Congregationalists	Methodists	Episcopalians	Disciples of Christ	Presbyterians	American Lutherans	American Baptists	Missouri Lutherans	Southern Baptists	Sects	Total Protestants	Catholics
Percentage answering:												
"I am quite certain and I pretty much grew up knowing these things."	23	26	20	30	29	39	34	43	44	49	31	49
"I am quite certain although at one time I was pretty uncertain."	16	16	25	22	25	19	28	27	46	36	25	19
Percentage certain	39	42	45	52	54	48	62	70	90	85	56	68
"I am uncertain whether or not I have found them."	36	32	29	32	28	23	24	18	5	5	25	17
"I am quite sure I have not found them."	11	8	8	0	5	6	3	3	0	1	5	4
"I don't really believe there are answers to these questions."	12	14	14	10	10	10	5	6	4	1	10	8

constitute the modal type. In all, 25 per cent of the Protestants and 19 per cent of the Roman Catholics classified themselves as converts.

Adding together these two types, since they share a present certainty about the meaning and purpose of life, striking denominational differences emerge (see boldface percentages in the table). Thirty-nine per cent of the Congregationalists, 42 per cent of the Methodists, 62 per cent of the American Baptists, and 90 per cent of the Southern Baptists consider themselves "certain" about the ultimate interpretation of existence. Thus, the degree to which their religious faith provides a clear solution to questions of ultimate meaning varies greatly among the Protestants.[13]

The doubtful are those who replied they were "uncertain whether or not" they had found the answers. This is the modal type of Congregationalist (36 per cent), Methodist (32 per cent), and Episcopalian (29 per cent) church member, but is found much less commonly among the more conservative groups. Overall, 25 per cent of the Protestants and 17 per cent of the Roman Catholics doubted the religious perspectives presently available to them. Likely, some of these people are incipient converts who will eventually embrace a religious explanation of life. However, they are probably relatively available for recruitment to other systems of belief. In any event, it seem significant indeed that so large a proportion of actual church members are unconvinced of the validity of Christian perspectives.

The disaffected candidly admit they are "quite sure" they have not found a satisfactory interpretation of ultimate meaning. This is the least common religious stance (5 per cent of all Protestants, and 4 per cent of Roman Catholics), yet a meaningful proportion of those from the more liberal denominations fit this type. These persons, too, are potentially recruitable to some system of ultimate explanation. It must be made clear that such recruitment need not be to religious outlooks, but could as well be to some humanistic *Weltanschauung,* such as those offered

---

13. One caveat must be offered about these findings. It should not be automatically assumed that persons who remain uncertain about the meaning of life are necessarily anxious or estranged from conventional values as a result. While it remains a question for further, careful study, we may report that despair, as measured by the Srole Anomia Scale, is more frequent among the conservative and fundamentalist groups than among the liberals. We would ˋxpect the opposite findings if uncertainty of ultimate meaning produced anxiety.

by science, radical politics, or a variety of other philosophical systems.[14]

The unavailable not only do not accept any ultimate solutions to the question of meaning, they also reject the existence of such answers. We have used the term 'unavailable' to indicate that, unlike either the doubtful or disaffected types, such persons are not currently available for conversion to any ultimate meaning system, since they discredit the validity of all such existential explanations. This type is found among both Protestants (10 per cent), and Catholics (8 per cent), and is somewhat more common in the liberal than in the conservative groups. Although they continue a formal affiliation with a religious body, about one out of ten church members rejects the possibility of explanations for the meaning and purpose of life.

Having examined empirical data on the religious outlooks of the contemporary Christian denominations, we may now return to the question posed at the beginning of this chapter: Is religion in modern America accurately characterized as unified? Do such concepts as 'common core Protestantism,' and 'common American religion' bear any important resemblance to reality?

We suggest that they do not; that differences in the religious outlook of members of the various denominations are both vast and profound. On the basis of our data it seems obvious that American religion has indeed undergone extensive changes in recent decades, but it seems equally obvious that these changes have been greatly misperceived and misinterpreted. In order to clarify the meaning of these religious changes and the new pattern of denominationalism they seem to have produced, we shall begin by considering the question of a secularization of American religion. As was noted in Chapter 4, and again in the present chapter, many commentators have claimed that American religion has become increasingly secularized; that the mystical and supernatural elements of traditional Christianity have been replaced by a demythologized, ethical rather than theological, religion.

In light of the data we have just examined, it seems clear that important changes of this kind have indeed occurred in *some* American denominations. While it is true that we have no comparable data on the theological outlook of church members in times past, there seem compelling historic grounds for assuming

---

14. See Chapters 10, 11, and 14.

that the typical Episcopalian or Congregationalist in the mid-nineteenth century firmly believed such tenets as the Virgin Birth and Biblical miracles that we have just examined. If this assumption is warranted, then it is clear that substantial changes of the kind called 'secularization' have indeed taken place in these religious bodies, for today only a minority of their members adhere to these beliefs. On the other hand, in groups like the Southern Baptists and the various sects, it would appear that commitment to traditional Christian theology has been virtually impervious to change. The fact that these more evangelical and traditionalist denominations have been growing at a faster rate than the mainline denominations suggests that two simultaneous trends have been taking place in American religion: Some portions of the public have been staying with or turning to 'old-time Christianity,' while other portions have been, to a greater or lesser extent, transforming their theological outlook into a less supernatural and miraculous and more naturalistic view of the world. These countervailing trends seem to hold significant implications for future relations among the denominations.

The historic schisms in Christianity were largely marked by subtle doctrinal distinctions and disagreements on proper organizational forms and ritual procedures. All observers generally agree that these issues have lost much of their relevance and divisive potential in contemporary America. Our data confirm these judgments. But while these historic bases for denominationalism seem to have largely subsided, the data we have just examined suggest that new and relatively unremarked cleavages have emerged within the Christian community that may well hold a greater potential for factionalism than did older disputes.

Although earlier disagreements that accompanied the fragmentation of Christianity were bitter, nevertheless they took place among men who, for the most part, shared commitment to such basic components of Christian theology as the existence of a personal and sentient God, the Saviourhood of Christ, and the promise of life-everlasting.

But today, our data indicate that the fissures which map what might well be called the 'New Denominationalism' fragment the very core of the Christian perspective. The new cleavages are not over such matters as how to worship God properly, but whether or not there is a God of the sort it makes any sense to worship; not over whether the bread and wine of communion become the actual body and blood of Christ through transubstantiation, or are only symbolic, but over whether or not Jesus was merely a man. These disagreements, it much be emphasized, are not between Christians and secular society, although this is certainly true as well, but exist substantially *within* the formal boundaries of the Christian churches.

In the light of these findings it seems difficult to account for the hopes and activities directed towards general ecumenicalism. For groups falling close together on the theological continuum from modernism to fundamentalism, such a possibility may well exist. At least there seem no overwhelming theological barriers to merger. But how are we to interpret exploratory talks between Roman Catholics and Episcopalians, or between Methodists and Baptists? Do the participants in the ecumenical dream simply misperceive one another's theological position, or do they consider such matters unimportant? To a degree, both of these factors may be operating, but there are also signs that church leaders are becoming slightly aware of the doctrinal chasms that separate them.

It seems to be the case that the major source of general ecumenical rhetoric, despite these profound doctrinal schisms, is from the most secularized mainline denominations. It is plausible that the theological changes in these bodies have been accompanied by a lessening of concern for theology itself. Thus, these bodies may not view theological barriers to church unity as especially significant, and indeed such barriers hardly pertain to relations among these particular denominations. But it must not be supposed that the more conservative groups are similarly unconcerned about doctrine. A relevant illustration is provided by relations between the National Council of Churches and the fundamentalist bodies. Although continually and bitterly denounced by the more fundamentalist denominations, the National Council retains its composure and continues to encourage these hostile groups to become members.[15]

---

15. An example of awareness among conservative Christians of the doctrinal differences with liberal denominations and their hostility on the point is provided by a recent article in *Christianity Today,* IX:4 (November 20, 1964), which commented on the findings presented here following their appearance in a national wire-service story. The data were used to support a vitriolic attack on "liberal" denominations for "Coddling Atheists," and went on to denounce ecumenicalism.

It may be of some importance that the bodies least amenable to the idea of ecumenicity are those in which there is the greatest consensus on matters of religious belief. Among the Southern Baptists and the various sects, for example, from 90 to 99 per cent of the members take a similar position on major articles of faith. In bodies most concerned about ecumenicity, however, such as the Congregationalists and Episcopalians, members tend to be spread across a wide range of views on theology. Looking at these apparent conflicts on doctrine within these liberal bodies raises the question of how they manage to remain united. Examination of other aspects of these data suggests several factors may be operating. For one thing, persons in the more liberal bodies place considerably less importance on religion and on their own church participation than do members of the more conservative bodies. Thus conflicts over belief may not develop, simply because religion is of relatively low salience to these people. Second, persons in the liberal bodies who do hold traditional beliefs have many of their friends in the congregation, while persons with more secularized theological outlooks report that very few of their friends belong to their congregation. In addition, the sermons preached in these denominations tend to be topical and ethical rather than doctrinal in content while confessions and other ritual aspects of the service retain their traditional form and content. Thus it seems possible that the orthodox minority tends to remain unaware that the majority of their fellow congregants do not share their beliefs because the people they know in the congregation, their friends, do share these beliefs. Meanwhile, the majority, not being linked into the congregation by friendship bonds, may remain largely unaware of the fundamentalist segment of the congregation.[16] In sum, the low salience of religion and differential patterns of association may largely prevent the potential conflicts from coming into the open. There are signs, however, such as the recent rise of theologically conservative lay groups within the more liberal denominations, for example, the current growth of 'tongues-speaking' groups, that strains are developing in these bodies because of their theological differences.

One further aspect of these new denominational cleavages ought to be mentioned in passing. The liberal bodies that have

---

16. See Chapter 6.

most transformed their doctrines generate the least participation and concern among their members. In such matters as attendance at worship services, membership in church organizations, private prayer, and acknowledging religion as playing an important role in their daily lives, the less orthodox Protestant bodies show strikingly lower levels of commitment among their members than the more conservative groups. Furthermore, even within these more secularized denominations, those members who nevertheless retain a traditionally orthodox theological outlook are consistently the more active in the life of the church. This suggests that if a denomination is going to adopt new theological forms, it may well have to find new organizational and ritual forms as well or run the risk of simply settling for a less significant role in the lives of men. Mission societies, the ladies aid, and other traditional church activities may be inappropriate and even distasteful to persons who bring an ethical rather than theological concern to church, and who are perhaps more interested in the social betterment of mankind than in worldwide conversion to Christianity. Similarly, such persons may be more attracted to sermons raising moral questions about social problems than in messages of peace of mind in Christ. In any event, the churches are presently failing to obtain much participation from members with the most modernist religious views.

Returning to our data, at least four and probably five generic theological camps can be clearly identified among the American denominations. The first, which we shall call the *liberals,* comprises the Congregationalist, Methodists, and Episcopalians, and is characterized by having a majority of members who reject firm belief in central tenets of Christian orthodoxy. It seems likely that the changes that have gone on in these bodies, since they are among the highest status and most visible Protestant groups, have largely produced the impressions that Protestantism in general has shifted towards a secular and modernized view of the world.

The second group, the *moderates,* is composed of the Disciples of Christ and the Presbyterians. This group is less secularized than the liberals, but more so than the *conservatives,* who are made of the American Lutheran groups, and the American Baptists. The *fundamentalists* include the Missouri Synod Lutherans, the Southern Baptists, and the host of small sects

Because of historic differences with Protestantism, the Roman Catholics are perhaps properly left to form a fifth distinct group by themselves. But on most theological issues—those presented here and many more—the Roman Catholics consistently resemble the conservatives. Only on special Protestant-Catholic issues such as Papal infallibility (accepted by 66 per cent of the Roman Catholics and only 2 per cent of the Protestants) were the Catholics and the conservatives in any extensive disagreement.

Merging the various denominations to form these five theological groups is the greatest degree of clustering that is statistically permissible. It seems likely that ecumenical clustering would face similar restrictions.

In conclusion, a subsidiary finding in these patterns of belief among the denominations ought to be pointed out. The data seriously challenge the common social science practice of comparing Protestants and Roman Catholics. While Protestant-Catholic contrasts are often large enough to be notable, although often, too, remarkably small, they seem inconsequential compared to differences found *among* the Protestant groups. Indeed, the data indicate that the overall impression of American Protestantism produced when members of all denominations are treated as a single group (the Total Protestant column in the tables) at best bears resemblance to only a few actual denominations making up the Protestant collectivity. Indeed, in some instances these 'average' Protestants do not closely correspond to any *actual* denomination.

This suggests that, to a great extent, when we speak of 'Protestants,' as we so often do in the social sciences, we spin statistical fiction. Thus, it seems unjustified to consider Protestantism as a unified religious point of view in the same sense as Roman Catholicism. Not that Roman Catholicism is monolithic either; clearly there are several theological strands interwoven in the Catholic church too, but there is at least some justification for treating them collectively since they constitute an actual, organized body. Protestantism, on the other hand, includes many separately constituted groups and the only possible grounds for treating them collectively would be if they shared in a common religious vision. Since this is clearly not the case, we shall have to change our ways.

This change in the way we should conceive of Protestantism seems to offer considerably more interesting prospects for future research. It ought to be much more significant to discover what Protestant groups Catholics are similar to and different from on particular issues then to focus on the crude comparisons between the average Protestant and the average Roman Catholic which is characteristically what past studies have done. Furthermore, the data we have presented in this chapter illustrate the importance of examining differences *among* Protestant bodies, for denominationalism seems still to be a major fact in American religious life.

Chapter 6

The Dilemmas of the Parish Church

THIS chapter constitutes an analysis of the contemporary parish church from the perspective of the social sciences, particularly sociology. Its purposes are to exemplify what is meant by this perspective, to report what the social sciences have already learned about some aspects of the church both as a community and as an organization, and to highlight some of the organizational strains confronting the parish church as it seeks to operate effectively in an increasingly complex society.

The evidence reported in the previous chapter raises some fundamental questions about the functioning of the church, particularly in those denominations where heterogeneity rather than homogeneity characterizes what parishioners believe. How does the church at the parish level cope with and contain the diversity? What are the tensions which are introduced? And, more generally, to what extent is the parish church, as it is now organized, appropriate to its traditional goal of making religion the central focus of people's lives. This chapter offers no final answers to these questions. Rather, its purpose is to highlight the dilemmas of the parish church as it struggles for survival in a society which no longer unquestioningly acknowledges its authority.

The chapter considers, in turn, four elements in the structure and function of the parish church: its leadership, its government, its program, and its constituency. The model which is addressed is the typical American Protestant church. However, while the details will vary, the major thrust of what is said is seen to be applicable to Roman Catholic parishes and to Jewish congregations as well.

THE PARISH MINISTRY

The minister is in many respects the central figure in the life of a church, and it seems appropriate, therefore, to begin with some observations on his role. One obvious fact is that it is a multi-faceted role. The minister, in the course of his work, must don many hats and perform in various and sundry ways. Less obvious perhaps is the role's unique symbolic quality. In a very special sense, the minister stands as a man apart, representing for others a symbol of the divine. Finally, the minister is also an organizational man bound by and responsible to a bureaucracy, whose traditions are rooted in denominational history. Each aspect of the ministerial role has its implications for what the minister is, for how effectively he performs, and for the authority he exercises.

The multi-faceted character of the ministerial role is most evident in the parish church. There, typically, the minister is the only full-time, professionally-trained person on the staff. Consequently the burden of responsibility for the church falls primarily on him. In the exercise of this responsibility, the minister is at once pastor and preacher, administrator and organizer, counselor and educator. His multi-faceted role poses a number of problems to him. One is the problem of acquiring the competence to perform these many functions, another the problem of judging the relative importance of each function and dividing his time accordingly, and a third the related problem of resolving the cross-pressures which inevitably arise where there is more to be done than can effectively be done.

The background, training, and skills required of the contemporary minister stand in sharp contrast to what was demanded of him only so short a time as twenty or thirty years ago. The changes have come about not so much in his role as preacher and priest but in his role as pastor, administrator, organizer, and educator. It is becoming increasingly incumbent on the minister to bring an understanding of psychology and psychiatry to his role as a pastoral counselor and of sociology to his task of organizing the church's program to meet the problems of rapid

urban change and surburban development. Nor can he reasonably ignore the fact that administration, too, is increasingly becoming a science and that the philosophy and techniques of
education are constantly changing.

But can anyone, much less the minister, be expected to
prepare himself in all of these manifold areas? The implicit
premise of the contemporary church seems to be that he can—at
least, this would seem to be indicated by the proliferation of
courses in psychology and education in theological schools, by
the establishment of specialized institutes in pastoral counseling,
and by the pressures from denominational headquarters to have
the minister give more attention to parish education and to the
problems of the changing city. How realistic it is to hold this
premise is an open question.

The difficulty, however, is to perceive any reasonable alternative. In other professions, the desirability of specialization is
being increasingly recognized. But there is has been possible to
foster the changes in organizational structures which allow
specialization. This may become possible for the church if the
ecumenical trend continues and there is a consequent decrease
in the number and a concomitant increase in the size of churches.
Presumably, large churches could afford professional staffs
with personnel trained in specialized areas such as religious
education or counseling. There is little evidence of planning for
such an eventuality; nor, for that matter, is very serious attention being given to the desirability and feasibility of greater
specialization within the ministerial role.

For the foreseeable future, it seems likely that the typical
Protestant parish will be relatively small, there will be but one
minister, and he will play a multi-dimensional role. It seems
reasonable, therefore, to pursue the analysis with this model in
mind. Give his manifold functions, deciding how to divide his
time among them becomes a formidable task for the minister.
What decision is made (and for what reasons) is likely to have
significant influence on the character of the parish church.

How the minister actually does divide his time has recently
been studied by the sociologist Samuel Blizzard,[1] who finds that
the average minister spends most of his time, about 40 per cent
of it, in performing the administrative duties of the parish—at-

1. "The Minister's Dilemma," *Christian Century,* LXXIII:17 (April 23,
1957), 00–000.

tending staff meetings, handling publicity, supervising and actually doing clerical and stenographic work, and administering the church's finances. About a quarter of his time, on the average, is devoted to pastoral duties – visiting, ministering to the sick and distressed, and counseling. The functions of preacher and priest take up about 20 per cent of his time, including the time devoted to sermon preparation. The remaining 15 per cent is divided between organizational work and parish education.

These statistics raise two questions: Is this the way the average minister *wants* to spend his time? and, Is this the way he feels he *ought* to spend his time? Generally speaking, ministers are inclined to answer both questions in the negative. They feel that how they spend their time is largely out of their own hands and is dictated by the functional demands of the parish. What they feel they ought to be doing is devoting more of their energies to reflection, contemplation, and planning in connection with the more clearly religious aspects of their role. Whether ministers, given the opportunity, would actually do other things, than they are doing or whether they merely feel that they ought to be doing different things is not answered in Blizzard's research.

A more fundamental issue concerns the basic values which guide the minister in allocating his time. This question has not been subjected to research, but even the casual observer of the American religious scene cannot help but note the great attention given to arranging programs, to meeting budgets, to increasing membership, and to maintaining harmony in congregations. These activities apparently are highly valued and perhaps need to be. What matters, however, is the effect that emphasizing these activities has upon the fulfilment of other church goals. While it would be difficult to argue that attracting new members is not a desirable goal, it may very well be that this task has been given so much attention as to have important negative consequences for other aspects of the church's objectives. Directing evangelistic effort to the unchurched may mean that the task of internal evangelism is neglected. In order to continue to win new members, the church may increasingly compromise the degree of authority which it seeks to exercise over the lives of its members.

What the church holds dear and to what ends its resources

are allocated are not, of course, for the minister alone to decide. He is bound by the traditions of his church and by the prevailing attitudes of his parishioners. To be sure, he is a part of these traditions and exercises an influence over these attitudes. But that his influence is limited is indicated by his own testimony that he is unable to do the things he feels he ought to be doing.

In a constantly changing society, freedom to break with tradition, to alter old ways of doing things and to innovate new ones, is almost a prerequisite to serving communities which have been disrupted by urban redevelopment or in which shifts in racial, religious, and social composition have occurred. How much freedom parishioners and the church-at-large are inclined to permit their ministers in meeting the challenge of social change is thus of more than academic importance. Judging from several recent studies which touch on this issue, the answer for parishioners is "not very much."

In one study done by sociologist Frank Santopolo,[2] a sample of Roman Catholic laymen were presented with a series of drawings depicting a priest in different settings. Some were traditional settings—the priest was shown offering mass, for example—while others were quite nontraditional—in one drawing the priest was playing ball, in another he was helping someone dig a hole. Laymen were asked to interpret what they thought the priest might be doing in each of the drawings and to express their reaction to it. Generally speaking, there was little tolerance for any but the traditional roles. It is of more than passing interest that Santopolo found the clergy considerably more tolerant of nontraditional behavior than the laity.

As will be shown in Chapter 7 present day parishioners place highest value on three aspects of the ministerial role—preaching, visiting members, and visiting nonmembers. Parishioners are most concerned that their ministers not spend too much of their time on administration or working for the church-at-large. In sum, parishioners are most pleased with their ministers when they behave in traditional ways.

That parishioners are particularly hesitant to grant their ministers authority to engage in a partisan way in social, eco-

---

2. So far as is known, Dr. Santopolo has not as yet published the results of his study, which it was done several years ago while he was on the faculty of Fordham University.

nomic, and political affairs is documented by a study of a national sample of Episcopalian parishioners.[3] Parishioners expressed a willingness to have the clergy speak out on issues only where they were related to a traditional concern of the church, for example, prayers in schools.

The results of these studies appear to be related to the observation made earlier that the minister, to some degree, stands as a symbol of the divine. In part, this is reflected in the inclination of the parishioner to impose, implicitly at least, more rigid moral standards on the minister than on himself. It is also reflected in the apparent propensity to perceive the minister in traditional terms and to see any sharp break with tradition as a threat to the symbol. Insofar as ministers must break with tradition to cope with contemporary life, it appears that the church faces a major educational job to encourage an atmosphere in which the minister is allowed greater freedom in defining his role.

The issue would not thereby be wholly resolved, however. The minister is beholden not only to his parishioners but to a denomination whose policies and practices also influence the amount of freedom he can exercise. It is the unusual minister who has no concern for his career and for the standards of promotion set by his denomination. Where these standards are based on traditional values, he is not likely to feel encouraged to try to establish new ones, except perhaps where their impact will be quickly shown. Thinking particularly of ministers serving city churches, denominations would appear to be desperate for new ideas which would make the church's work in the inner city effective. It is suspected, however, that new ideas will not be accepted if they seriously challenge tradition. A minister may see his problem as a long-range one and undertake to institute a program whose fruits may not be apparent for many years. If, in the interim, the minister fails to meet his budget or flaunts the tradition that churches are to be evaluated by the number of new members they recruit each year, his efforts are not likely to be applauded or his work encouraged.

These observations and the research undertaken so far barely begin to illuminate the ministerial role. On many important

---

3. Benjamin B. Ringer, and Charles Y. Glock, "The Political Role of the Church as Defined by its Parishioners," *Public Opinion Quarterly*, XVIII (1954–55).

questions concerning the role and performance of the minister, there is hardly even a basis for speculation. The extent of the moral and religious authority which the minister exercises over the lives of his congregation is a case in point. In the United States alone, the clergy attempts to communicate some message to fifty million people every Sunday. Although the numbers have varied, this communication process has been going on for many years. Yet the church, much less the social sciences, cannot say with authority what has been communicated, with what effect, or to whom.

To the questions which have been raised concerning ministerial performance could be added many more concerning recruitment and training. It is not known systematically what selective processes operate in the recruitment of seminary students. The importance of denominational as against nondenominational colleges in recruitment is another problem deserving exploration. Some have noted the relatively high drop-out rate in theological schools, but no one has sought in a sound empirical way to find out the cases. And there is, of course, very little knowledge available on the educational process in the seminary.

In pointing to these gaps in current knowledge of the ministerial profession, the intention is not to assert that it is the only profession suffering from an absence of information necessary for self-understanding. But the other professions do not seem to be quite as ignorant of themselves. The difference seems to be that the latter are more concerned about their ignorance and more systematic in self-inspection.

PARISH CHURCH GOVERNMENT

Within American Protestantism, three forms of church organization and government may be distinguished — the episcopal, the presbyterian, and the congregational. Theoretically, each of these traditional structures implies a different form of church government at the parish level, a fundamental difference being the amount of authority vested in the hands of the congregation. Formally speaking, American denominations are organized within one or another of these three basic structures. It seems evident, however, that the lines are no longer so sharply drawn as in the past and that, in its quest for autonomy, the average parish church has tended to move toward the congregational model. As between denominations, the similarities in the formal structure of church government at the parish level now outweigh the differences.

In the typical congregation, the reins of government lie in the hands of a church council (vestry, session) usually presided over by the minister. The council varies in size depending on a variety of factors, most often the size of the parish membership. Generally speaking, it will comprise twelve to twenty members drawn (almost always) from the male membership of the church. A formal distinction in council membership between elders and deacons is often made, but this distinction, though sometimes sharply drawn, is more frequently only symbolic so far as the exercise of authority is concerned. The council, under the minister's guidance, is responsible for carrying on the business of the church, and in most matters has authority to act without conferring with the congregation as a whole.

Insofar as the entire congregation participates in church government, it does so at an annual meeting where work of the past year is reviewed and the succeeding year's plans, including the budget, are set forth. The organization of the annual congregational meeting is the responsibility of the council working in collaboration with the minister, who usually presides. The term of office of council members varies but three-year terms are the most common and are usually rotated so that there is never a complete turnover in council membership. The procedure for nominating councilmen also varies, but as a rule the responsibility is given to a nominating committee chaired by a member of the council. The entire congregation participates in voting for councilmen, and individual members have the right to make additional nominations from the floor.

Between congregational meetings, the council ordinarily meets once a month. In most churches, the council is augmented by a group of committees, each charged with some particular responsibility, such as the worship service, finances, education, plant maintenance, evangelism, or stewardship. Committees are most often presided over by a member of the council, and he recruits the membership, usually with the assistance of the pastor. Committee reports are a basic part of the agenda at most council meetings.

The minister is the central figure in church government and, while the amount of control he exercises will vary from congregation to congregation, he is nevertheless ultimately responsible for the conduct of the affairs of the church. He generally plans the agenda for council meetings, chairs the meeting, has the right to sit in on committee meetings, and, formally or informally, has a good deal to say about who is elected to the council and appointed to committees.

Very briefly, this is the typical structure of church government. In examining this structure, the social scientist is likely to ask the following kinds of questions about it: Who constitutes the congregational leadership? How representative is the leadership of the membership of the church? Where does the power lie, and for what purposes is it being exercised? What are the implications of the way in which church government is structured and the way in which it functions for ministerial performance, for the church's program, for the church's role in the community?

The limited research attention that has been given to these questions has been focused on examining the membership composition of governing councils in order to evaluate its effect upon the program of the church. It is possible to point to only two studies in this connection, however, and one of them was done in 1928. That study,[4] conducted by Jerome Davis, investigated the social composition of the boards of control of 387 Protestant churches representing seven denominations. Davis considered his most significant finding to be that "on the whole the membership of the boards of control is made up overwhelmingly of the favored classes." He felt this to be a consequence of the fact that the church of his day was largely a white-collar institution. It was Davis' opinion that such domination of church governing councils resulted in a basically conservative viewpoint on the church's part, a reinforcement of the *status quo,* and a resistance to change and innovation.

There is no evidence that Davis' study had any significant impact on the nation's churches. Since 1928, there has been no other study which has given attention to these questions. However, James Swift has recently examined data from twelve urban Lutheran congregations in a way roughly comparable to that adopted by Davis. Swift's work has not been published, but his findings were made available for summation in this chapter.

The procedure adopted by Swift was to investigate the de-

4. "The Social Action Pattern of the Protestant Religious Leader." *American Sociological Review,* I (February, 1936), 105–114.

gree to which different subgroups of parishioners are represented in leadership positions in the church. In this way, he was
able to provide some insight into the selective processes operating in the election and appointment of church leaders. He
found that these processes differ somewhat from congregation to
congregation but that certain generalizations are warranted and
are applicable to most, if not always to all, of the twelve congregations studied.

It is well known, of course, that women are more often
church members than men, and this was the case in each of the
twelve congregations studied. However, men were consistently
more often represented in leadership positions of the church, the
discrepancy being most marked in the composition of the church
councils of these churches. Membership was exclusively male in
all but two of the councils, and in those there was only one
woman council member in each. This discrepancy has its historical roots, of course, and is reflected in the fact that women
represent but a small minority in secular governments as well.

In his 1928 study, Davis had reported that the median age
for members of the church boards of control was between 45
and 49. Breaking down the data on Lutheran churches for the
purpose of checking this observation in as comparative a way as
possible, Swift found that the leaders of the Lutheran congregations tend to cluster in the forty-to-fifty age group. However, this
was in large part a reflection of the fact that a substantial proportion of the membership as a whole came from this group.
Making comparisons on the basis of the degree to which different age groups were represented in leadership positions, Swift
found great variations from congregation to congregation and
concluded that a generalization on this score was not warranted.
Apparently there were idiosyncratic factors in each congregation which influenced the age composition of the leadership.

Since Davis' study was completed, there has been a marked
upward shift in the educational level of the general population.
It is not surprising, therefore, that Swift found the average
Lutheran leader in the twelve congregations to be much more
highly educated than were the leaders in the Lutheran churches
in Davis' sample. To be sure, the comparison is not entirely
valid, since there were differences in the samples of churches
studied. However, it is of more than passing interest that the
leaders of these twelve churches were divided educationally as

follows: 11 per cent had an elementary school education only, 40 per cent had a high school education, and 46 per cent had had some college training.[5] Generally speaking, the leaders tended to be more highly educated than the general membership, more so, interestingly enough, in the case of women than of men leaders. While pointing to exceptions in some of the congregations studied, Swift concluded that there is a general tendency to turn to the more educated members for leadership.

That this is so is further reflected in the additional finding that the leadership of these churches was predominantly drawn from members who were in the professions or who held managerial positions. And, when leaders were in blue collar occupations, they were likely to be skilled craftsmen rather than unskilled workers. Thus, while acknowledging that there were some congregations which do not entirely fit the pattern, Swift concluded that the general propensity which Davis noted some thirty years ago for congregations to turn to their better educated and more well-to-do members for leadership continues to hold true today, at least insofar as these twelve Lutheran churches are concerned.

These findings are unlikely to come as a surprise. It seems eminently reasonable that a minister should seek out his more talented members to take on major responsibility for guiding the destiny of the parish. Nevertheless, Davis' old questions as to what this implies for the role of the church in society, for its program, and for its impact on the community are still highly relevant. Like his answers, any contemporary evaluation of the significance of church leadership patterns must continue to be speculative, for the necessary data upon which to base a reliable opinion are still absent. But the issue is important enough to justify speculation, if only as an incentive to further research.

It is by now reasonably well established that class differences in society are associated with different ways of looking at the world. In general, the more well-to-do a person is, the more conservative he is likely to be. Living in a world which has satisfactorily served his ends, he is understandably reluctant to see things changed. The less well-to-do person, on the other hand, when he aspires to improve his position often finds that, with things as they are, it is extremely difficult if not impossible

---

5. The remaining 3 per cent failed to report their educational status.

for him to do so. He is naturally, therefore, more open to change which promises to afford him a better life. To be sure, this is a gross oversimplification of a complex set of relationships. Nevertheless, it makes the central point that some basic differences in values distinguish people at different socio-economic levels.

The church, more than most other institutions in society, is committed to serve everyone without regard to sex, age, economic position, race, or ethnic group membership. The question arises as to whether its ability to fulfill this commitment is enhanced by a situation where the commitment is not reflected in its government. It would seem that the relative exclusion of certain groups from church government can only serve to reduce the church's capacity to follow out its commitment in practice.

First of all, the church is likely to become identified with the values of those who are in control. And, if its leadership is conservative and resistant to change, the church is not likely to be able effectively to meet the problems posed by a constantly changing culture, particularly in urban places. The dilemma is well illustrated in the situation faced by many urban congregations where changes in the class composition of church neighborhoods are occurring. Such a situation demands creative innovation of a high order if the church is to survive. Yet even with the best will in the world, the chances are that, because its values are different, a middle-class church council will not understand how to reorient the church's program so that it can adapt to an increasingly lower-income neighborhood.

The hesitancy of the churches to deal effectively, if at all, with the social problems of their communities—juvenile delinquency, crime, alcoholism, drug addiction—is perhaps made more understandable by these observations. These are social disorders which are usually associated with the more deprived groups in society. Middle-class church council members are unlikely to have come into contact with such disorders, to be particularly concerned about them, or to know how they might be dealt with effectively.

The solution is not an easy one, of course. It is not simply a matter of insuring that church councils more adequately represent all segments of the congregation. This might conceivably help but only if some way could be found to develop understanding among different social classes and groups. Here, society-at-large has itself failed to pursue the dialogue, and it seems unlikely that the church can entirely remedy the deficiency. But if the church is to regain its vitality, it is here that there is probably most to be accomplished.

THE CHURCH PROGRAM

The church is unique among voluntary associations in its commitment to serve everyone. While many reject its appeal, the commitment nevertheless has its effect. For, truly, the church includes within its membership a rich assortment of human kind—young and old, rich and poor, informed and ignorant, doctor, lawyer, beggar man, and thief. The degree of heterogeneity varies, to be sure, from parish to parish. There are parishes whose membership is drawn largely from older age groups, others where the proportion of female members is extremely high, still others which appeal predominantly to one or another social class, and many where the members are all of one race. Even in these parishes, however, similarities in one respect are likely to be counterbalanced by differences in others. Generally, the parish church, when compared with other voluntary organizations, is distinguished by its heterogeneity rather than by its homogeneity.

This heterogeneity has a profound implication for the task of organizing the church's program. In effect, it defines that task as developing a program which in one way or another will appeal to and involve many different kinds of people. Carried to an extreme, this would mean developing a complex programmatic apparatus which would take into account the entire range of interests and concerns, habits and customs, values and attitudes which are represented in the varied membership of the average church. This is clearly beyond the capacity of the smaller one-minister parish and would strain the resources of even the most well-endowed larger church. Some compromise is obligatory. In the average church, age and sex are taken to be the two most important characteristics determining members' interests and capabilities, and church programs are organized primarily around age and sex distinctions.

This decision is reflected in the church's program in many ways. At the most general level, it is exhibited in the distinction made between children and adults, Sunday school being the principal source of contact with the former and worship services and Bible classes with the latter. Beyond this, many other aspects of the church's program are organized around finer age distinctions. There is the cradle roll for the very young, junior and senior Scouts for the next age levels, the young people's society for the next, the young couple's club for the newly married, and so on up to the Golden Age society for the aged. Some of these activities are open to both boys and girls, both men and women. Many of them are not, however, and next to age, sex becomes the primary characteristic for organizing the church's program. Here, particularly at the middle and older age levels, the emphasis is given to women's activities presumably because women ordinarily have more time to devote to the church.

It is the unusual church which will organize the bulk of its activities around other than age and sex differences. There are some that recognize the need for programs that take account of differences in parishioners' level of sophistication and educational background. There are others which take cognizance of differences in recreational interests despite similarities in age and sex. In making assignments to church committees, differences in personality, in interests, in background and ability are likely to be taken into account. And, in the counseling activity carried on by the minister, some provision is made for meeting the idiosyncratic needs of individual members of the church. By and large, however, age and sex loom largest in their influence on the organization of the formal program of the church.

That this is so is not surprising. Age and sex are indicators of basic differences in capabilities, in interests, and in attitudes, and it would be difficult as well as foolish to ignore them in the development of parish programs. Their importance is reflected in the structure and program of many secular organizations as well—in schools, lodges, welfare groups, youth organizations, and so on. The crucial differences, however, is in the degree of their influence over programs. In most secular organizations age and sex tend, paradoxically, to have less influence precisely because these organizations are open to or attract members of like age and of one sex. As a consequence, they are in a better position to consider other factors over and above age and sex in the development of their programs. Because its membership is so heterogeneous, the church is in no position to ignore the importance of age and sex in the construction of its program. But it cannot easily take account of other differences because its resources are so limited, particularly in the one-minister parish.

There is no intention here to suggest a resolution to this dilemma. It is altogether possible that there is no solution. It is nevertheless important to be aware of the many possible implications of parishioner heterogeneity, especially in the pursuit of the churches educational aims. Here, more than in other areas, differences in the abilities, interests, and values of individuals make it almost obligatory that all educational programs not be cut from the same cloth. What constitutes effective education for the plodder may alienate the gifted. Conversely, education aimed at the gifted will not be easily communicated to the less talented. This is a basic problem faced by educational institutions generally. Ordinarily, however, the school, the college, and the university are able to make some provision for adjusting the level of education to the level of the pupil. This is much more difficult to accomplish in the church. Most Sunday schools are not large enough to organize classes into sections. It is not feasible to present different sermons to different parish groups. Nor is it usually possible to have a varied enough adult education program to meet the interests and needs of all. To be sure, there is no evidence that parishioners are particularly motivated by educational considerations to join the church. However, the church has an educational objective and, if it is not realized, its overall program suffers even if it still manages to retain its membership.

A further consequence of parishioner heterogeneity may be to inhibit creative innovation in programing except where it may have a mass appeal. A minister may feel it highly desirable, for example, to form a group to discuss and develop the church's resources for dealing with community problems. If only a small number of members exhibit an interest in such a group, the minister is hard pressed to justify devoting his time to it rather than to programs having a broader appeal. Under pressure, he is likely to forego the experimental program in favor of one which generates more widespread interest. Where resources are limited, the temptation is to program something which will have the broadest appeal. Whether this is the most satisfactory criterion for programing is an open question.

Judged by a number of criteria — having a religiously literate and committed membership, dealing effectively with social problems, having a significant impact on the community, exercising authority over the basic values of the society — the church can scarcely be said to be meeting its potential. In part, the gap is undoubtedly a consequence of the way in which the church's program is (and perhaps must be) organized. The church's commitment to a heterogeneous membership probably will not be abandoned, but it might be pursued in ways less destructive to the church's programmatic activity.

THE PARISHIONER AND HIS CHURCH

In the final analysis, the nature, the significance, and perhaps even the destiny of the church is determined by the kind and degree of commitment which it expects and receives from its parishioners. Recalling Chapter 2, there are five ways in which the parishioner is expected to manifest commitment: ritually, ideologically, experientially, intellectually, and consequentially.

Presumably, churchmen as well as parishioners are in agreement that these are all relevant dimensions of commitment. The truly committed parishioner would be expected to evince his commitment in all of them. What is not so clear is precisely what the church expects from its parishioners in each of these dimensions. Most agreement would probably be secured in the realm of religious practice. Regular church attendance would be universally more highly valued than irregular attendance; praying every day would be more highly approved than doing so less frequently or not at all. But, even in this area, disagreement may arise as, for example, in the continuing discussion of 'high church' versus 'low church' practices.

On the belief dimension, the importance of religious belief as a manifestation of commitment is not likely to be questioned. Disagreement does arise, however, in defining what beliefs the committed parishioner ought to hold. We have seen in the previous chapter that not only do denominations differ in this regard; there is also great variation within denominations between and among both clergy and laity. Similarly, the importance placed on knowledge about one's church, its traditions, rituals, beliefs, and history varies among churchmen.

In the realm of religious experience there seems to be disagreement as to both the importance of this dimension and the kinds of religious experience necessary to manifest commitment. Thus, for example, some religious groups place high value on the expression of religious emotion while others are embarrassed by any display of religious feeling.

Finally, while there is a general expectation that commitment in practice, belief, knowledge, and experience ought to have consequences for other aspects of behavior, precisely what these should be is very much open to debate. Whether, for example, the committed Christian has a responsibility to live up to certain traditional moral codes (such as were exemplified in the 'blue laws') continues to be an abiding question.

The lack of agreement about what is or should be expected of the committed parishioner in each of these dimensions is paralleled by considerable disagreement concerning the emphasis to be accorded to each. Within Lutheranism, for example, the theological emphasis on 'salvation by faith' has tended to lead to a de-emphasis on 'works,' irrespective of what Luther may have actually intended. The debate between those who would have the church 'stick to religion and stay out of politics' and those who take the view that 'everything in the sight of God is a responsibility of the church' is another indication of the relative lack of accord.

It is recognized that these observations highlight the disagreements and overlook the existence of and the necessity for some degree of consensus if the church is to exist at all. Certainly, at the parish level, these differences will not all be in evidence. Nevertheless, even at this level, incipient disagreement, as noted in the previous chapter, can be great enough to limit seriously the kind and amount of authority which the church seeks to have and is capable of exercising in both the lives of its parishioners and the life of the community-at-large. Standards which are not explicit and not uniformly expressed are not likely to be convincing or to provide effective guides for behavior.

Irrespective of the variations in expectations, parishioners do differ in the kind and strength of their commitment to the church. No minister would argue otherwise. This raises a number of empirical questions about the parishioner's ties to his church which also have their implications for defining the church's nature. How do parishioners, in fact, differ in their commitment? What accounts for the difference? Why, for example, are some parishioners more ritually observant than others? And what difference does the kind and the strength of the parishioner's commitment make for other aspects of his behavior—for his life goals, for his relationships with others, for his morality, for his mental health, for his perceptions of the social world? While these questions have still to be given systematic attention, some preliminary answers are beginning to come from a study now in process of differential 'involvement' in the church based on data collected from a national sample of the membership of the Protestant Episcopal Church.[6]

This study does not include information on the religious beliefs of Episcopalians. It does, however, provide data on their ritual observance as measured by attendance at worship services and participation in the sacrament of Holy Communion, their participation in the organizational life of the church as represented by the proportion of their total organizational life devoted to church groups, and their 'intellectual' interest in religious matters as represented by the extent of their reading of religious periodicals and Scripture. There is a relatively high degree of association among these three different indicators of involvement, i.e., the more ritually observant Episcopalians are, the more active they are in the organizational life of the church and the more attention they give to religious literature.

The fact of this high relationship between different indicators of involvement made it possible to combine them into a single composite index of involvement. The analytical questions which were then asked were concerned with how the more involved parishioners differ from the less involved and what accounts for the differences.

The data show a greater involvement for female than for male parishioners at every age level from twenty years up. Not only is the church more successful in attracting women than men to membership; among present members it is more successful in involving women in its activities. This is perhaps not too surprising since it is to be expected that women have more time to devote to the church. However, the difference holds even when the comparison is made simply on the basis of attendance at worship service.

Involvement also varies greatly with different periods of the life cycle. Before they are married, both men and women exhibit a relatively high involvement, which declines with marriage and decreases even further when the first child is born. As children grow older, there is a resurgence of interest in the church—how-

---

6. Charles Y. Glock, Benjamin Ringer, and Earl Babbie, *The Social Sources and Consequences of Church Involvement* (New York: The Free Press of Glencoe, 1966).

ever, it is now greater for women than for men. As they get still older, women tend to become even more involved, reaching the highest point in the later years of life. Men also show a slight increase as they get older but the difference between men and women becomes greater rather than smaller. The fact that older parishioners exhibit higher involvement than younger ones may possibly contribute to what many have observed as the conservatism of the contemporary church. Older people are generally more set in their ways and feel less comfortable about change. And if they are more involved in the church, presumably they have a greater influence on its affairs.

It was also possible to consider the bearing of marital and family status on involvement. Among both male and female Episcopalians thirty years of age and older, those with both a spouse and children are consistently less involved than those with neither or with one but not the other. Those who are both spouseless and childless are the most highly involved. This finding contrasts sharply with the general propensity of the church to picture its members in the image of the nuclear family. That its membership includes persons without complete family ties is seldom recognized in sermons, church literature, church programs. Whether this has had the effect of alienating some without or with only partial family ties is not known. It would certainly seem to be the case where partial ties or the absence of ties is a result of divorce. But where the church does succeed in winning those with incomplete families to membership, it would appear that these people tend to be among its more loyal members.

An examination of the relationship between involvement and the parishioner's social class revealed that social status is less strongly related to involvement than sex, age, or family ties. Insofar as any generalization is warranted, parishioners having upper-class status tend to be the least involved. The differences between those classified as middle and lower class are neither significant nor highly consistent when differences in age and sex are taken into account. As was mentioned earlier, the church tends to draw on its more well-to-do members for positions of leadership. There is, then, the possibility that positions of leadership in some parish churches go to those who are least religiously involved.

This is as far as the analysis of the concomitants of involvement has been pursued. The results would appear to be useful in affording some limited descriptive information on what kinds of people are more likely to be involved in the church. The problem of explaining differential involvement, however, is left largely untouched. A clue which may contribute to an explanation is suggested by the fact that those characteristics associated with low involvement are all more highly valued by the society-at-large than the characteristics associated with high involvement. Society affords greater opportunities to the male than to the female. It values youth more highly than old age. Like the church itself, it places a high regard on the family. Those without complete family ties are, at least to some extent, deviants. And that society highly esteems wealth requires no documentation. The extremes of the discrepancy are best visualized by seeing the wealthy young man with a family at one end and the poor elderly widow at the other. Clearly, all of the rewards and gratifications which society has to offer are readily accessible to the former while they are almost wholly withheld from the latter.

What these observations suggest is that a strong factor influencing deep involvement in the church may be a feeling of being rejected by general society. Where it rejects, the church is there to offer a helping hand. Thus, involvement in the church affords a source of gratification for those who cannot find it in society-at-large.

The speculative character of these observations must, of course, be recognized. Insofar as they may be true, they point to a central and important function which the church may be serving in society. At the same time, they pose additional dilemmas for the church. The church's mission, though it includes serving those who feel rejected by the world, is not identical with this service. What is at issue, however, is whether the church can have a significant influence on society if its strength lies in its appeal to those who feel some sense of estrangement from that society.

It is important, obviously, that these speculations be tested with a high degree of scientific rigor before they are acted upon. In whatever testing may be done, some attention must necessarily be given to elaborating the concept of rejection beyond what has been attempted here.[7] One of the issues to be considered concerns the question of whether turning to the church represents an attempt to escape from the world or a way to deal rationally with it. Both possibilities exist. Some credence is

---

7. This task is pursued in Chapter 13.

given to the latter possibility as the more salient one by an additional finding of the Episcopal study.

In this study, parishioners were distinguished by whether they preferred having the church remain aloof from the affairs of the world or whether they preferred it to play an active role in public affairs. It was hypothesized that if high involvement represents a desire to escape from the world then the more highly involved parishioners would tend to want the church to remain aloof from social, economic, and political affairs. If the involved parishioner was attempting to escape from the world, presumably he would want the church to escape with him. The results do not confirm this possibility. Rather, they indicate that the more highly involved feel about the same as the less highly involved on the issue of church participation in public life. The absence of a relationship lends some support to the notion that involvement, rather than representing an escape from the world, represents a means to live comfortably within it. There remains the question of what the consequences of differential involvement may be for other aspects of the parishioner's behavior and attitudes. Clearly this is a matter of some importance to understanding the nature of commitment.

CONCLUSIONS

The course that has been followed has pointed to a number of dilemmas of the contemporary church: the dilemma of reconciling the religious and secular functions of the ministerial role; the dilemma of recruiting talented congregational leadership while still representing the membership in church government; the dilemma of organizing, with limited resources, an effective parish program in the face of parishioner heterogeneity; the dilemma of developing consensus on commitment in an atmosphere of incipient disagreement.

Underlying and implicit in all of these is the more fundamental dilemma of defining the church's task in contemporary society. It is here, of course, that the church is confronted in the broadest sense with the complexities of modern culture. In that confrontation, traditional answers stated in abstract terms are not likely to suffice. The church has still to say explicitly what its objectives are and what values it is dedicated to in ways that are meaningful not only in principle but in practice in today's world. There will be occasion in Part III to examine this matter somewhat more fully.

Chapter 7

Parishioners' Views of How Ministers Spend Their Time

HAVING considered some of the general problems facing the parish church in its efforts to generate and mobilize human resources, we shall now examine certain problems of the ministerial role. Specifically, we shall be concerned with the tensions that derive from the multiple roles the minister must perform: administrator, pastor, preacher, teacher, and private citizen.

As noted in the preceding chapter, the minister typically must perform a large variety of functions—more, perhaps, than any other professional. He must be able both to serve his parishioners in many different ways and to operate a voluntary organization—the parish church—almost singlehandedly. Except in larger churches, his only paid assistance will be for music and custodial duties.

Allocation of time thus becomes a central problem for the minister, and the decisions he makes partly determine the character of his church. In turn, the decisions of many ministers contribute to shaping the character of a denomination and of the ministerial profession itself. Blizzard, as noted earlier, has gone extensively into the question of time allocation.[1] On the basis of interviews with 480 urban and rural ministers, he distinguishes

---

1. Samuel Blizzard, article in *The Christian Century*, April 25, 1956.

six basic ministerial functions and has the following to say about how the minister's time is distributed among them:

> The professional work day of the cooperating ministers averages a few minutes less than ten hours . . . almost two fifths of their total work day was spent as administrator. Slightly more than one fourth was devoted to the pastor role. Preaching and priestly activities took up almost one fifth of the work day. Organizing consumed more than one tenth of the work day. The residual time (about one twentieth) was devoted to teaching.

In commenting on these figures, Blizzard goes on to say that ministers

> . . . actually spend most of their time doing those things they feel are least important. Denominational goals and programs and local parish needs determine the use of their time. But these activities bring the least satisfaction. Hence the various offices of the ministry are normatively in one order of priority and functionally in another order of priority.

The present chapter follows in the tradition of Blizzard's work but approaches the problem of the allocation of the minister's time from the perspective of the parishioner rather than from that of the minister. It is concerned with two questions. What are parishioners' estimates of how their ministers spend their time? And what estimates generate the most approval?

The study is based on the secondary analysis of 2,729 questionnaires received in 1956 from a sample of the membership of twelve urban Lutheran congregations located primarily in the East and Middle West.[2] In the questionnaire, parishioners were asked the following questions, the responses to which form the basis of our analysis:

> 1. As far as you know, what two kinds of work does your pastor spend *most* of his time on? What two kinds of work does he spend *least* of his time on? (Eight alternatives were offered: preparing sermons, visiting members, visiting nonmembers, attending church meetings, office work, work for the church at large, giving people advice, his own recreation.)
> 2. For each of these activities, check whether you think your pastor spends too much, too little, or about the right amount of time on each? If you feel you can't answer, check "Don't know."

---

2. The initial analysis was reported in Walter Kloetzli's *The City Church – Death or Renewal* (Philadelphia: The Muhlenberg Press, 1961).

PERCEPTIONS OF MINISTERIAL ACTIVITY

As might be expected, opinions about how ministers spend their time varied from congregation to congregation; nevertheless there was a high degree of consistency among them. How the twelve congregations ranked the eight activities is reported in Table 7–1. The numbers represent how many of the twelve congregations assigned the indicated rank to each activity. In this table, the modal rank appears in boldface. The mean rank is reported in the column to the far right.

Sermon preparation is most often ranked first as the activity on which ministers spend most of their time. All congregations were agreed that their ministers spend least time on their own recreation. Between these two extremes, work for the church at large and attending church meetings ranked second and third, respectively, whether the comparisons are made using the modal or the mean rank. Office work, giving people advice, visiting nonmembers, and visiting members come next in that order based on the modal rank. The mean ranks suggest, however, that parishioners perceive little difference in the relative emphasis given these four activities.

Unfortunately, no parallel data are available from the ministers reporting how they actually do distribute their time among

TABLE 7-1

Parishioners' Ranking of Time Spent on Eight Activities by Ministers in Twelve Lutheran Congregations*

Activity	Most time 1	2	3	4	5	Least time 6	7	8	Mean rank
Sermon preparation	**8**	2	2	–	–	–	–	–	1.5
Work for church at large	2	**5**	3	1	–	1	–	–	2.6
Attending church meetings	2	2	**5**	2	1	–	–	–	2.8
Office work	–	–	–	**5**	2	2	3	–	5.2
Giving people advice	–	–	1	2	**6**	2	1	–	5.0
Visiting nonmembers	–	1	1	1	1	**5**	3	–	5.4
Visiting members	–	2	–	1	2	2	**5**	–	5.4
His own recreation	–	–	–	–	–	–	–	**12**	8.0

*Ranks were based on scores for each activity computed by subtracting the number of "least" responses from the number of "most" responses and dividing by "n." "Don't know" responses, which ranged from 27 to 52 per cent of the parishioners in the twelve congregations, were omitted in the computation of this table.

these eight activities. We cannot, therefore, compare parishioners' perceptions with the ministers' actual behavior. However, Blizzard reports for his study that time devoted to sermon preparation averages 36 minutes out of a ten-hour day. This scarcely jibes with our parishioners' general judgment that ministers spend most of their time on sermon preparation.

Though we can only speculate about what contributes to parishioners' estimates, it would appear that the number of parishioners to whom an activity is visible largely determines how it is ranked. Parishioners' primary contact with their ministers is at Sunday worship services at which the sermon is featured. Since this is the one activity that parishioners are regularly exposed to, it seems not surprising that sermon preparation should loom large in their awareness. On the other hand, even where a minister gives a great deal of his time to office work, counselling, and visiting, these activities do not bring him into sustained contact with many parishioners at frequent intervals. This relatively infrequent contact may well lead parishioners to believe that these activities do not take much of the minister's time.

Except for worship services, organizational meetings are the most frequent occasion for regular contact of parishioners with the minister. That this activity tends to rank high is in line with our visibility hypothesis. Work for the church at large, though the least visible of the eight activities, nevertheless ranks second in parishioners' estimates of the activities on which ministers spend most of their time. It may be, of course, that ministers are careful to report this kind of activity to the membership. It is also a possibility that, somewhat perplexed as to how the minister manages to find enough to do, parishioners are led to guess that he does things which are outside their purview. To be sure, they could just as well decide that the minister spends his time on his own recreation. To do so, however, would be in serious conflict with parishioner expectations about ministerial behavior.

When compared to Blizzard's findings, these observations suggest that the church and its ministry have perhaps failed to communicate effectively to the membership just what the ministerial role entails in practice. They also suggest the hypothesis that the image of a profession among its clientele will be largely informed by what is visible in professional activity.

PARISHIONERS' EVALUATIONS OF MINISTERIAL ACTIVITY

How a parishioner perceives his minister is one thing; how he evaluates what he sees turns out to be another. Table 7–2 shows that the degree to which ministers elicit congregational approval varies considerably depending on how they are thought to spend their time, i.e., whether they are thought to spend most, least, or neither most nor least of their time on an activity. The approval scores reported in the table were weighted to insure equal representation of each congregation, regardless of size. The scores range from 0 to 1; the higher the score, the greater the approval.

Table 7–2 tells us, in effect, whether it is 'better' for a minister to be thought of as spending most, least, or neither most nor least of his time on each activity. Approval is most likely to come where the minister is perceived as devoting considerable time to visiting members and nonmembers, as not spending much time on office work, and as striking a reasonable balance in the amount of time spent in sermon preparation, work for the church at large, attending church meetings, and giving people advice. If he fails to strike a proper balance in these last four

TABLE 7-2

Index of Parishioner Approval of Eight Ministerial Activities According to Parishioner Conceptions of Time Spent on Them

Activity	Approval score* for parishioners who perceive their ministers as spending:		
	Most of their time on an activity	Least of their time on an activity	Neither most nor least of their time on an activity
Sermon preparation	.65	.05	.80
Work for church at large	.25	.55	.70
Attending church meetings	.45	.50	.55
Office work	.00	.85	.65
Giving people advice	.60	.10	.80
Visiting nonmembers	.80	.10	.65
Visiting members	.85	.00	.65

*Scores should not be interpreted as representing proportion of parishioners approving an activity. In fact, a majority of parishioners were uncritical of their ministers.

activities, he is better off to emphasize sermon preparation and giving people advice and to de-emphasize working for the church at large. Mild approval is given to attending church meetings almost regardless of perceptions of time spent on it.

The two activities—visiting members and nonmembers—on which the minister is generally thought to spend least of his time are nevertheless those two activities most approved when they are believed to occupy most of his time. On the other hand, sermon preparation—though generally conceived to occupy most time—is most highly approved when it is believed to take only a middling amount of time. The conclusion appears to be that parishioners would like ministers to spend more time on visits and less time on sermon preparation.

The relatively high emphasis which members would have their ministers give to counselling is undoubtedly, in part, a reflection of the fact that this function has had a traditional place in the church. It may also be a sign of the impact which the development of psychotherapy has had on perceptions of the ministerial role.

Most ministers would probably applaud the parishioners' view that they should not spend too much time on office work, while at the same time wondering what sacrifices members would be willing to make to relieve them of this burden. At the same time, they may be perplexed by the finding that how much time ministers spend attending church meetings makes little difference in congregational approval. Here, the relative lack of a clear-cut parishioner preference may be a result of some ambiguity in interpreting what attending church meetings means —the wording could mean meetings of parish organizations or meetings outside the church at the conference, synod, or denominational level. That ministers receive slightly greater approval if they are perceived as spending least rather than most of their time on this activity perhaps suggests a parishioner propensity to make the latter interpretation.

This is given some confirmation by the finding for work for the church at large. Here, work outside the parish is clearly implied, and having the minister spend least of his time on this activity is clearly preferred to his spending most of his time on it. However, parishioners appear to recognize this as an appropriate ministerial function assuming that it is given a reasonable

KANSAS SCHOOL OF RELIGION
University of Kansas
1300 Oread Avenue
LAWRENCE, KANSAS 66044

amount of time. Comparing the results of Tables 7-1 and 7-2, ministers are thought to give somewhat more time to this activity than parishioners would like.

CONCLUSIONS

These results suggest that the pastoral (including evangelistic) and preaching functions of the ministerial role are paramount to the parishioner, that he wants his minister to focus his energies on these tasks, and that he is prone to be critical where these expectations are not met. Ministers, according to Blizzard, give precedence to preaching rather than to the pastoral function, but both functions take precedence over all other activities. The two—ministers and laity—are not far apart in their preferences.

In practice, Blizzard's ministers acknowledge that they are obliged to de-emphasize these functions under the pressure of other parish duties. The parishioners in this study recognize the neglect of the pastoral function at least. In a sense, both minister and parishioner are pleading for a greater specialization in the ministerial role in the face of an institutional situation which inhibits specialization. This is one dilemma for the church posed by the two studies.

Another, and perhaps more subtle, dilemma has to do with the role of an institution strongly committed to tradition in a constantly changing society. Among the activities both studies have examined, it is the preaching and pastoral functions which are the most traditional to the church and it is here that primary commitment—both ministerial and lay—appears to lie.

Chapter 8

Social Contexts and Religious Experience

CHAPTER 3 developed a set of theoretical types for classifying religious experience. Building on that scheme, the present chapter attempts to assess the degree to which such felt encounters with the supernatural are a product of social situations. We shall also see how commonly members of contemporary Christian churches in America have such religious experiences, and how much this varies from one denomination to another.

The classic works on religious experience were all written from a psychological point of view.[1] Whether the phenomenon was considered 'normal' or 'abnormal,' to the degree that an effort was made to explain the occurrence of religious experiences, primary attention was paid to various aspects of the human psyche. Such terms as "auto-eroticism," "hysteria," "neurasthenia," "instincts," "guilt," "pathological unhappiness" and "querulous melancholy," characterize the variables used and the rhetoric in which they were cast. To a lesser extent these writers also credited certain individual statuses such as age, sex, or "insecurity of natural goods,"[2] as affecting the propensity for religious experience.

---

1. The three major works on religious experience are: James H. Leuba, *The Psychology of Religious Mysticism* (New York: Harcourt, Brace, and Co., Inc., 1925); Edwin Diller Starbuck, *The Psychology of Religion* (New York: Charles Scribner's Sons, 1899); and, of course, William James, *The Varieties of Religious Experience* (New York: Mentor Books, 1958), first published in 1902.

2. James, *op. cit.*

We do not mean to suggest that such social-psychological qualities of individuals are unimportant for an understanding of religious experience; yet it seems obvious that the most significant single cause of felt encounters with the divine was overlooked by these early psychologists. If we adopt a cross-cultural view of human affairs for a moment, it is apparent that the vast majority of instances when human beings have thought themselves confronted with supernatural agencies occurred in social situations where, far from being unusual, such experiences were considered normal. Indeed, in many such situations, failure to manifest religious experience would have been deemed atypical, perhaps even bizarre. The early psychologists regarded religious experience as problematic or even unusual on the basis of their conceptions of what was customary in modern societies. Had such a social science enterprise sprung up among the Indians of the Southwest, for instance, the question would probably have been posed in a rather different way: Why do some persons *fail* to undergo religious experiences?

The point we are trying to emphasize is that some social situations are structured to produce religious experiences among participants. In such circumstances, it is as irrelevant to seek the causes of such behavior in purely individual terms as it would be to search for a personality syndrome to account for the fact that Roman Catholics typically genuflect when passing in front of an altar. The primary causes for such normative behavior are understood to be located in the social environment, not to be an additive outcome of unrelated individually motivated actions.

All this is elementary. But we are proposing a somewhat more radical criticism of the psychological explanations of religious experience than merely to point out that such theories break down when applied cross-culturally. We mean to challenge the basic assumption that religious experience is problematic and is primarily an individually motivated act in *our* society. Such an assumption, it would seem, is predicated on a simplistic view of our modern society as homogeneous and on a corresponding failure to perceive the great tangle of subgroups and subcultures which make an American Society something of a fiction unless it is defined with a good deal of sophistication. By ignoring the complex social character of modern societies, these psychologists applied a rhetoric of abnormality to religious experience prematurely, that is, without first distinguishing persons for whom such behavior could be considered "unusual" from those for whom such behavior must be classed as "normal" (i.e., norm-governed).

As pointed out in Chapter 3, certain of the conservative and fundamentalist denominations and sects in America have well-organized and institutionalized mechanisms for generating and channeling religious experiences, particularly of the salvational variety. Anyone who has attended a revival meeting has observed a social situation where definitions concerning the appropriateness and character of particular varieties of religious experience are fostered and maintained, and where persons present are subjected to great pressure and inducement to conform to these normative expectations and consummate an encounter with a divine agency. Consider, for example, the collective nature of religious experiences among the mountain folk of Tennessee in this account by H. L. Mencken:

> [after a long harangue by a revival preacher and some witnessing by various members on the efficacy of the Holy Ghost, the group began to sing hymns] . . . Suddenly a change of mood began to make itself felt. The last hymn ran longer than the others, and dropped gradually into a monotonous, unintelligible chant. The leader beat time with his book. The faithful broke out with exultations . . . At a signal the faithful crowded up to the bench [on which a young girl lay repentant for having "bobbed" her hair] and began to pray—not in unison, but each for himself. At another they all fell on their knees, their arms over the penitent . . . Suddenly [the leader] rose to his feet, threw back his head and began to speak in the tongues—blub-blub-blub, gurgle-gurgle-gurgle. His voice rose to a higher register. The climax was a shrill, inarticulate squak, like that of a man throttled. He fell headlong across the pyramid of supplicants.
>
> From the squirming and jabbering mass a young woman gradually detached herself . . . Her head jerked back, the veins of her neck swelled, and her fists went to her throat as if she were fighting for breath. She bent backward until she was like a half a hoop. Then she suddenly snapped forward . . . Presently her whole body began to be convulsed—great throes that began at the shoulders and ended at the hips. She would leap to her feet, thrust her arms in air, and then hurl herself upon the heap . . . [Her behavior] seemed to be contagious too, for soon a second penitent, also female, joined the first, and then came a third, and a fourth, and a fifth . . . [one of these] was bounding all over the place . . . Every time her head came up a stream of hosannas would issue out of it. Once she collided with a dark,

undersized brother, hitherto silent and stolid. Contact with her set him off as if he had been kicked by a mule. He leaped into the air, threw back his head, and began to gargle as if with a mouthful of BB shot. Then he loosed one tremendous stentorian sentence in the tongues, and collapsed.[3]

From the point of view of sedate, middle-class church-goers and of Mencken's urban readers, such goings-on were a source of mirth or disgust, to be regarded as bizarre, strange, foolish, and somewhat demented. But this is not the case viewed from the perspective of these backwoods participants. To them, Mencken, who lurked in the shadows smoking a cigar, was the 'abnormal' man.

Not only is religious experience appropriate in some contexts, but some groups foster and maintain norms concerning religious experiences which members will seek and undergo in private. Considering the existence of such social situations in contemporary America, it seems likely that for some persons religious experience is not problematic but simply conformity to the norms of relatively stable social groups.

For this reason, a search for the sources of religious experience must begin with an examination of the prevalence and effects of such social settings. By discovering how much religious experience is accounted for by compliance to norms, we would be in a position to search for the factors which elicit such behavior among persons in social contexts where religious experiences are indeed problematic or even regarded as deviant. Furthermore, we could then seek to explain why persons join or remain in groups which sanction religious experiences.

Chapter 3 developed a detailed series of types for classifying religious experience, which was defined as *some sense of contact with a supernatural agency.* Four general types of religious experience were postulated:

The confirming type: The human actor simply notes (feels, senses, etc.) the existence or presence of the supernatural actor, but the supernatural is not perceived as specifically acknowledging the human actor.

The responsive type: Mutual presence is acknowledged, the supernatural actor is believed to specifically note (respond to) the presence of the human actor.

---

3. H. L. Mencken, "The Hills of Zion," in Alistair Cooke, ed., *The Vintage Mencken* (New York: Vintage Books, 1956), pp. 158–159.

The ecstatic type: The awareness of mutual presence is replaced by an affective relationship akin to love or friendship.

The revelational type: The human actor perceives himself as becoming a confidant of or a fellow participant in action with the supernatural actor.

Within each of these types several subtypes were specified. Of these, only two subvarieties of the responsive type need concern us in the present chapter. These subtypes are:

The salvational: being acknowledged as especially virtuous; 'chosen,' 'elect,' or 'saved' by the divine actor.

The sanctioning: experiencing the displeasure of the supernatural actor; being chastised or punished by the supernatural.

The primary feature of this conceptual scheme is order. The underlying assumption on which the types were developed was that religious experience is a systematically progressive phenomenon; that the diverse instances when men believe they have encountered the divine follow a patterned sequence. This development was likened to the pattern through which normal interpersonal relations build up along a continuum of increasing intimacy. It was recognized that such development could be arrested anywhere along the way; but however much men may differ in the degree of intimacy they experience with supernatural agencies, they start at the same place and move along the same route.

As was pointed out in the earlier chapter, this ordering of religious experiences into a series of generic intervals along a dimension of intimacy coincides with the order suggested by several other criteria, including the normative definitions attached to the various types by both religious and secular standards. Nevertheless, the case for this order must rest primarily on statistical grounds. If religious experience is a unidimensional phenomenon in the manner specified, then the relative frequency with which the various types occur in the population must decrease from the less to the more intimate varieties. Similarly, men who have experienced more intimate types should have undergone the less intimate. Furthermore, the relative frequency of the types should decrease within the experience of individuals. That is, men who periodically undergo several varieties of religious experience should manifest the less intimate more often than the more intimate. They should also experience the less intimate prior to ever experiencing the more intimate. Of these various tests of the postulated order, the last two cannot be assessed with the data at hand.[4] Since respondents were not asked to date the first occasion of any particular religious encounter, the case will have to rest on the relative frequency of types within the sample and by determining that persons who report more intimate experiences also report the less intimate varieties. The data we shall examine to determine whether or not such an assumption of order is warranted will also enable us to get some estimate of how common religious experience is among Christian church members in contemporary America.

Before proceeding to this examination, several remarks must be made about the quality and form of the data. The materials available on religious experience in this study are of two sorts. Several structured questions asked respondents whether or not they had undergone various kinds of religious experiences. In addition, an open-end question sought voluntary reports of religious experience, some of which were quoted in the earlier chapter. The open-end data are rich in detail, but are badly incomplete. Although they are probably reliable as far as they go, there is no way of knowing what additional experiences were omitted from these reports, since the space provided was limited and respondents were not asked for a complete recounting of all incidents. Thus, many who wrote about being saved may also have had confirming or ecstatic experiences, for example, which were omitted. In examining the questionnaires, many instances were discovered when experiences acknowledged in the structured items were not mentioned in the free response. Indeed, unless respondents had been attempting to be definitive (and also shared our definition of what should be considered a religious experience), there is no reason to expect the open-end responses to provide adequate data. For these reasons, the open-end data seem best suited to provide qualitative materials on religious experience, and are of little use for quantitative purposes.

The structured items, on the other hand, avoid this incompleteness, but are inadequate in another way. For the varieties of religious experience to which they were directed, the structured items required respondents to indicate whether or not they

---

4. The data are from the same study, conducted by the authors, on which Chapters 3 and 5 are based. For further details of sampling see footnote 6 in Chapter 3.

had ever undergone such an encounter with the supernatural. These items provide a basis for classifying all respondents. But not all of the types of religious experience postulated were explored by structured items. No items were included which would have tapped the ecstatic or the revelational.

One reason for these omissions, aside from the fact that the lack of a clear conceptual scheme at the time made the choice of items somewhat fortuitous, was that it was little imagined how frequently modern Christians would report religious experiences. Items aimed at the more complex and intimate types of religious encounters seemed, then, as too extreme to be credible. Given these limits on both kinds of data, the burden of the analysis will have to rest on the structured items. Our quest for the social situational roots of religious experiences will be limited to the confirming and responsive varieties. The question of the frequency of the types of religious experience may now be taken up.

One structured item in the questionnaire is a straightforward inquiry about confirming experiences — an awareness of the presence of divinity. Respondents were asked whether they had ever, as adults, had "A feeling that [they] were somehow in the presence of God."

Looking at the data in Table 8 – 1 we may see how commonly American Christians have undergone confirming experiences. Forty-five per cent of the Protestants and 43 per cent of the

TABLE 8-1

Confirming Experiences among Christian Church Members

Confirming	Protestants	Roman Catholics
"A feeling that you were somehow in the presence of God."		
Percentage who responded:		
"Yes, I'm sure I have."	45	43
"Yes, I think that I have."	28	23
"No."	20	25
Did not answer	7	9
	100	100
N=	(2,326)	(545)

Roman Catholics reported they were "sure" they had experienced such a feeling of divine presence. Additionally, 28 per cent of the Protestants and 23 per cent of the Roman Catholics thought they'd had such an encounter. Overall, more than two-thirds of the Christian church members in this sample at least thought they'd had a confirming experience, and nearly half were certain of it.

The absolute frequency of even this least intimate variety of religious experience seems something of a surprise. There are few cues in the culture which would lead an observer to predict so high a rate of supernaturalism in what seems to be an increasingly modern, scientific, and secularized society. For example, characters in contemporary literature rarely undergo such encounters with the divine; and when they do, it is usually clear that they are odd people, old-fashioned, simple, demented, and the like. Furthermore, a recent Gallup survey of a national sample of Americans found only 20 per cent felt they had undergone a religious experience of some variety.[5] Of these, most were of the confirming variety. The great discrepancy between Gallup's findings and those we are now examining must be in large part produced by differences in the populations sampled. While about one-fifth of the general population reports divine encounters, these proportions increase greatly among a population drawn entirely from members of Christian churches. This differential strongly suggests that having such an encounter is intimately connected with participation in religious situations. We shall shortly take up this question in detail; but in any event, it is clear from the data in Table 8–1 that an investigation of religious experience among Christian church members is not a quest to understand a rare phenomenon. For all that religious experiences may be strange, they are not unusual. Indeed, *most* of the persons in our sample at least thought they might have undergone a confirming encounter with the Divine.

It has been postulated that confirming experiences are more common than responsive experiences. The data in Table 8–2 support this assumption. Responsive experiences of both the salvational and sanctioning variety were considerably less often reported than were confirming experiences. Furthermore, the data reveal some interesting contrasts between Protestants and Roman Catholics.

5. American Institute of Public Opinion, poll of April, 1962.

TABLE 8-2

Responsive Experiences among Christian Church Members

	Protestants	Roman Catholics
Responsive (Salvational)		
"A sense of being saved in Christ."		
Percentage who responded:		
"Yes, I'm sure I have."	37	26
"Yes, I think that I have."	23	22
"No."	29	33
Did not answer.	11	20
	100	100
Responsive (Sanctioning)		
"A feeling of being punished by God for something you had done."		
Percentage who responded:		
"Yes, I'm sure I have."	16	23
"Yes, I think that I have."	25	30
"No."	44	33
Did not answer.	15	13
	100	100

To seek an experience affirming one's salvation is a much more familiar part of the rhetoric of Protestantism than of Catholicism. This difference in emphasis is reflected in the data. Thirty-seven per cent of the Protestants were certain they'd had "A sense of being saved in Christ," while only 26 per cent of the Roman Catholics were certain they'd done so. An additional 23 per cent of the Protestants and 22 per cent of the Catholics thought they'd had such a sense of salvation.

Looking at the second item in the table, sanctioning experiences, the Catholics seem much more consistent that the Protestants. Many fewer Protestants were sure they'd had a "Feeling of being punished by God for something you had done," than reported a salvational experience. Catholics reported sanctioning experiences virtually as frequently as they reported the salvational. Hence, while 37 per cent of the Protestants were certain they'd had a salvational experience, only 16 per cent were sure they'd been sanctioned. The same comparison among Catholics is 26 versus 23 per cent. These contrasts seem to match differences in the conceptions of God held by Protestants and Catholics. For many Protestants, God seems endlessly benevolent—indeed, many Protestants believe in heaven, but deny there is a hell—while the Catholic God is more often depicted as the judge who punishes as well as rewards. Similarly, virtually all Catholics in this sample who believed there was a heaven also believed in hell. In any event, either subtype of responsive experience is, as expected, less frequently reported than are confirming experiences. Table 8–3 gives further statistical support for the proposed ordering of the types. Of those persons who were sure they'd had a salvational experience, 81 per cent were certain they'd undergone a confirming experience and an additional 15 per cent thought that they had done so. Thus, 96 per cent of those who reported a salvational experience acknowledged a confirming experience. Seen in reverse, however, many who reported a confirming experience did not also report a salvational experience (only 66 per cent were certain they'd had one). These findings increase the confidence which may be placed in the hypothesis that the manifestation of the more intimate types of religious experience presupposes previous encounters of a less intimate variety.

Aside from theoretical considerations, this confirmation is methodologically fortunate. For, implicit in the discussion of the ordering of types was the expectation that religious experience has a cumulative or scalar quality; that encounters with the supernatural follow a developmental sequence along a single dimension. These data display this hypothesized scalar character.

Given this outcome, we may briefly discuss the summary measure, or index, of religious experience that will serve as the basis for analysis in the remainder of this paper. The three items discussed above were used to classify respondents through a simple indexing procedure.[6] In the subsequent analysis, initially

6. The scoring was as follows: 2 points for each answer of "Yes, I'm sure I have," 1 point for each answer of "Yes, I think I have," and 0 points for each "No." Persons who failed to answer one or more of the three questions were omitted from the analysis. Study of nonresponse indicated these omissions in no way changed the findings.

TABLE 8-3
Virtually All Who Reported A Salvational Experience Reported A Confirming Experience*

| | Since you have been an adult have you ever had . . . | | |
| | A sense of being saved in Christ? | | |
A feeling that you were somehow in the presence of God?	"Yes, I'm sure I have."	"Yes, I think that I have."	"No."
Percentage who responded:			
"Yes, I'm sure I have."	81	36	20
"Yes, I think that I have."	15	50	27
"No."	4	14	53
	100	100	100
N =	(941)	(642)	(850)

*Persons who failed to respond to either item have been omitted.

the index was used in its original form, ranging respondents from a score of zero (earned by answering "No" to all three questions) to six (earned by answering "Yes, I'm sure I have" to all three). These tables revealed that all the relationships were isotropic—no matter what cutting points were chosen to collapse the index, the direction of relationship was unchanged—hence, the index was collapsed into three categories for ease in presentation. The first category, High, contains all respondents who *at least* answered "Yes, I think that I have," to all three questions (combining scores of 3 through 6). The Medium category contains persons who thought they might have had one or two of these experiences (scores of 1 or 2). The None group includes only persons who were certain that they had *not* had any of these experiences.

We may now return to the question raised at the beginning of this chapter: To what extent are religious experiences normal, that is, the product of compliance to the norms of social contexts?

Turning to the data in Table 8–4, we may see that the propensity for religious encounters is greatly influenced by the denomination to which a person belongs. While 24 per cent of

TABLE 8-4
Religious Experience Among The American Denominations

| Denomination | Index of Religious Experience | | | | |
	High	Medium	None	Total	N***
Congregational	24%	48%	28%	100%	119
Methodist	40	42	18	100	325
Protestant Episcopal	50	30	20	100	341
Presbyterian	52	34	14	100	403
Lutheran*	56	30	14	100	169
Disciples of Christ	61	31	8	100	39
American Baptist	74	17	9	100	117
Lutheran-Missouri Synod	76	21	3	100	211
Sects**	94	6	0	100	211
Southern Baptists	97	3	0	100	78
TOTAL PROTESTANT	58	28	14	100	1875
Roman Catholic	57	25	18	100	422

* A combination of members of The Lutheran Church in America and The American Lutheran Church.
** Included are: The Assemblies of God, The Church of God, The Church of Christ, The Church of the Nazarene, The Seventh Day Adventists, The Foursquare Gospel Church, and one independent tabernacle.
*** Persons who failed to answer any of the three questions on religious experience were dropped from the analysis.

the Congregationalists are classified as high on the index of religious experience, 76 per cent of the Missouri Synod Lutherans, 94 per cent of those in sects, and 97 per cent of the Southern Baptists scored high. Religious experience increases systematically from the more liberal groups on the top of the table to the more fundamentalist groups on the bottom.

Overall, these data indicate that, while religious experience tends to be uncommon or at least problematic among members of the more liberal denominations, the overwhelming majority of fundamentalists believe they have encountered some supernatural agency. These rather impressive differences reflect contrasts in the degree to which religious experience is explicitly sanctioned and fostered by the various religious bodies.

But let us push these findings further. One important way in which these denominations differ is the degree to which they constitute quasi-primary groups. The more liberal bodies resemble occasional audiences or focused crowds, while the more conservative groups tend to resemble moral communities in the Durkheimian sense of the word. That is, the conservative respondents not only attach great importance to their church membership, as indeed the liberals do too, but their congregation serves as a *primary source of informal social relations*. For example, only 29 per cent of the Congregationalists and 38 per cent of the Episcopalians reported that more than one of their five best friends were members of their church congregation, while 63 per cent of the Southern Baptists and 81 per cent of those who belong to sects have more than one of their best friends in their congregation. Indeed, 45 per cent of those in sects report that four or more of their five best friends belong to their congregation.

What can such differences in the nature of one's informal social ties to a religious community tell us about the social character of religious experience? Let us examine the relationship between denomination and religious experience with these friendship bonds controlled in Table 8–5. First of all, we can observe a mild specification. Among persons who have four or all of their five best friends in their congregation, denominational differences are moderately reduced. Furthermore, the joint effect of social integration and denomination accounts for somewhat more of the variance in religious experience: from 100 per cent of the Southern Baptists who have four or more friends in

TABLE 8-5
Denomination, Friendship Ties, and Religious Experience
Per Cent High on Index of Religious Experience

Denomination	Number of person's 5 best friends who are members of his congregation		
	0-1	2-3	4-5
Congregational	18% (84)	40% (25)	— (10)
Methodist	36 (200)	49 (94)	52 (29)
Protestant Episcopal	45 (214)	53 (88)	76 (33)
Presbyterian	41 (239)	57 (113)	78 (49)
Lutheran	57 (88)	83 (35)	80 (19)
Disciples of Christ	61 (18)	— (13)	— (8)
American Baptist	70 (53)	71 (38)	88 (24)
Lutheran-Missouri Synod	68 (60)	90 (31)	— (7)
Sects	81 (36)	94 (78)	94 (91)
Southern Baptists	92 (25)	100 (24)	100 (19)
Roman Catholics	55 (213)	57 (113)	65 (90)

— Cells with less than 15 cases were not percentaged.

the congregation down to 18 per cent of the Congregationalists who have one or none of their five best friends in the congregation. Friendship seems to matter in all groups, but much more so in the liberal groups.

But there is an even more significant finding to be read in this table. Among the liberal denominations, religious experience tends to be concentrated among a minority subgroup which constitutes a socially integrated community of believers existing within the loose context of the audience-like, unintegrated majority of the congregation. Thus, within the liberal churches there are groups of members who resemble fundamentalists, both by virtue of their reliance on the church as a primary source of friendship and by their propensity for religious experiences. Hence, even in denominations where religious experiences are somewhat unlikely or at least problematic, such behavior tends to be a social phenomenon—the property of an integrated subculture. Among the fundamentalists, however, where the congregations are in general highly bound by friendship ties and where religious experience is the norm, persons who are not enmeshed in a friendship network within their congregation nevertheless report a high proportion of religious experience.

This finding suggests that when the group in general offers marked support for religious experience, such behavior can be induced in the absence of significant affective bonds, simply through general exposure to the prevailing religious climate. The unintegrated members of the liberal bodies also tend to conform to the prevailing religious climate by *not* undergoing religious experiences.

These relationships were not affected by sex, social class, education or age, although each was modestly related to religious experience.

While these findings seem quite revealing, they leave a good deal unanswered. For example, why is religious experience encouraged in some of these denominations and not in others? Obviously the mere names, Baptist, Congregational, etc., do not in themselves mean much. What is it then that distinguishes these religious bodies? When asked, churchmen have generally said that the primary differences among these groups are theological. In the past, social scientists have been somewhat reluctant to accept such an answer and to thereby credit theology with any great causal importance. They have been inclined, instead, to concentrate on such cleavages as social class, ethnicity, and the like. Indeed, social scientists have typically regarded theological disputes among the denominations as rhetorical 'superstructures' produced by and obscuring the 'real' reasons —such as class—behind their conflicts.[7] Thus, theology has been left to languish as a perpetual dependent variable, always a consequence, never a cause.

Recently, we have been rediscovering what should always have been obvious, that religious beliefs have important implications for the ways men evaluate, respond to, and act upon the world. In a matter so intimately religious as feeling in contact with some supernatural agency, theology ought to play a crucial

---

7. The classic work in this tradition was, however by a theologian, H. Richard Niebuhr. See his *The Social Sources of Denominationalism* (New York: Henry Holt, 1929). We do not mean to deny the importance of non-theological factors in religious schism and conflict. However, these have too often been seen as sufficient conditions, when it seems clear enough that they are merely necessary. Granted that Luther would simply have been an obscure monk punished for disobedience, had the social and political conditions conducive to a reorganization of German states independent of papal control not been present. But it must not be forgotten that the German princes would have been hard pressed to reject papal authority had they lacked the new source of nonpapal religious legitimacy with which Luther provided them.

role. Clearly, such behavior presupposes that persons have some conception of an active supernatural.

As we have seen in Chapter 5, these denominations differ greatly in the degree to which they are committed to traditional conceptions of Christianity, including belief in an anthropomorphic God with whom one may communicate. To what extent, then, are denominational differences in religious experience a function of these theological differences? If theology does play an important role in generating religious experience, then we would expect the denominational differences to be reduced among groups sharing a similar belief system.

The Index of Religious Orthodoxy, employed in Table 8 – 6,[8] is based on questions concerning belief in a personal God, belief in the divinity of Jesus, belief in Biblical miracles, and belief in the Devil. Each of these items posits a conception of an active supernatural realm.

Turning to the data in Table 8 – 6, we see that theology does significantly interpret the relationship between denomination and religious experience. In all theological groupings, the relationships shown in Table 8 – 4 are reduced by nearly half. For example, among those high on the belief index, 63 per cent of the Methodists are high on religious experience, as compared with 100 per cent of those Southern Baptists who are high on belief. This is a 37 percentage point difference, rather smaller than the 57 points separating these groups in Table 8 – 4. Among persons medium on belief, 47 per cent of the Congregationalists and 84 per cent of those in sects scored high on religious experience. This 37 percentage point difference is also markedly smaller than the 70 points between them in Table 8 – 4. Similar reductions occurred among those low on the belief index.

Nevertheless, sizable denominational differences remain. This should be no surprise. For even though theology importantly interprets the denomination-experience relationship, we ought to expect this linkage to be highly limited by social context. That is, an ideology appropriate for warranting religious experience ought to in fact generate such divine encounters most frequently when it is the *prevailing, normal* outlook of a

---

8. Details of construction and validation of this index will be presented in a volume on religion and anti-Semitism by the authors scheduled for publication in the spring of 1966 by Harper and Row.

TABLE 8-6
Denomination, Religious Orthodoxy, and Religious Experience

| | Per Cent High on Index of Religious Experience | | |
| | Index of Religious Orthodoxy | | |
Denomination	High	Medium	Low
Congregational	— (4)	47 (36)	7 (73)
Methodist	63 (27)	58 (130)	25 (151)
Protestant Episcopal	74 (37)	63 (129)	31 (146)
Presbyterian	67 (69)	54 (171)	39 (141)
Lutheran	80 (68)	45 (56)	31 (39)
Disciples of Christ	— (3)	55 (22)	— (10)
American Baptist	94 (47)	65 (45)	45 (22)
Lutheran-Missouri Synod	82 (59)	64 (30)	— (6)
Sects	94 (175)	84 (30)	— (2)
Southern Baptists	100 (59)	— (8)	— (0)
Roman Catholics	70 (241)	47 (107)	28 (53)

social group; and the impact of such a theology ought to be muted when it is held by persons embedded in a social situation where their religious beliefs are somewhat deviant and where religious experience is itself problematic.

We have considered the fact that religious experience in the liberal bodies was concentrated in a subgroup for whom the church functioned as a basic source of the social relations. The majority of the members of these congregations, who do *not* draw their friends mostly from the church and who thus resemble members of audiences rather than moral communities, exhibit little propensity for religious experience. To this finding we may now add the information that in the liberal churches it is particularly those persons for whom the congregation is a primary group who not only are inclined towards religious experience but are also those who hold orthodox beliefs concerning the supernatural. Thus, one could say that there are sects within these churches—amid the liberal and loosely integrated Protestant bodies are encysted subcultures of fundamentalist believers, united by affective bonds, and for whom religious experiences are relatively common.

It seems plausible to suppose that in these subcultures a

system of norms encouraging religious experience is maintained. In short, we can regard a good portion of the religious experience that occurs even among members of liberal denominations as basically a social phenomenon.

CONCLUSION

It is now clear that the reservations raised at the beginning of this chapter about the danger of prematurely considering religious experience in terms of individual, rather than social, behavior were justified. The data indicate that a good portion of religious experience can be attributed to norm compliance within enduring social situations. To have applied an individually oriented conception of causality without having first extracted those for whom this behavior is 'normal' would have simply clouded the findings, and perhaps obscured actual individual effects.

As indicated earlier, it is hardly our intention to deny the relevance of individual factors in motivating religious experience. Psychiatric and other social-psychological theories may indeed prove useful in extending our understanding of this variety of human behavior, but *only* when applied in appropriate instances. Many persons may well undergo felt encounters with supernatural beings because they are caught in some disintegrating psychic conflict, as Leon Salzman has suggested;[9] but clearly such a state cannot be reasonably attributed to the majority of persons participating in some stable social context. Hence, the social context within which a person engages in religious experiences must be examined before it is possible to assess the meaning of his act or assess his individual motivation. Only in relation to a man's context can we know whether his behavior classifies him as the most docile conformist or as a strange deviant.

---

9. Leon Salzman, "The Psychology of Religious and Ideological Conversion," *Psychiatry,* XVI (1953), pp. 177–179.

PART III:

RELIGION AND SOCIAL CHANGE

The role of religion in social change has been subject to considerable confusion. On the one hand it has been widely recognized that religious institutions frequently seek to preserve the *status quo* and lend support to the prevailing elites. Yet the religious, sometimes even millenarian, character of revolutionaries has also been remarked. Does religion integrate societies, or does it foster conflict? In this section, we shall attempt to sort out these seemingly contradictory functions of religion.

Chapter 9

Religion and the Integration of Society[1]

CLASSICAL sociological theory of religion places great emphasis on religion's integrative functions in society. This chapter seeks to clarify the meaning of this assertion, and specifically considers religion's changing role in the integration of American society. The chapter further exemplifies the need for conceptual clarification of the ways in which religion is defined, a theme already introduced in Part I.

One of the abiding general propositions of sociology is that religion serves the central and crucial function in society of supporting what has been variously called social integration, social solidarity, and social cohesion. Underlying this proposition is a still more general one, namely, that, in order to maintain itself, every society must achieve some consensus around a set of basic values, an agreement upon ultimate meaning that affords an appropriate basis for social organization and common action.

The concept of social integration is an ideal-typical one. It does not imply that every society achieves universal consensus or that every one of a society's members shares precisely the same set of values. It is argued, however, that considerable consensus must exist if a society is to withstand diversity and cleavage without breaking down. Where consensus is at a minimum, collective social action becomes more and more difficult to

1. This chapter owes much to ideas first suggested by Robert Bellah in an unpublished paper, "Some Suggestions for the Systematic Study of Religion."

achieve, and eventually a state of disintegration or social disorganization sets in.

The term 'integration' has a favorable connotation in our language, 'disintegration' an unfavorable one. However, as the term is being used here, to say that a group or a society is highly integrated is not necessarily to express approval of it. There are instances in history of highly integrated societies which have been judged, by outsiders at least, as opprobrious. Hitler's Germany, for example, was for a time highly integrated; there existed a high degree of consensus around a set of basic, though questionable, values. While it certainly cannot always be associated with the 'good,' integration nevertheless appears to be a necessary condition to effective social organization and control.

Religion has been especially singled out as the prime force in the creation and maintenance of social integration. A number of scholars, Durkheim among them, have expressed the belief that religion is so important to social integration that without it social disintegration would inevitably follow. This integrating role of religion is seen as manifold: One, through its belief system, it gives basic support to social and individual values; Two, through its ritual, its repeatedly reinforced identification with and commitment to these values; Three, through its system of eternal rewards and punishments, it helps to insure the embodiment and acting out of values in behavior.

We have lived with these notions for a considerable time now. Developed at the turn of the century, they have continued to be salient, with little modification, ever since. As we attempt, however, to apply them to contemporary American society—or for that matter to any existing society, whether primitive or modern—we are confronted with a number of difficulties.

For one thing, we find it difficult to reconcile the general theory with the considerable evidence of religious conflict. On every side, it would seem that religion threatens social integration as readily as it contributes to it. Some scholars have recently suggested that it is religion which today divides Americans most. Not only does the present situation seem not to jibe with the theory, but neither does the historical situation. The history of Christianity, with its many schisms, manifests the great power of religion not only to bind but to divide.

It is also difficult to find evidence that, with increasing secularization, there is a general decay of social and personal values. To be sure, the values of Western society have changed during the past centuries and are still changing. Some observers have lamented that the changes in America reflect a gradual departure from the values of the Judeo-Christian heritage and attribute many of our social ills to this fact. At the same time, however, our society appears to be maintaining itself with a reasonable degree of success. Moreover, many of the pathologies of contemporary society are paralleled by significant advances in social responsibility and individual ethical conduct. Though only the future can decide the question, there seems to be no immediate danger of the disintegration of our society or the wholesale retrogression of our moral life.

What seems evident, certainly in modern complex societies and probably in most primitive ones as well, is that religion is not the only source and support of social values. It may be making a contribution in this respect, but the contribution is clearly not an exclusive one. Indeed, defining religion as we have in Chapter 1, as entailing a supernatural referent, it is clear that religion has never been the only possible source of social cohesion. Still, religious perspectives have obviously been the most common source of support of social integration; hence, it becomes relevant to ask: What are the ways in which religion enters into and influences human values and human action? And, more parochially, What contribution is religion currently making to the value structure of American society? At this juncture, let us consider several defining concepts.

NORMS, VALUES, AND BELIEFS

Social integration requires and presupposes consensus on three distinct levels. First of all, there must be agreement on norms. Norms are prescriptions for action; they formulate the accepted ways of doing things. Second, there must be agreement on the values which the norms embody or further. Values underlie norms in the sense that they sum up what makes the norm worthwhile and a proper and good way of behaving. Third, there must be considerable agreement in belief concerning the nature of man and the world, that is, as noted in Chapter 1, there must be agreement that the nature of reality makes a particular set of values both viable and rational.

In a stable society, most action follows directly from the norms. The norms prescribe what is to be done in given situations and action follows almost automatically without any question being raised explicitly as to the meaning of the action. For example, we get up in the morning early enough to allow us to get to work on time. We tip our hat when we greet a lady. Ordinarily, we do these things without hesitation and without even contemplating possible alternatives.

This kind of rote action is very important to social integration and to the integration of the personality. If we paused to consider the meaning of every act, our ability to make decisions would be seriously hampered; we should certainly find ourselves frustrated and confused and eventually unable to act at all.

The ability of norms to function in and of themselves as effective guides to behavior is a consequence, of course, of the socialization process. From earliest childhood we are indoctrinated in the norms so that acting in conformity to them becomes almost instinctive. Indoctrination in the norms also involves, however, indoctrination in values and beliefs, subtly as this may be done. We come to learn what is expected of us, but we also develop a sense, however vague, of the meaning and value-import of these expectations.

If norms are described as prescribed ways of behaving, then a value can be defined as a preference for some state of being. Americans value democracy insofar as they prefer democracy over other forms of political organization. Beliefs, often confused with values, are to be distinguished from them in that they are not preferences but constitute statements about the true nature of things. As we shall see shortly, values *and* norms may be raised in a society to the status of beliefs, that is, they may be seen not as preferences but as unalterable elements of the nature of things. Ordinarily, however, the indicated distinction holds.

The three concepts may also be distinguished in the following way: Norms deal with means, values with ends, and beliefs with their rationale. One norm of our society, for example, prescribes that Americans vote on election day. Voting, then, is a means for the realization of the end-value of democracy. Democracy, in turn, is rationalized by belief—that all men are created equal, for example, or that ability is not always equivalent to status at birth. This suggests that norms are derived from values, and values from beliefs. This is frequently the case, but it is not always so. Values and beliefs may also follow from norms, rather than the other way around.

NORMS IN CONFLICT

Theoretically, all action would automatically follow the norms in a fully integrated society. There, occasion would never arise for questioning the norms since complete consensus would exist at all three levels—norms, values, and beliefs. In reality, of course, such complete integration probably never exists. Almost inevitably, circumstances arise in which the norms are not sufficient to govern action in and of themselves. This will be the case when contradictory norms exist, when traditional norms are challenged by new ones, when for one reason or another norms do not further the ends for which they were designed, or when norms have been inadequately internalized.

Norms are often contradictory even in simple and homogeneous societies, but in complex and pluralistic societies some contradiction almost always exists. Consider, for example, the situation of a recently married Roman Catholic girl whose husband, a Protestant, wishes to practice contraception. The girl is being faced with clearly contradictory norms: the practice prescribed by her Church and the practice her husband wishes to follow.

A society may be homogeneous and consistent in its norms and yet have its traditional norms challenged by a new set of norms coming in from outside. The present situation in the South, in which the traditional norm of segregation is being challenged by the norm of integration imposed from the outside, is a case in point. Another is represented by the situation in rural India, where recent government edicts threaten the traditional norms of the caste system.

Norms can also lose their self-warranting character when they turn out to frustrate rather than to further some basic value of a society. This can happen because underlying values are changing and are rendering traditional ways of doing things obsolete and irrational. However, it can also happen that a devised norm turns out to have been ill-advised for one reason or another. This is especially the case with legal norms. In the thirties, the relatively permissive divorce laws in Russia were abandoned as destructive of the stability of the state despite the fact that they were theoretically consonant with Marxist ideals.

Finally, norms are not always so thoroughly internalized that they are automatic. Though the power of society is great, it is not absolute. Norms are always more or less internalized, and therefore always more or less open to doubt and challenge.

In situations of these kinds, some understanding of the import of the norm in question for basic values and beliefs is essential if doubt is to be resolved. Doubt may be overcome and a choice of norms made through a rational consideration of the values and beliefs underlying contradictory rules of behavior. The Southerner may rationally weigh the values and beliefs supporting segregation and those supporting integration and decide where he wishes to commit himself. More often, a choice for or against a norm merely reflects training so deeply ingrained as to be, in effect, irrevocable. In such cases, alternative norms, values, and beliefs are not seriously considered. Instead a norm is chosen or rejected because it is prescribed or forbidden by a particular institution in society to which commitment has become absolute.

THE NATURE OF COMMITMENT

The concept of commitment has a central bearing on social integration. In our theoretical model of the wholly-integrated society, there would be total consensus as to where primary commitment lies just as there would be consensus on norms, values, and beliefs. In actual societies, the locus of commitment becomes a problem wherever action does not directly follow from a norm. When conflicting norms imply distinct values and beliefs, then resolution of conflict can be achieved only through a decision as to where primary commitment lies: on the level of the norm itself or on other and deeper levels.

Locating one's primary commitment may be entirely relative to a particular conflict situation. Commitments to given norms, values, or beliefs may all be relative and insisted upon only in some contexts and not in others. At the same time, we can nevertheless conceive of ultimate commitments, i.e., commitments which are inexorably held under all circumstances and conditions. Commitments of such kinds may be said to be 'sacred' in two senses: One, they are held to be unalterable and, two, any sacrifice will be endured in order to withstand a threat to the commitment.

The locus of a commitment, whether 'sacred' or otherwise, may be a belief, a value, or a norm. Where, for example, the commitment is to a value, beliefs and norms as well as other values become subject to change whenever they undermine that value. Thus, in time of war, the norm, Thou shalt not kill, and the belief in the sanctity of the individual are sacrificed in order to sustain the commitment to what is more ultimately valued — the nation. The ability of a nation to wage war — and presumably therefore to maintain itself — is dependent upon a high degree of consensus that in fact the nation represents an ultimate commitment. Were ultimate commitment to be attached to the belief that human life is more sacred than national identity, war would not be possible.

But, as we have suggested, ultimate commitment may not always be at the level of beliefs or values. It may exist at the level of the norm. In such cases, values and beliefs are subject to change in the service of maintaining the norm. The norm of segregation is a case in point. The members of the White Citizens' Councils in the South have their primary commitment to the 'norm' of segregation. The values and beliefs which are conceived to give meaning to this norm are relatively unimportant. In fact, the way in which the norm is rationalized may shift and change. Thus, the White Citizens' Council member may argue that his adherence to segregation is a consequence of his belief that God ordained segregation, as is shown in the Biblical story of Ham. Yet, his commitment to this belief is weaker than his commitment to the norm. Faced with a different interpretation of the Biblical story, he will find another belief to support what to his mind is an unquestionable norm. Where norms are ultimate, beliefs are their servants.

Ultimate commitment is likely to be at the level of the norm wherever the norm is deeply imbedded in the traditions of a society or group. Norms have become so much a part of a way of life that they come to be perceived as 'sacred.' In such instances, the values and beliefs which originally gave meaning to the norms may no longer be applicable; they may indeed be irrelevant to contemporary adherence to them. The meaning of the norms, insofar as it exists and is rooted in other than bare self-interest, is supplied by the high value placed on tradition or custom itself. The difficulty which the Indian government is experiencing in abolishing the caste system is illustrative of the point. For the Indian peasant, the beliefs and values which produced the caste system many years ago may be entirely forgotten and lost in history. Nevertheless, the commitment to the norm is as strong as if past values and past beliefs were still operative.

It might be argued that in cases like these not the norms but tradition itself is regarded as 'sacred' and that ultimate commitment is to traditionalism as an end in itself. It is important to recognize, however, that conformity to traditionalism as a 'sacred' ideal is largely achieved through an insistence on conformity to specific ways of behaving, that is, to norms.

AUTHORITY AND SANCTIONS

In sum, it is important to social integration that the members of a society share commitments to certain norms, values, and beliefs and that some of these commitments be ultimate in character. The question arises as to how commitments are generated and sustained. It is not enough to say that what must operate is, in effect, a collective conscience. Left to themselves, the members of a society would not exhibit the kinds of commitments to collective means and ends necessary to produce social solidarity and stability. The United States, or any other country, would probably not succeed, for example, in recruiting the necessary defense forces in time of war on a completely voluntary basis. The commitment to the nation is not that strong.

Essential to producing commitment is some form of authority with the power of constraint over the members of a society. Societies depend not on one but on a number of sources of authority to produce the kinds of commitments necessary to assure that norms are acted out in practice. Four kinds of authority may be identified, each of which includes its own sanctioning or reward-and-punishment system.

First, there is *legal authority* and its sanctioning system. In every society, implicit and sometimes explicit judgments are made that certain norms, and sometimes certain beliefs and values, are so crucial to the social order that nonconformity in these respects cannot be tolerated. It is these crucial elements of a social order that are ordinarily covered by its laws, which specify illegal actions and their punishments. Punishment for breaking a legally established norm frequently takes the form of depriving the law-breaker of the rights and privileges which the society values most highly. Imprisonment, for example, now denies him freedom of action; in ancient time, banishment from one's country expressed punishment by revoking a different but similarly valued privilege.

Akin to the legal authority of the state manifested in its laws is the authority of private bodies to formulate and enforce their rules and regulations. Thus, in any society, legal authority will be lodged within some government to which everyone is subject, but it will also be lodged in private associations — business firms, labor unions, universities — to whose authorities employees or members are subject and which constitute in effect private governments.

Not all norms, even basic ones, are incorporated into formal laws and regulations. Societies also depend upon the force of social authority and its sanctioning system to sustain commitment. Societies differ, of course, in the relative degree to which legal and social authority are relied upon to secure adherence to the norms. The more traditional the society, probably the greater the reliance on *social authority*.

Social authority is no more or less than the authority of the group to exercise a degree of control over the behavior of its members. Like legal authority, social authority includes a sanctioning system — a much more informal one to be sure — through which 'good' conduct and beliefs may be rewarded and 'bad' conduct and beliefs punished. This is most clearly seen in the group's power to reward through acceptance and punish through rejection.

Social authority may be uni- or multi-dimensional depending upon the complexity of the society. In anything but the most primitive societies, there are usually many sources of social authority, often in conflict with one another — membership and interest groups of all kinds which are capable of imposing sanctions not only upon their own members but upon others as well.

A third type of authority is the suprasocial one, which too has its accompanying sanctioning system. Here, beliefs, values, and norms derive their authority from a transcendental referent. *Suprasocial authority* operates most clearly through institutionalized religion. Like legal and social authority, it also has the power, theoretically at least, to reward and punish. The rewards and punishments, however, are not immediately imposed but are promised for the future. To be sure, the church is capable of exercising its authority to reward or punish in the present. When it does, however, it is exercising legal rather than suprasocial authority, just as the corporation may reward or punish its executives for adherence to or infraction of the rules.

The transcendental referent from which the suprasocial authority of institutionalized religion is derived is always a divine being or beings. But, suprasocial authority may also rest in a secular ideology where that ideology has been assigned "sacred" status in the sense that, like God, it is seen as eternal, trans-social, and immutable. The transcendent authority of the Marxist dialectic working throughout history is a clear example. Marxism, like Christianity, postulates a millenium where the faithful will be rewarded and the unfaithful punished. Both Marxism and Christianity, therefore, postulate a suprasocial authority which is capable of imposing sanctions as a means to generate compliance with beliefs, values, and norms. In this sense, the God of Christianity is functionally equivalent to the transcendent ideology of Marxism.

There is still a fourth authority—the *authority of the* self as manifested in the *individual conscience*. It does not seem to be arbitrary to say that the individual conscience can exercise authority and is capable of rewarding and punishing. The authority it exercises is not entirely independent of legal, social, or suprasocial authority, but neither are the other three entirely independent of each other. To point to self-authority is to point to the obvious fact that societies differ greatly in the extent to which they produce individuals more or less free to choose their commitments for themselves. All human beings are members of some society and all are socialized in some way or other through the force of some authority or other. When circumstances are right, genuine individuality emerges; that is to say, though external rewards and punishments are taken into account, they do not determine behavior.

In any given society, the relative saliency and influence of these various authorities and their sanctioning systems will vary. Furthermore, they will not all be relevant to every situation. Social integration is maximized, however, where different sanctioning authorities reinforce rather than contradict each other in the values, beliefs, and norms they support.

RELIGION AND SOCIAL INTEGRATION

With these defining concepts in mind, we now wish to return to the first of our two original questions, namely, the place of religion in social integration. From what we have learned, it is evident that, if we define religion as a 'sacred' or ultimate commitment to some set of norms, values, and beliefs, then religion is indeed essential to social integration. Though society is not capable of maintaining itself when it lacks a high degree of consensus as to what is it ultimately committed to, what is essential is not the kind of authority from which the commitment's 'sacred' quality is derived but the simple fact that the commitment exists.

Hence, as was pointed out in Chapter 1, traditional sociological theory concerning religion's contribution to social integration, though highly general, does not appear to be general enough. What contributes to social integration is not necessarily institutionalized religion, but what society defines as 'sacred,' that is, a value orientation. The reinforcement is not necessarily provided by religious ritual; it may be provided by entirely secular forms of social support. Indeed, Leni Riefenstahl's famous documentary film, "Triumph of the Will," shows the proliferation of effective secular ritual in Nazi Germany. And, though the acting out of the 'sacred' requires a sanctioning system, it does not demand that it be a specifically religious one.

It follows from what has been said that institutionalized religion is not essential to social integration; theoretically, a high degree of social integration may exist without it. Where it exists, institutionalized religion may or may not contribute in large or in small measure to social integration. Where it is in conflict with other moral authorities, it may indeed contribute to social disorganization.

How much of a contribution tradition makes to social integration, and the direction of that contribution, depend upon a number of factors. First of all, there is the degree to which suprasocial authority is granted precedence over other forms of authority as the source and support of norms, values, and beliefs. Theoretically, if there were consensus on the primacy of the suprasocial authority and its sanctioning system, institutionalized religion could play a central role in social integration.

Secondly, there is the degree to which suprasocial, social, and legal authority support the same values. Where they do, the contribution of institutionalized religion to social integration is dependent on whether it informs and influences other sources of authority or is influenced and molded by them.

Thirdly, the role of transcendental authority is dependent upon the degree to which a society is ruled by tradition. Where custom and habit form the primary basis of social organization, the belief system of organized religion can play an important role in rationalizing tradition. However, it must be pointed out that, insofar as institutionalized religion is tied too closely to one set of secular norms and customs, it can quickly lose its moral authority when new norms gain acceptance. When this happens, there is a propensity either to abandon traditional religious belief or to empty it of all practical application.

Fourth, organized religion's integrating role depends upon the degree of consensus which exists in the religious community itself. Where internal dissent pervades organized religion, it is not likely to contribute to the integration of the society at large, though it may heighten the cohesion of particular groups. At the same time, however, unless there is dissent, the commitment to organized religion may well be so slight as to have little influence on the value structure of the society.

In the very nature of things, religion can never serve as the exclusive basis for social integration; it can only be more or less important. There have been societies in which religious authority was dominant; we know of many today in which its role is negligible. There is good reason to believe that, where religious authority is accepted, its power to generate and sustain commitment in the face of opposition, and even of persecution, is very great. Historically, revolutionary political movements have often been closely associated with revolutionary religious movements. In contemporary society, this is not usually the case. Yet, because they also require commitments that are difficult to carry out in practice, present-day revolutionary movements construct secular ideologies that have much of the flavor and many of the characteristics of transcendental religious belief.

Little is known of the empirical circumstances under which religious authority gains dominance and under which its influence decays. Perhaps a crucial factor in the acceptance of religious authority is the capacity of religious institutions and their personnel to organize society, that is, to provide the institutional framework in which the on-going everyday life of a society is carried on. This happened in medieval Europe but the history of Western society is the history of the gradual spread of wholly secular institutions.

These theoretical considerations still leave open the question of the actual role of religion in influencing the value structure of particular societies. We turn now to a brief examination of the situation in America.

RELIGION AND VALUES IN AMERICAN SOCIETY

The basic normative structure of American society derives in large measure from the high value placed on democracy as a basis for political and social organization. At the present time, this commitment to democracy rests primarily on secular beliefs and values. It is nevertheless fair to say that the respect for human individuality which underlies democratic conviction is rooted in and has been informed by the Judeo-Christian heritage as it has been interpreted in the light of history.

This capacity of religion to inform the secular normative structure seems to be largely a thing of the past. In a complex society, and particularly in a democratic one, contributions to the normative structure come from many sources—the body politic, the economic order, the mass media, labor unions, and private citizens, as well as the church. These sources at once inform the norms and values of our society and are informed by them. The process is a dialectical one but it is not necessarily a matter of even exchange. Any particular institution may at times be influenced by the surrounding value structure considerably more than it is able to exercise influence over it.

Organized religion in the United States, we would assert, is currently much more on the receiving than on the contributing side of the value process. This is not because of lack of opportunity to make explicit what secular values should be, to elaborate on the implications of religious faith, or to question the existing normative structure. The avenues open to the church for making a contribution are many—sermons, church periodicals and educational materials, official pronouncements, church programs, discussion groups. The available audience is large; the majority of the population is regularly exposed to the church's influence through Sunday worship as well as in other ways. Yet, the evidence indicates that the church is not availing itself of its manifold opportunities. It is not, in fact, seeking to make explicit how men ought to behave, to what ends, and for what reasons.

This is not to say that norms and values are ignored in what the church seeks to communicate. On the contrary, they are the major themes of much that it talked and written about. But the level of abstraction at which the topic is pursued has the consequence of leaving to other sources the final say in determining everyday norms and values. The church's emphasis is overwhelmingly on man's relationship to God. The implications of the faith for man's relation to man are left largely to the individual to work out for himself, with God's help but without the help of the churches. Man is exhorted to be a steward of God; to exercise choice and initiative in his use of leisure time in keeping with the new life in Christ; to manage economic wealth in terms of Christian responsibility and leadership; to accept the political responsibilities of Christian citizenship on the basis of his citizenship in the Kingdom of God.

However well grounded these injunctions may be theologically, and whatever symbolic or psychological functions they may serve in the lives of individuals, the result from the standpoint of influencing concrete behavior is very little. How the majority of Americans behave, and what they value, is not informed by religious faith but by the norms and values of the larger society of which he is a part. Confronted on the one hand by the abstract prescriptions of religion and on the other by the concrete norms and values made explicit by law, by the context in which they labor, and by secular groups, men are almost inexorably led to follow the latter—partly because these sanctioning systems are more salient, but also because the nature of a religiously inspired choice is not clear.

There are good and perhaps sufficient reasons, aside from theological ones, to account for the church's failure to contribute significantly to informing present-day values. The implications of the faith are simply not clear enough to be expounded authoritatively and unequivocally. Also relevant, most noticeably on the contemporary scene, is the high value which the church appears to place on harmony and the avoidance of conflict. Wherever choice is between maintaining harmony and taking a stand on an issue which would produce conflict, the church most often chooses harmony. This is seen in the way that local congregations are governed as well as in situations where the church has an opportunity to inform the general community, for example, in the recent events in Little Rock, Arkansas. What is being here spoken of is perhaps no more than another facet of the frequently commented upon 'dilemma of the churches.' Were the church to insist upon strict obedience to a set of norms, values, and beliefs, it would probably lose whatever power it now exercises in the larger society.

Because of this dilemma, it is unlikely that the church could succeed in generating a general commitment to its standards even were it to make explicit the behavioral and attitudinal implications of the faith. Insofar as it has made its position explicit on given issues, its constituency has not widely adopted its values, at least not in situations where there are conflicting secular norms. Witness, for example, the relative failure of the churches to foster racially integrated congregations though this is an issue on which most major denominations have spoken out in unequivocal terms.

That the church is being informed by, more than it is informing, the values of the larger society is an indicator that our society no longer appeals to religious suprasocial authority and its sanctioning system to validate its norms. It is also a sign that organized religion is committed, implicitly at least, to maintaining the society as it is rather than to fostering its regeneration along lines formulated by the church. In this latter sense, religion is indeed making a contribution to social integration though perhaps on terms which compromise its distinctly religious character.

It is not being suggested that the contemporary church can not inform the lives of individuals and exercise an influence on society through them. Nor can it be said that, within particular minority religious movements, suprasocial authority may not still have precedence over other forms of authority. Looking at American society as a whole, however, organized religion at present is neither a prominent witness to its own value system nor a major focal point around which ulitmate commitments to norms, values, and beliefs are formed.

Chapter 10

Class, Politics, and Religious Involvement

THE conservative role of religion in the process of social change—its commitment to maintaining the status quo—*has been dealt with at a theoretical level in the preceding chapter. The present chapter deals with the same theme empirically, through an examination of the relationship between political and religious commitments.*

A long tradition in Western thought has viewed religion, and Christianity in particular, as a haven for the dispossessed. From its beginning, the special salience of the Christian faith for those disappointed and frustrated in this world has been remarked, and, according to Biblical accounts, even the Apostles were aware of this special feature of their movement.[1] Modern historians of the early church agree that it had great appeal and support among the deprived classes in the Roman world—the slaves, the poor, and the subject peoples.[2]

This conception of religion, as functioning to assuage the suffering of those near the bottom of the social hierarchy, provided a ready solution for social theorists who first pondered the role of religion in society and the reasons for variation in reli-

---

1. St. Paul wrote to his converts that "not many of you were wise according to worldly standards, not many were powerful, not many were of noble birth." I *Cor.* 1:26 (RSV).

2. For example, see Ernst Troeltsch, *The Social Teaching of the Christian Churches,* 2 vol., translated by Olive Wyon (New York: The Macmillan Co., 1931), esp. I, 45–46, 86–87.

gious involvement. Such an interpretation was central to the analyses of Weber[3] and Nietzsche,[4] and certainly it was the basis for Marx's angry comment that religion was an "opiate of the people," a pain-killer for frustration and deprivation that interfered with their attaining "true class consciousness." Similar views are held by many current social theorists. The clearest recent statement is by Kingsley Davis:

> The greater his [man's] disappointment in this life, the greater his faith in the next. Thus the existence of goals beyond this world serves to compensate people for frustrations they inevitably experience in striving to reach socially acquired and socially valuable ends.[5]

Max Weber shared this view and described how religion glorified the suffering of the dispossessed, but he also reported the opposite. In *The Protestant Ethic and the Spirit of Capitalism* he noted that Calvinists took worldly success as a sign of Divine Election, which in turn justified exploiting those with less material success, since they were not Elect.[6] Surely this theology was no comfort to the lower classes. Instead of heavenly glory in recompense for their suffering, Calvinism offered them only the prospect of damnation in the next world too. Yet, social theorists have been virtually unanimous that religion does indeed comfort the poor.

The only significant dissent from this 'opiate' view of religion was entered by H. Richard Niebuhr.[7] His historical studies indicated that though all the major religious movements during the Christian era grew up as solutions to lower-class frustrations, they failed to meet those needs adequately for very long. Instead, all were shortly transformed into middle-class institutions. Thus, Niebuhr concluded, except when the lower classes were briefly swept by religious movements, they have generally been uninvolved in, and outside of, religious institutions.

---

3. H. H. Gerth and C. Wright Mills, eds., *From Max Weber: Essays in Sociology* (New York: Oxford University Press, 1958), Chapter 11.

4. Frederick Nietzsche, *The Genealogy of Morals,* in *The Philosophy of Nietzsche* (New York: Modern Library, 1927), pp. 617–807.

5. Kingsley Davis, *Human Society* (New York: The Macmillan Co., 1948), p. 532.

6. Max Weber, *The Protestant Ethic and the Spirit of Capitalism,* translated by Talcott Parsons (New York: Charles Scribner's Sons, 1958).

7. H. Richard Niebuhr. *The Social Sources of Denominationalism* (New York: Henry Holt, 1929).

With the surge in empirical social research following World War II, the question of whether or not the church compensates for economic deprivation has been partly settled. A series of investigators have called the roll and found that the lower classes are least, rather than most, likely to be church members or attend Sunday worship services.[8] Thus, a long-cherished theory of social behavior was dealt a major disconfirmation. But, despite the flurry of research activity that unearthed these surprising findings, little effort has been made to explain them satisfactorily. Why aren't the lower classes more often in pews on Sunday morning?

Gerhard Lenski[9] has suggested that lower-class persons tend to participate less than middle- and upper-class persons in *all* types of voluntary organizations, but instead limit their social round to informal and primary group relations, particuarly those built on family and kinship. On these grounds Lenski argues that lower-class absence from church services does not raise specifically religious questions, but instead simply reflects this general nonparticipant syndrome. This interpretation assumes that participation in religious organizations is not importantly different in quality from participation in voluntary organizations generally. But in accepting this assumption, Lenski ignores the central thesis of his own work, namely, that religion has important and distinctive consequences for human behavior, which surely suggests that participation in religious organization is a distinctive experience.

Fortunately, empirical data are available to test Lenski's explanation. If class differences in church attendance actually reflect nothing more than a general lower-class tendency not to participate in any kind of voluntary organization, then we would

8. Among these studies are: Hadley S. Cantril, "Educational and Economic composition of Religious Groups," *American Journal of Sociology,* XLVIII (March, 1943), 574–579; August Hollingshead, *Elmtown's Youth* (New Haven: Yale University Press, 1949); Louis Bultena, "Church Membership and Church Attendance in Madison, Wisconsin," *American Sociological Review,* XIV (June, 1949), 385–388; Harold Kaufman, "Prestige Classes in a New York Rural Community," *Cornell University Agricultural Experimental Station Bulletin,* March, 1944; Lee G. Burchinal, "Some Social Status Criteria and Church Membership and Church Attendance," *Journal of Social Psychology,* XLIX (February, 1959), 53–64; and Gerhard E. Lenski, "Social Correlates of Religious Interest," *American Sociological Review,* XVIII (October, 1953), 533–544.

9. Gerhard Lenski, *The Religious Factor* (Garden City: Doubleday & Co., 1961), p. 44n.

expect church-going differences between classes to disappear when organizational participation is controlled.[10] Table 10–1 shows that this is not the case. Differences in church attendance between white- and blue-collar workers persist regardless of organizational participation. Whether they belong to several organizations or to none, blue-collar workers are less likely than white-collar workers to attend church. The table is based on data from a national sample of American adults, interviewed in February, 1960, by the Gallup organization.[11]

TABLE 10-1

Among American Adults, Class Differences in Church Attendance Remain When amount of Activity in All Kinds of Voluntary Organizations is Held Constant

| | Number of Organizations Participated In:* | | | | | |
| | None | | One | | Two or More | |
Breadwinner's Occupation:**	White Collar	Blue Collar	White Collar	Blue Collar	White Collar	Blue Collar
Church Attendance:						
Attended in past week	53%	45%	54%	46%	56%	52%
Attended in past year	34	38	39	40	38	31
Not attended for a year or more	13	17	7	14	6	17
Total	100	100	100	100	100	100
(N)	(22)	(367)	(132)	(132)	(103)	(58)

*Church organizations excluded to prevent contamination with dependent variable.
**Farmers, service workers, and those not in the labor force were excluded.

10. The methodological procedure used here is what Paul F. Lazarsfeld has called a test of spuriousness. If an observed association between two variables, X and Y, is actually an artifact of their joint association with some third variable, T, then the association between X and Y should disappear under conditions of T or *not-T*. In this instance, Lenski has argued that church attendance is simply one facet of organizational involvement in general, and hence, that no independent association of social class and church-going ought to obtain when this general organizational activity is controlled.

11. Study Number 625K. IBM cards and codebook were furnished by the International Data Library and Reference Service, Survey Research Center, University of California, Berkeley.

A second explanation of apparent class differences in church involvement has been offered by the writers working from the recent conceptualization of religious involvement as a multidimensional phenomenon presented in Chapter 2. It will be recalled that five general kinds of involvement which religious institutions expect of their adherents were identified, and that each was seen as an analytically discrete dimension along which persons may differ in their degree of conformity to this kind of institutional expectation. The five dimensions are: the *ideological* (beliefs); the *intellectual* (knowledge); the *ritual* (religious participation, e.g., church attendance); the *experiential* (feelings of contact with divinity); and the *consequential* (acts in everyday life that follow from the ideology). It was suggested that some of these dimensions may be independent of one another, and that several may even be negatively correlated.

Building on this conceptual scheme, Yoshio Fukuyama[12] and Jay Demerath[13] found in their studies of church members data suggesting that class differences in religious involvement are primarily of kind, rather than of degree. Specifically, they found the middle and upper classes were more likely to 'do' their religion (attend worship services, etc.), while the lower classes were more likely to 'feel' or 'believe' their religion. This suggests that religion does provide a haven for the dispossessed after all, but that it does not show up when involvement is measured on the single dimension of ritual participation.

Note, however, that because both these studies were based on samples composed exclusively of church members, their findings may represent a special case, applicable to church members alone.[14] It may well be true that lower-class persons who are sufficiently involved in religion to belong to a congrega-

12. Yoshio Fukuyama, *Styles of Church Membership* (New York: United Church Board for Homeland Ministries, 1961), esp. p. 16.

13. N. J. Demerath III, *Social Class in American Protestantism* (Chicago: Rand McNally & Co., 1965).

14. Similar findings have been reported for a general population (Columbus, Ohio) by Russell Dynes, "Church-Sect Typology and Socio-Economic Status," *American Sociological Review*, XX (October, 1955), 555–560. However, failures in both sample design and return rate make Dynes' descriptive findings of questionable validity. The sampling frame was the city directory, obviously biased against the geographically mobile and the lower classes. A mail questionnaire obtained a 53 per cent return rate, yielding 360 cases, but only 33 per cent of those in the lowest occupational category responded. Presumably, since the study concerned religious attitudes, the more rather than the less religiously-involved lower-class persons replied.

tion (so they could be included in these samples) are more likely to hold traditional religious beliefs and to have various religious experiences than are middle- and upper-class persons. But it would be curious indeed if people who are less likely to be church members were more likely to have beliefs and feelings which ought to motivate church participation, and which are culturally transmitted mainly by the churches. If Demerath's and Fukuyama's findings are in fact specific to church members, then the economic deprivation theories of religious involvement hold, given some minimum degree of involvement to begin with, but they do not account for the behavior of a general population where such commitment is problematic. Hence, we must seek further to explain the religious apathy of the lower classes in general.[15]

ECONOMIC DEPRIVATION, RADICALISM AND RELIGION

A number of early socialist leaders, including Marx and Engels, noticed that radical parties of the left seemed to compete with the churches in offering opposite solutions to the deprived, the one calling for change, the other for acceptance. Leon Trotsky was so aware of the similarity of revolutionary Marxism to sectarianism that in the late 1890s he successfully recruited the first working-class members of the South Russian Worker's Union among adherents to religious sects.[16] This competition has also been remarked by theologians. H. Richard Niebuhr pointed out that no important sectarian movements have occurred among Western working classes since the rise of Methodism, and suggested that since the end of the eighteenth century

---

15. While all of the investigations reviewed treat deprivation in purely economic or class terms, some theorists, including Kingsley Davis, clearly meant much more than this when they wrote about the effects of deprivation on religious involvement. The authors extensively broaden the scope of deprivation theory and clarify a number of kinds and circumstances of deprivation in Chapter 13. There, it is suggested that religious involvement is highly related to several kinds of deprivation, though not directly to economic deprivation, although such deprivation may lead to the formation of new sects. This suggests that traditional theories concerning the effects of deprivation on religious involvement will prove fruitful when adequately formulated. None of this bears directly on the fact that economic deprivation fails to predict religious involvement, however; hence the scope of the present chapter is restricted to this specific problem.

16. Reported in Seymour Martin Lipset, *Political Man* (Garden City: Doubleday & Co., 1960), pp. 107–108.

working-class dissatisfactions have been mainly channeled into radical politics instead.[17]

The mechanisms available to party and church for dealing with the problems of the dispossessed are strikingly different. The church, basically, offers relief to those near the bottom of the social hierarchy in two related ways: (1) *transvaluation,* or redefinition of earthly values as valueless on a grander level, which is largely justified on the basis of (2) *heavenly rewards* which are contrasted with the transient pleasures of this world to show the relative unimportance of material well-being. Religion has perennially counselled the poor to endure their deprivations happily because they are thereby piling up riches in the eternal world to come.

Just as clearly as the church can offer other-worldly promises to mitigate earthly deprivation, it cannot, usually, offer changes in material rewards in this world. Radical political movements, on the other hand, offer to change things here and now—to create "a paradise on this planet, unlike Christianity, which promises a paradise after death."[18]

While radical Utopias and theological heavens may be equally chimerical, hope for the former lies in the material world, thus posing a potential threat to existing institutions, while the latter imply no social overhaul. This distinction is intimately connected to the different stances religion and radicalism take toward the legitimacy of the prevailing social arrangements. As noted in the last chapter, that religious value systems characteristically sanction prevailing institutions, thus contributing to social stability and integration, is a major tenet of current social theory. From this view, religion not only bids the deprived to accept their lot, but maintains that it is the just outcome of rules that are the best possible, indeed, in some instances divinely inspired.

---

17. Niebuhr, *op. cit.* In America, however, widespread sectarian movements have continued to appear, and widespread radicalism has correspondingly failed to develop. Robert Blauner, for one, has argued convincingly that the high level of sectarianism in the South impeded the development of a labor movement there. See his "Industrialization and Labor Response: The Case of the South," *Berkeley Publications in Society and Institutions* (now the *Berkeley Journal of Sociology*), IV (Summer, 1958), 29–43.

18. Nikita S. Khrushchev, remarks at a reception in Moscow given by the West African Republic of Mali, as reported by the United Press in the *San Francisco Chronicle*, May 30, 1962, p. 9.

This commitment of religious institutions to the *status quo* poses a specifically religious problem for radical movements. We shall sketch this problem in a very general way. First, the greater the proposed changes in the distribution of power, status, and wealth in any given society, the more likely these proposals are to call into question the values, often religious, that legitimize these arrangements. For example, to challenge the absolute political rule of a monarch is by implication to challenge any institutions that attribute the monarch's authority to a divine source.

If by radicalism we mean the proposal of such changes,[19] then it follows that the greater the degree of radicalism, the greater the tendency for the movement to conflict with prevailing values, and hence with the institutions and elites primarily concerned with maintaining these values. Although a radical movement may claim a purely political character, it is likely to engender opposition on religious grounds.[20]

Finally, the greater the conflict between radicals and religionists, the more likely the radicals are to be denied religious legitimacy, and, as a consequence, the more likely they are to fashion and promulgate an alternative value system, or new religion, under which they are legitimate. Thus, radicals may be transformed into active heretics. And whether their new value system is a new theology or 'dialectical materialism,' involve-

---

19. Admittedly, the word 'radicalism' is usually reserved for political movements on the far left, particularly those in a Marxist tradition. But in attempting to formulate our theoretical notions it became necessary to adopt variable language, and to speak of dissatisfaction with prevailing social arrangements in terms of degree. Of the possible common-language terms to describe such a variable, 'radicalism' seemed the most apt. Hence, we have decided to employ the term in this rather broad sense. Actually, it seems a useful way to use the term generally, for in everyday speech, as well as in the language of social science, we too often use nominal categories that tend to obscure an important underlying continuum.

20. A clear instance is the Peruvian Aprista Movement, which has constantly tried to define itself as a purely political movement having no concern with religious matters, while the Catholic hierarchy attacks it on primarily religious grounds. Through the years this denial of their religious legitmacy has led the Aprista to denounce the 'high' clergy as irreligious while claiming the support of a 'low' clergy, thus substituting a folkish Catholicism for the prevailing church. See Harry Kantor, *The Ideology and Program of the Peruvian Aprista Movement* (Berkeley and Los Angeles: University of California Press, 1953), esp. p. 96.

ment in a movement sanctioned by heterodox values ought to preclude commitment to the orthodox value system.[21]

If the foregoing speculations are approximately correct, then we ought to expect modern radicalism and religion to be mutually corrosive kinds of commitment, plausibly conceived as competitors for lower-class support. But are radical political movements in Western nations actually draining off the discontent once manifested in religious movements? This seems likely when we consider the implications of the well-known correlation between class and leftist politics, which presents us with an ecological correlation: as class falls, radicalism is more widespread and church involvement declines. The empirical question remains, however, whether these are the same people. Are the radicals the irreligious, and those who accept the *status quo* as legitimate, the ones involved in religion? And, if this is true, does it account for an important portion of the class differences in religious involvement?

We shall seek empirical answers to these questions by reanalyzing data collected from a national sample of British adults in 1957 by Social Surveys, Ltd., the British Gallup organization.[22]

CLASS, POLITICS, AND CHURCH ATTENDANCE

On the basis of the many studies previously cited, we would expect church attendance to be highly related to social class. This is strikingly confirmed by Table 10–2, where the proportion attending church at least "now and again" markedly declines with subjective social class — the respondent's self-rating of his class membership. Seventy-three per cent of the upper-class respondents reported attending church at least now and again, while only 39 per cent of the working class responded similarly. The relationship was replicated in direction and magnitude when occupation was used as a class measure.[23] The class differences

---

21. The theoretical perspective employed here owes much to the recent work of Neil J. Smelser. See his *Theory of Collective Behavior* (New York: The Free Press of Glencoe, 1963), esp. Ch. 10.

22. Study Number 1717. The sampling was by usual quota techniques. IBM cards and the codebook for the study were made available by the International Data Library and Reference Services, Survey Research Center, University of California, Berkeley.

23. Subjective class was used in subsequent analysis because the fewer categories involved made it possible to examine more complex relationships and still preserve sufficient bases for stable percentages.

TABLE 10-2
Church Attendance Declines with Subjective Class

Class	Percentage Attending at Least "Now and Again."
Upper	73 (26)*
Upper-Middle	71 (138)
Middle	56 (474)
Lower-Middle	52 (283)
Working	39 (748)

*Parentheses contain the total number of respondents in each class category on which the percentages were based.

in church going were not reduced by age, sex, or denomination, although each of these factors was related to attendance.

How much of this class difference in church attendance can be accounted for by political radicalism? We have suggested that disaffection with the existing social order brings radicals into conflict with the values sponsored by the prevailing religious institutions. Conversely, those who accept these religious values are constrained to acknowledge the legitimacy of the social *status quo.* Thus, radicals may be expected to be 'irreligious,' while the religious ought to be politically conservative. Since the two major British parties in 1957, Tory and Labour, are predominantly class-based and represent conflicting attitudes toward existing arrangements for distributing power, status, and economic well-being, it seems reasonable to expect supporters of these two political viewpoints to exhibit contrasting religious involvement. That is, Tories should not only accept the *status quo* as legitimate but should also be attached to the religious values associated with these arrangements, while the Labourites should tend to reject both the *status quo* and the religious values.

This interpretation is supported by the data. Table 10-3 shows that Labourites are much less likely than Tories to report attending church even now and again, with the politically intermediate "Don't Knows" and "Others" taking a middle position on church attendance. Clearly political affiliation is markedly related to church attendance. How much does this account for class differences in church going? In Table 10-4, party preference, representing approval or disapproval of the *status quo,* does intervene between class and church attendance. Regardless of class, church attendance is greatly influenced by political

TABLE 10-3
Party Preference and Church Attendance

Party	Percentage Attending at Least "Now and Again."
Tory	62 (546)
Labour	36 (631)
Other and Don't Know	50 (373)

outlook; those who cast their lot with political change are consistently less likely to participate in church. And within both Tory and Labour groups, particularly in the latter, the relation *between* class and church attendance is reduced, though the original class effect persists in the undecided group. Thus radical politics, perhaps functioning as an alternative outlet for feelings of status deprivation, do seem to provide a key to understanding the low church attendance of the lower classes.

While these findings support out thesis, they are far from the whole story. Marked class differences in church attendance still remain. How can they be further explained? The answer may lie in the manner in which the church attempts to redress deprivations as compared with the relief promised by radical parties, *and in the way different classes perceive this comparison.* The church offers to make things better in the next world, while leftist parties offer change in this world. The greater the felt deprivation, the more pressing are grievances in this world,[24] and perhaps the less probable that other-worldly solutions will suffice when radical parties offer an alternative to waiting. Thus, the propensity of the lower classes for politics of change, and their lack of religious involvement, suggest that they view polit-

---

24. Under stable circumstances, great objective deprivation may be accompanied by little or no felt deprevation, because there is no discrepancy between aspiration and the actual state of affairs. In an improving situation, felt deprivation may increase even though objective deprivation is lessening, because aspirations are being raised. In modern Western societies, however, felt deprivation appears to vary with objective conditions of deprivation. This seems to be a consequence of a generalization or homogenization of status aspirations, perhaps partly produced by the impact of mass media on the world-view of the lower classes. See Raymond Aron, *Le Développement de la Société Industrielle et la Stratification Sociale,* (Paris: "Les Cours de Sorbonne," no date), II, 48–49, 139.

TABLE 10-4
Subjective Class, Party Preference, and Church
Attendance

	Percentage Attending at Least "Now and Again."		
Class	Tory	Labour	Other and Don't Know
Upper	82 (17)	* (1)	* (8)
Upper-Middle	74 (96)	* (13)	79 (29)
Middle	62 (255)	40 (94)	53 (124)
Lower-Middle	56 (101)	47 (120)	57 (62)
Working	54 (122)	33 (449)	43 (177)

*Following the usual convention, no cell with fewer than 15 cases has been percentaged.

ical action as more relevant than religion to their problems.
This is confirmed by the data. Respondents were asked:

> Speaking generally, which would you say has more influence on
> the way people live and their circumstances: religion or politics?

Lower-class respondents were much more likely than those
from the upper classes to say that politics is more important
than religion, and Labourites were much more likely than Tories
to choose politics. Understandably, those who picked politics
were much less likely to attend church than those who picked
religion, or didn't know, or thought they were about the same.
These different perceptions of the relevance of politics vis-à-vis
religion tend to interpret the church-going differences between
both classes and parties. As shown in Table 10-5, party and
class differences in church attendance are markedly reduced
within groups sharing a similar view of the relevance of politics
and religion; differences within parties and classes *across* these
groupings are large and consistent. For example, 55 per cent of
the working-class Labourites who think religion is more important than politics attend church at least now and again, as compared with 25 per cent of their class and party peers who think
politics more important. The same comparison among working-class Tories is 63 per cent versus 38 per cent. As would be
expected, party and class differences are least reduced among
those who see little or no difference between politics and religion.

TABLE 10-5
Subjective Class,** Relevance of Religion Vis-a-Vis Politics, Party Preference, and Church Attendance

	Percentage Attending at Least "Now and Again."		
Class	Tory	Labour	Other and Don't Know
Religion more important than politics			
Middle	75 (93)	62 (31)	67 (45)
Lower-Middle	73 (29)	62 (29)	* (10)
Working	63 (58)	55 (105)	55 (54)
Politics more important than religion			
Middle	43 (91)	33 (49)	44 (52)
Lower-Middle	49 (39)	43 (60)	45 (33)
Working	38 (39)	25 (210)	21 (69)
They are about the same, or don't know			
Middle	72 (71)	* (11)	52 (29)
Lower-Middle	51 (33)	39 (31)	56 (18)
Working	60 (25)	31 (134)	44 (71)

*Not percentaged.
**Lack of cases precluded comparisons for upper and upper-middle classes; members of these classes were omitted from the table.

Thus, we have isolated an important link between radical politics and religious apathy: Radicals are more inclined than conservatives to see politics as the more relevant answer to their status difficulties. In summary, lower-class preference for the this-world solutions associated with radical politics accounts for a considerable portion of the class differences in church attendance.

CLASS, RADICALISM, AND RELIGIOUS BELIEF

To enhance confidence in these findings, we shall now consider religious involvement of another kind. Both Fukuyama[25] and Demerath[26] found that among *members* of church congre-

25. Fukuyama, *op. cit.*
26. Demerath, *op. cit.*

gations, class differences in religious involvement were in kind rather than degree. Specifically, they showed that the middle and upper classes were more likely to attend worship services, but that the lower classes were more likely to hold the traditional beliefs of the church. As suggested earlier, these findings seem unlikely to apply to lower classes generally, and are probably only characteristic of lower-class church members. Table 10–6 warrants this interpretation. The proportion of persons believing that Jesus was actually the Son of God, that the Devil exists, and that there is a life after death diminishes down the class hierarchy. All three qualify as central elements of traditional Christian theology, but the Devil is generally regarded as a pivotal belief for separating fundamentalists from modernists in the religious world. Yet the upper is more likely than the working class to report belief in the Devil. This suggests that the upper classes are more sect-like than the lower, a reversal of the findings for church members.

The most important of these three beliefs, for this chapter, is life after death. Clearly, a major mechanism by which religion can assuage economic deprivation is to promise rewards in the world to come. But unless the lower classes believe that another world exists beyond the grave, church promises can only seem irrelevant and spurious. What consequences does radicalism hold for belief in the hereafter? Surely those who opt for changes in this world should be less likely to accept the reality of the next, and those who believe in the hereafter should be

TABLE 10-6

Religious Beliefs are Less Widely Held the Lower the Social Class*

Class	Per Cent Who Believe In:		
	Life After Death	The Devil	Christ's Divinity
Upper	85 (26)	50 (26)	88 (26)
Upper-Middle	60 (138)	40 (134)	79 (138)
Middle	56 (474)	33 (474)	72 (474)
Lower-Middle	54 (284)	34 (279)	67 (285)
Working	49 (767)	32 (758)	70 (768)

*The fluctuations in case bases are due to fewer responses on some items.

TABLE 10-7

Subjective Class, Party Preference, and Belief in Life After Death

Class	Per Cent Who Believe in Life After Death		
	Tory	Labour	Other and Don't Know
Upper	88 (16)	* (1)	* (8)
Upper-Middle	61 (96)	* (12)	63 (30)
Middle	64 (255)	43 (94)	50 (126)
Lower-Middle	61 (100)	48 (120)	58 (64)
Working	58 (122)	45 (451)	50 (194)

*No cell with fewer than 15 cases has been percentaged.

more likely to accept the prevailing condition of this world. This expectation is confirmed by Table 10–7. In all social classes where comparisons are possible, Labourites are considerably less likely to believe in life after death than are Tories or the "Other" and "Don't Know" group. But class differences in belief all but vanish among Tories and Labourites and are drastically reduced in the third group.[27] Thus, radicalism clearly accounts for an impressive portion of the class differences in this religious belief. A similar effect occurred when beliefs in the divinity of Christ and in the existence of the Devil were examined by class and party.

SUMMARY

These data provide considerable support for the thesis that radical solutions for economic deprivation imply a lessening of religious involvement, and that the strength of lower-class radicalism in Great Britain partly accounts for lower-class religious apathy. Thus, the failure of long held economic deprivation theories to account for the religious alienation of the working classes may well be laid to failure to consider alternative outlets for dissatisfaction. To avoid a similar oversight in interpreting this chapter, we should point out that these dissatisfactions probably find many outlets besides religion and radical politics.

27. This disregards the upper-class Tories where the number of cases is so small that the reliability of the percentage is low.

Alcoholism, suicide, crime, insanity, television viewing, vicarious identification with the rich and famous, and adult education all recommend themselves as possibilities that ought to be explored in this connection.[28] We have tried to show only that religion and radicalism may both function in this manner, and that the choice of one tends to preclude the other. No general explanation has been offered as to *why* some people adopt a religious solution, while others turn to radical politics, although this question surely merits careful investigation. The data suggest, however, that the future and character of traditional religious institutions may be linked with the future course of radical politics. In the next chapter, we shall shift the main focus of our attention to this relationship.

---

28. An attempt will be made in Chapter 13 to specify some of these alternatives in greater detail.

Chapter 11

Religion and Radical Politics: A Comparative Study

IN the previous chapter, an attempt was made to examine the impact of commitment to the moderately radical British Labour Party on religious involvement. It was clear in our theoretical discussion that we conceive of radicalism as a variable, that political movements may differ from mild to wild radicalism depending on the degree to which they seek to alter existing economic, status, and power arrangements. However, in Great Britain the political variable essentially only takes two values: Tory and Labour. In this chapter, we shall seek to examine the relationship between religion and radicalism in nations where a variety of parties provide for many degrees of radicalism.

The tendency for religious and political institutions in all societies to be mutually supportive is a central proposition in current social theory. But little attention has been given to the argument advanced in the previous chapter, namely, that there is necessarily a corresponding tendency for political radicalism to come into conflict with religious institutions.

The survey data from Great Britain which we have just examined strongly suggest that religious involvement and political radicalism, even the mild brand represented by the British Labour Party, tend to be mutually exclusive commitments. This lent support to the generalizations offered about the intimate interconnection between faith and politics.

However, there is an obvious difficulty in making assertions about general social processes on the basis of observations of only one society at one historical moment. Although the data may conform to theoretical predictions, it is always possible to offer plausible explanations of these findings on the basis of idiosyncratic historical developments, and thus deny that they illustrate an instance of some general social tendency. Such difficulties can only be overcome through a comparative approach.

If expected relationships can be shown to obtain in a number of societies, then *ad hoc* explanations must be multiplied until an implausible string of historical coincidences is required to discount the operation of some general social processes. Having previously examined a single nation, we shall now adopt a comparative strategy.

Recalling the last chapter, it was argued that the commitment of religious institutions to the *status quo* poses a specifically religious problem for radical or even mildly reformist movements. Such movements, by proposing changes in the distribution of power, status, and wealth in any given society, call into question the values, often religious, that legitimize these arrangements. Hence, although radicals may conceive of themselves in a purely political way, they tend to engender opposition on religious grounds. The more they come into conflict with religious institutions, the more likely radicals are to turn away from the prevailing religion and develop a value orientaton of their own to legitimize themselves.

On these grounds we would expect that modern radicalism and traditional religion are mutually corrosive kinds of commitments. While this may seem clear enough for extremist radical groups such as the Communist Party, which takes an avowedly antireligious line, we mean to suggest that such effects are also associated with moderate and even very mild degrees of proposed political innovation: *To the degree that men seek to alter existing stratification arrangements, they are likely to have turned away from the prevailing religious institutions of their societies.*

It was reported in the last chapter that the moderate radicalism of British Labour was associated with a considerable tendency to reject religious beliefs and not to attend church worship services. On the basis of the hypothesis above, it would be predicted that in nations where the left-right differences on the political spectrum are greater than in Britain, differences in religious involvement between the left and right would be correspondingly greater, and where differences between left and right are slight, differences in religious involvement will similarly be slight. In order to test this hypothesis empirically we shall draw on survey data from France, The Netherlands, and the United States. Suggestive findings from data on students in Colombia, South America will also be briefly reported.

RELIGION AND RADICAL POLITICS IN FRANCE

In modern France there are two major religious statuses: Catholic and ex-Catholic. A nationwide survey in 1956 found that 86 per cent of French adults said they had been born Catholics, 3 per cent were born Protestants, 10 per cent reported they had never had a religious affiliation, and less than one-half of 1 per cent were Jewish. But of those who said they were born Catholics, only 45 per cent said they were now practicing Catholicism, 38 per cent were not practicing, and 14 per cent said they were indifferent.[1]

Thus, it is clear that to the degree that France is religious, it is Catholic; but that the greater proportion of French adults consider themselves to be generally irreligious. It is well known that French leftists are heirs to a radical tradition of anticlericalism and irreligiousness with its roots in the humanistic values of the revolution. The question that concerns us, however, is whether or not, and to what degree, contemporary French irreligiousness is related to French radicalism.

In Table 11–1 respondents have been classified along a left-right political continuum according to the party they indicated they would vote for in the next election. The relative positioning of the Peasant and Independent group and the Gaullists is arbitrary since both groups were about equally right-wing at the time of the studies. The presence of a Catholic left-of-center party causes some apparent confusion in ordering, and this group is meant to lie off the scale, as indicated by the

---

1. Conducted by the National Institute of Demographic Studies, in May, 1956, survey number 072. Codebooks and IBM cards for this and all other studies used in this essay were made available by the International Data Library and Reference Service, Survey Research Center, University of California, Berkeley.

line in the table. Yet a religious, leftist party is not a contradiction of our theoretical notions, when two features of such parties are considered. First, they are launched in circumstances where, far from challenging a church-dominated *status quo*, they represent a bid by the church to regain power in a society where it has lost its link to the Establishment or to establish such a link where none has ever existed. Second, such parties are leftist only on what Lipset has called "economic liberalism"—bread and butter issues—and are rightist on noneconomic or procedural issues.[2] Furthermore, the suggested model concerning the support given prevailing social arrangements by *established* religious institutions must not be interpreted as implying that religions will never be implicated in radicalism or even revolution. On the contrary, we mean to emphasize the tendency for radical movements to take on a 'religious' character, and to suggest that when a radical movement has access to an equally disinherited religious institution, an alliance between them ought to be expected. Such is often the case with anticolonial radicalism, where the indigenous religion often provides leadership and legitimacy to the political movement. Indeed, Great Britain's centuries of failure to subdue Irish independence efforts was greatly due to the continued support given Irish rebelliousness by Roman Catholic clergy who were excluded from the British Protestant Establishment. But, while they advocated revolt, the Irish clergy have never been known as advocates of changing economic, status, and power arrangements *within* the Irish community.

Thus, while religious parties may seek to enlist mass support through bread and butter issues or may back anticolonial revolts in order to establish the power of the church, they retain rightist attitudes on matters of status and authority. For example, while Catholic parties in modern France have typically supported programs to mitigate economic deprivations, they have continued to support an hereditary view of status and authoritarian qualities in government. In this way religious parties resemble many successful radical rightist movements in the twentieth century, which have enlisted mass support through 'bread and circuses' in the tradition of the Caesars, while retaining tyrannical powers.

---

2. See: Seymour Martin Lipset, *Political Man* (Garden City: Doubleday & Co., 1960).

Immediately following World War II, the Catholic M.R.P. in France did take a legitimately radical stand on both economic and procedural questions. Indeed, it briefly joined a united front with the Socialists and Communists. This seems to have been possible because the influence of prewar Catholic political leaders and the Church hierarchy had been destroyed by their collaboration with the Nazis during Vichy and the occupation. Thus, rank and file young Catholic liberals were able to assert control over the party without much interference from above. As an unanticipated function of their success in creating an honorable image for the M.R.P., they created the conditions for the hierarchy to again assert influence in political life, and, by 1950, the M.R.P. was again on the right in its stance on questions of status and authority, and once again under the hierarchical domination.[3] Despite these grounds for placing the M.R.P. on the right, we shall restrict the testing of the hypothesis to parties whose political stance is unambiguous. Data on M.R.P. supporters are presented, but only for their intrinsic interest.

Turning to the data, does political radicalism predict religious estrangement?

Politics and Ritual Involvement

In Table 11–1 we may compare the proportion of persons who report they are currently practicing religion among the supporters of each of the major French parties. The data are from two national samples of the adult French population gathered at a four-year interval.[4] The enormous impact of radicalism on religious practice is immediately apparent reading across the table from left to right. While 7 per cent of the Communists in the 1956 sample report they are practicing a faith, 67 per cent of the Gaullists and 68 per cent of the Peasants and Independents report religious practice. Furthermore, the differences *increase systematically* from left to right. And, as expected, the supporters of the Catholic M.R.P. are overwhelmingly in the Church.

It is especially revealing to note the stability of the propor-

3. See François Goguel, *France Under the Fourth Republic* (Ithaca, N.Y.: Cornell University Press, 1952); and Paul-Marie De La Gorce, *The French Army: A Military-Political History* (New York: George Braziller, 1963).

4. National Institute of Demographic Studies, survey number 072, May, 1956, and Institute of French Public Opinion, survey number 90, August-September, 1952.

TABLE 11-1
Party Affiliation and Religious Practice in Two Independent French Samples

		Per Cent Who Say They Are Currently Practicing Their Faith					
		Communist	Socialist	Radical	Poujadists	Gaullist	Peasant & Independent	M.R.P. (Catholic)
May 1956 National Sample	N =	7% (210)	16% (389)	32% (205)	41% (78)	67% (57)	68% (308)	91% (229)
August-September, 1952 National Sample of Catholics Only		6 (77)	16 (130)	32 (53)	*	62 (95)	70 (85)	85 (198)

*Non-existent in 1952

tion of religious practitioners in each party between the two samples even though the relative strength of some of these parties has markedly *shifted* during the four-year interval between the first and second samples. Furthermore, the 1952 study contained *only* persons who said they had been born Catholics, all others were excluded from the sample (these being the few Protestants and the 10 per cent who never had a religion). But despite the absence from the 1952 sample of persons who claimed no faith, who are present in the 1956 data, the proportion claiming religious practice within each party remains essentially unchanged. These virtually identical findings are particularly important for this study since the 1956 data contain few usable items on religious behavior, while the 1952 study gathered extensive information on religion. Since the remainder of this section will use materials from the earlier study, it is reassuring to have an indication that a sample of only Catholics ought to be little different from a sample of French adults in general.

We may now turn our attention to more specific and sensitive measures of ritual involvement in religious institutions. For Catholics, great emphasis is placed on weekly attendance at Mass. In the mediational scheme of Catholic theology, grace lies only through the Church and its sacraments. Hence, salvation depends upon availing oneself of the formal mechanisms of the Church, for men may not seek God's mercy directly, but only through the sacrifice of Christ reenacted in the Mass. Continued absence from Mass puts a Catholic outside the Church, cut off from salvation.[5] The data in Table 11-2 show that radicalism greatly affects Mass attendance. While only 3 per cent of the Communists report they have been to Mass in the last two or three weeks, 60 per cent of the Independents and 56 per cent of the Gaullists have attended recently. The M.R.P. supporters, of course, show the very highest rate. Mass attendance systematically increases from left to right; differences are not just between Communists and right-wingers, but *within* the left, the Communists are less likely to attend than Socialists, who in turn are less likely to attend than are Radicals.

5. This importance of Mass for Catholics is readily demonstrated by marked differences in regularity of Sunday worship service attendance found between Protestants and Catholics in both Europe and America. Protestants, whose theology stresses the personal seeking of God, give church attendance less importance.

TABLE 11-2
Politics and Ritual Involvement (1952 study)

N =	Communist (77)	Socialist (130)	Radical (53)	Gaullist (95)	Peasant & Independent (85)	Catholic Party (M.R.P.) (198)
Church Attendance						
Percentage who attend Mass at least every two or three weeks.	3	11	21	56	60	82
Percentage who "in principle" go to Mass every week.	1	12	13	55	60	80
Ritual Obligations						
Percentage who received Communion recently.	8	27	28	65	77	91
Percentage who ever go to confession.	10	32	38	73	80	93
Percentage who regularly perform their Easter duty.	4	21	26	62	73	90
Percentage who always observe meatless Friday.	3	15	28	56	60	79
Prayer						
Percentage who ever pray outside of church.	22	52	68	84	90	96

A similar pattern is revealed in the proportions of the party supporters who say that in principle they consider themselves weekly Mass attenders, although they may have been a bit irregular recently. From this it is certain that we have uncovered relatively stable differences in patterns of Mass attendance, and not some differences which were idiosyncratic to the weeks of the interviewing. Leftists have not just missed the past several Sundays; they have stopped attending Mass.

This same pattern characterizes the performance of additional Catholic ritual obligations, such as receiving Communion, going to confession, performing Easter duty, and observing meatless Friday; the proportion fulfilling each of these ritual obligations increases drastically from left to right. Ritual involvement in the Church is the mode on the political right, while the overwhelming majority on the left are not involved.

It is possible, of course, that although French radicals have given up the ritual expectations of the Catholic Church, they have taken up a personal, Protestant-like faith instead and worship privately outside the Church. If this were so, then it could be convincingly argued that the effects of radicalism are not so much on religious values and commitment as upon formal institutional ties. Prayer would obviously be a central religious act of such a personal faith, and thus, by examining prayer we may resolve this possible alternative interpretation. It is apparent in Table 11 – 2 that personal religiousness, as indicated by personal prayer outside the church, is considerably more common among French adults than institutional participation. But this tendency to substitute a personal religion for the institutional *does not* account for left-right differences in religious involvement. For, while even Communists are much more likely to pray than to go to Mass or perform other ritual acts of the Church, they are still much less likely to do so than supporters of other parties. Moreover, differences in proportions of party supporters praying are about the same size as differences in institutional religious acts.

The interparty differences in ritual involvement were not reduced when sex was held constant. Although in all parties women were much more likely to be involved in religion than were men, among both males and females differences between political parties were similar and about the same size. Social class also had virtually no influence on party differences in religious involvement.[6] Thus, it seems reasonably certain that the differences we have observed are produced by a specifically political phenomenon: Value commitments tend to be mutually exclusive, and, thus, the more a party generates a concern with values, the less likely its supporters will adhere to competing value institutions. In the M.R.P., where political and religious ideologies are explicitly merged, party supporters are extremely likely to fulfill their religious obligations. In the Communist Party, where the ideology specifically presents an 'irreligious' value orientation, only the tiniest fraction of supporters have an attachment to the church.

So far, it seems definite that the French are likely to have turned away from ritual involvement in the church to the degree that their political commitments are radical. We would similarly expect radicalism to coincide with rejection of the central tenets of Catholic orthodoxy.

Politics and Religious Belief

The basic component of religious value-systems is some conception of a supernatural world, force, or being, and in traditional Christianity this involves a set of assertions about the nature and will of an all-powerful and sentient God. As the data in Table 11–3 indicate, belief in the existence of an all-powerful God is massively related to left-right differences in political affiliation: while 9 per cent of the Communists and 27 per cent of the Socialists are certain God exists, 75 per cent of the Gaullists and 88 per cent of the Catholic M.R.P. supporters are certain. Clearly radicalism has enormous implications for religious belief as well as for ritual involvement in the church. Further confidence is given this conclusion by the virtually identical patterns of belief in the soul and in the miracles at Lourdes. As with party differences in ritual involvement, these findings were independent of age, sex, and social class.[7]

So far, then, we have seen that French radicals tend to have lapsed from religious belief and practice. But these findings still tell us little about the attitudes and feelings radicals have about

---

6. The original relationship between social class and ritual involvement was reduced when political affiliation was held constant, thus replicating findings from Great Britain reported in the last chapter.

7. As with ritual involvement, the social class–religious belief relationship was reduced when party was held constant, again confirming the findings in the preceding chapter.

TABLE 11-3
Politics and Religious Belief (1952 study)

N =	Communist (77)	Socialist (130)	Radical (53)	Gaullist (95)	Peasant & Independent (85)	M.R.P. (Catholic) (198)
God						
The existence of an all-powerful God seems:						
Percentage Certain.	9	27	39	75	77	88
Percentage Very probable or Probable.	19	43	42	21	17	11
Percentage Unlikely or Impossible.	72	30	19	4	6	1
	100	100	100	100	100	100
The Soul						
The existence of an invisible soul within you seems:						
Percentage Certain.	10	24	35	68	70	85
Percentage Very Probable or Probable.	12	37	46	27	23	14
Percentage Unlikely or Impossible.	78	39	19	5	7	1
	100	100	100	100	100	100
Miracles						
Percentage who believe that miracles of Divine origin occur at Lourdes.	10	23	34	73	78	88

religion and the church. They could simply be disinterested. But if value conflicts are the key to understanding the religious apostasy of radicals, then we must expect radicals will harbor active resentment and hostility towards what they view as opposition values. Thus we need to know not only what they do not do and do not believe, but also what kinds of images and feelings radicals do have about religion.

As may be readily seen in Table 11–4, French radicals overwhelmingly do harbor animosity and contempt for religious ideology, the clergy, and church members. Ninety per cent of the Communists, and nearly two-thirds of the Socialists agreed that a just God would not let innocent people suffer as they do, while only a small proportion of the right wing and Catholic M.R.P. supporters would agree with this statement. This particular item seems fraught with implications that Catholic interpretations of justice as well as the sanctioning system on which it is based, are unacceptable to radicals. For, clearly, a central Christian tenet concerns the justice of God and the infallibility of his judgments. Radicals seem to be saying that if any such God does exist, he is not just. Such a God might inspire fear, but surely not love.

The clear identification of the Church with forces of conservatism is shown by agreement to the statement "Church is for rich people." Right and left markedly disagreed over the truth of this charge, precisely as we would expect. More interesting, however, is the belief of radicals that "the clergy does not live up to its standards." This hostility was extended to Catholic laity as well. Much more than the rightists, radicals were willing to agree that "I am disgusted by the wickedness and the strictness of certain so-called Catholics." Not only, then, are radicals likely to be apostate, but also to be hostile towards the prevailing religious system. Rightists maintain their ties with the church, their belief in religious ideology, and reject hostile statements about the Church and religion. Thus the predicted relationships between radicalism and religious commitment obtain in modern France as well as in Great Britain: The further left a man's politics, the more likely he is to have cast aside religion.

RELIGION AND RADICAL POLITICS IN THE NETHERLANDS

Although The Netherlands lies only a short distance north of France, the two nations differ in many important ways. While

TABLE 11-4
Politics and Hostility Towards Religion and The Church

Percentage Who Agree That:	Communist	Socialist	Radical	Gaullist	Peasant & Independent	M.R.P. (Catholic)
"One sees innocent people suffering every day. If God were just He would not let this happen."	90	66	35	16	11	12
"Church is for rich people."	100	57	22	11	6	8
"The clergy does not live up to its standards."	89	68	43	26	19	14
Religion is a superstition."	85	37	22	2	4	2
"I am disgusted by the wickedness and the strictness of certain so-called Catholics."	81	66	72	33	27	27

France is a Republic, the Dutch Queen still reigns as a constitutional monarch; while France is at least nominally Catholic, the Dutch are evenly divided between Protestantism and Catholicism and the nation and crown are traditionally Protestant; and while France experienced a violently anti-clerical revolution, The Netherlands was swept by the Reformation.

Despite these important differences between the two nations, they have a common feature which makes a comparison between them especially valuable: a multiple party system diversely spread across a left-right spectrum. Thus, the political variable we have examined in France is available for reexamination in The Netherlands in an importantly different social and historical context. This will allow us to make a more certain judgment whether the massive correlations between radicalism and apostasy found in France are mere artifacts of peculiar configurations of historical events, or whether some more general social process is at work. Our theoretical framework asserts that radicalism tends to be incompatible with commitment to the prevailing religion regardless of social context, and hence rests on the prediction that the similarity in left-right political dispersion between France and The Netherlands will be matched by similarities in religious commitment even though the nations are importantly different in other respects.

A study as rich as the French one in questions on religious beliefs and practices was not available for The Netherlands. The available data require us to settle for examining the single relationship between party affiliation and church attendance.[8]

Again, as in France, a Catholic left-of-center party, representing a church lacking participation in the traditional power structure, is placed off the left-right continuum as indicated by the line in the table. Nevertheless, Table 11–5 clearly shows the power of political affiliation as a predictor of religious involvement. While none of the Communists and 10 per cent of those supporting the Labor Party reported attending church in the past seven days, 79 per cent of those in the Anti-Revolutionary Party did so, and the proportions decrease systematically from politically right to left, down the table. Indeed, the size of

---

8. A combination of two surveys, numbers 619 and 620, conducted by the Netherlands Institute for Public Opinion in April and May, 1956. Survey 619 was a national sample of males, 620 a national sample of females; when merged they accurately reflect the adult population.

TABLE 11-5

Political Affiliation and Church Attendance in The Netherlands

	Party**	Percentage Attending Church in past 7 days
Right	Catholic People's Party	95 (331)
:	Anti-Revolutionary Party	79 (139)
:	Christian Historical Party	59 (109)
:	Liberal Party	12 (77)
:	Labor Party	10 (314)
Left	Communist Party	0 (11)*

*Because of the small number of cases, ordinarily no percentage would be reported. The percentage was included for descriptive interest only.

**Small parties have been omitted since they drew so little support no stable percentages on church attendance could be computed.

the relationship in terms of percentage-point differences is strikingly similar to that found in France (see Table 11-2). When denomination was controlled, the left-right effect remained among liberal and orthodox Protestants as well as the Catholics, even though members of the latter two groups tended to be concentrated in the rightist parties. Furthermore social class, age, and sex did not reduce the relationships.[9]

This replication of findings in The Netherlands strongly suggests that the French findings were not due to the peculiar historical development of French radicalism, but reflect a general functional arrangement among social institutions: Religious and radical commitments are mutually corrosive.

RELIGION AND RADICAL POLITICS IN THE UNITED STATES

Historical trends in the politics and religion of Western Europe and Great Britain are markedly discontinuous with developments in the United States. While, as Niebuhr[10] pointed out, no important sect movement has swept the European lower classes since the rise of Methodism at the end of the eighteenth century, in America sects have continued to erupt at a prodigious rate. Lower class 'awakenings' have produced such contemporary groups as the Nazarenes, the Free Methodists, the Mor-

---

9. Again an original relationship between social class and church attendance was reduced when political affiliation was controlled.

10. H. Richard Niebuhr, *The Social Sources of Denominationalism* (New York: Henry Holt, 1929).

mons, the Seventh Day Adventists, the Jehovah's Witnesses, and countless other perfectionist, millenarian, and pentecostal groups, some tiny and some large.[11] As a consequence, there are more than 250 separate, organized, religious bodies listed in the *Yearbook of American Churches*.[12] Thus, in contrast with Europe, the United States is characterized both by religious diversity and by the continuing generation of new religious movements.

While it is apparent that sect movements in America are eventually coopted by the middle classes (as were such European movements in the past) and thence transformed into institutions unsuitable for lower class frustrations, the dispossessed in America have continued to forge new religions to take the place of the old. This phenomenon has led American scholars to think of Troeltsch's[13] "church-sect" typology in terms of a *process,* through which a newly launched religious movement is transformed by organizational pressures into a middle-class 'church,' whereupon the lower class break away and initiate still another movement — an endless cycle of birth, growth, and schism. Such a process model no longer applies to Europe, and the coincidence of the death of sect formation and the birth of radical movements suggests that lower class frustrations — the dynamic of both sects and radical parties — were subsequently channelled into political radicalism.[14] The likelihood of such a connection is further suggested by American events: As sects have continued to emerge here, radicalism has been anemic and without appreciable lower class support.

Previously, we have examined rather impressive data from Europe which support the thesis that religious involvement is a negative function of the degree of political radicalism. But can such effects be detected within the American party system?

---

11. Elmer T. Clark, *Small Sects in America* (Nashville, Tennessee: Abington-Cokesbury Press, 1949).

12. Benson Y. Landis, ed., *Yearbook of American Churches for 1963,* New York: National Council of Churches of Christ in the U.S.A.

13. Ernst Troeltsch, *The Social Teaching of the Christian Churches,* 2 vols., translated by Olive Wyon (New York: The Macmillan Co., 1931). The fact that the church usually seems unable to function well in relieving status deprivations, as discussed in detail in the previous chapter, does not mean that the deprived are not a major source of support for *new* religious movements.

14. The sectarianism of extremist radical movements, however, seems somewhat analogous, as well as the mellowing of revolutions after the first generation rebels are replaced by a post-revolutionary generation.

Until the recent, and as yet unassessed, rise of Goldwater-ism, the most singular feature of American parties is the way they cut across classes and other lines of cleavage within the American polity, and to a great extent represent huge, multi-interest coalitions with a diversity of liberal and conservative elements within the ranks of each.[15] Because of their conglomerate makeup, the Republican and Democratic parties have tended towards the middle of the road, and thus towards one another. But, despite its moderate and Southern conservative elements, the Democratic Party has represented the forces of change, however mild, while the Republican Party has been identified with defense of the *status quo*. For this reason, combined with the virtual impossibility of successfully launching third parties, the more extreme left and right elements in America have been forced, through a doctrine of 'lesser evilism,' to affiliate with the party nearer their side of the road.

It is problematic, however, whether these conservative elements on the one hand, and radicals on the other, are of sufficient number to produce differences in religious involvement between the two American parties. Nevertheless, our theoretical formulations purport to make a general statement concerning the consequences of any degree of radicalism for religious involvement. We have seen that the predicted outcomes were easily observable in the extremely and moderately diverse political spectra of France, The Netherlands, and Great Britain. But, to be really adequate, a theoretical model must operate successfully when the values of relevant variables are near minimum and effects are subtle, as well as in gross circumstances where variables have maximum values. Thus, the United States provides an especially acute test of our theoretical notions.

---

15. This characteristic of American party politics has long been a source of amazement to European visitors. For example, Frederick Engels wrote in a letter to Sorge in 1892:

> The divergence of interest even in the *same* class group is so great in that tremendous area that wholly different groups and interests are represented in each of the two big parties, depending upon the locality, and almost each particular section of the possessing class has its representatives in each of the two parties to a very large degree, though *today* big industry forms the core of the Republicans on the whole, just as big landowners in the South form the Democrats.

From Karl Marx and Frederick Engels, *Letters to Americans: 1848–1895*, p. 239, quoted in Daniel Bell, *The End of Ideology* (New York: Collier Books, 1961), p. 67. Italics in the original.

Before turning to the data, several qualifications must be made. The political meaning of 'Democrat' is blurred by the Southerners, Catholics, and nonwhite minorities, who, more than other Americans, adopt the party label with little regard for class lines or political ideology. This tendency is confounded with the fact that these groups also form relatively distinct subcultures, and thus analysis among them must be carried on separate from the majority population. However, given the size of national survey samples, insufficient cases are available to permit separate analysis of Southerners and nonwhites. For this reason they are excluded from this section. The analysis will be separate for Catholics and Protestants, though among the former, historic reasons for Democratic affiliation may well make it impossible to use party affiliation to separate left from right.[16]

Turning to the data, it is apparent in Table 11–6 that among Protestants, Democrats are indeed less likely to attend church than are Republicans. The differences, as expected, are relatively small, but the findings are replicated in four independent national samples surveyed from 1957 through 1962.[17] Differences among Protestants range from 20 percentage points in 1962 down to 4 percentage points in the 1959 sample. This variation leaves in doubt the question of how great the differences between the two parties actually are, but the consistent direction of the differences indicates that some difference does exist. These findings strongly argue that—for Protestants—even the mild Democratic form of discontent with the *status quo* is accompanied by estrangement from religious institutions. Among Catholics, on the other hand, where party labels have considerably less meaning, differences are virtually zero and probably meaningless.

Although replication of the relationship between party and religious involvement on four independent samples gives strong assurance that the differences were not produced by chance, the question of spuriousness remains. In the European data, we found that social class did not reduce the size of party differences in religious involvement. As can be seen in Table 11–7,

16. See especially Seymour Martin Lipset, "Religion and Politics in the American Past and Present," in Robert Lee, ed., *Religion and Social Conflict* (New York: Oxford University Press, 1964), pp. 69–126.

17. American Institute of Public Opinion, national surveys, number 653-K, February, 1962; number 625-K, February, 1960; number 622-K, December, 1959; and number 580-K, March, 1957.

TABLE 11-6

**Party and Church Attendance Among Catholics and Protestants
(Southerners and Non-Whites Excluded)**

Study Number	Year	Attendance Measure	PROTESTANTS			CATHOLICS		
			REPUBLICANS	DEMOCRATS	Percentage-point difference	REPUBLICANS	DEMOCRATS	Percentage-point difference
653-K	1962	Percentage attended in past week	46 (265)	26 (266)	20	75 (40)	69 (210)	6
625-K	1960	Percentage attended in past 2 weeks	51 (267)	43 (190)	8	76 (78)	74 (193)	2
622-K	1959	Percentage attended in past week	43 (209)	39 (192)	4	72 (60)	74 (173)	−2
580-K	1957	Percentage in past week	48 (344)	35 (203)	13	78 (82)	78 (192)	0
					Average difference, 11.25			

TABLE 11-7
Party, Class and Church Attendance Among Protestants and Catholics (Southerners and Non-Whites Excluded)

Study	Attendance Measure	Class*	PROTESTANTS		CATHOLICS	
			REPUBLICANS	DEMOCRATS	REPUBLICANS	DEMOCRATS
653-K (1962)	Percentage attended in past week	White collar	49 (95)	32 (54)	72 (18)	79 (57)
		Blue collar	38 (69)	19 (108)	68 (16)	68 (104)
625-K (1960)	Percentage attended in past two weeks	White collar	64 (80)	57 (44)	81 (27)	81 (51)
		Blue collar	42 (81)	36 (88)	77 (23)	75 (92)
622-K (1959)	Percentage attended in past week	White collar	41 (112)	45 (40)	90 (27)	70 (50)
		Blue collar	36 (75)	32 (90)	53 (21)	75 (90)
580-K (1957)	Percentage attended in past week	White collar	48 (134)	43 (51)	93 (25)	84 (43)
		Blue collar	45 (105)	31 (102)	68 (34)	75 (108)

*Farmers, farm laborers, and service workers have been excluded from all tables based on American data in which occupation is used to indicate social class.

social class, as indicated by breadwinner's occupation, does not account for party differences in America either.[18] Among Protestants, of eight possible party comparisons with social class controlled, Republicans show a higher proportion of church attendance seven times. Among Catholics, as before, the pattern remains essentially meaningless.

The relationship among Protestants was also not reduced when sex and age were controlled.

Having thus made reasonably certain that we are dealing with a real political effect—that differences in church attendance were neither spurious nor a chance occurrence—we may attempt to sharpen these findings somewhat. In what follows, we shall not report further data on Catholics since no change in the findings already presented emerged in subsequent analysis.

As we have noted, left-right distinctions in American party labels, even outside the South and among white Protestants, are neither great nor altogether clear. Since the central concern of this chapter is with radicalism, which is here considered to be a continuum of satisfaction-dissatisfaction with existing status, power, and economic arrangements, we shall now examine the reasons Americans gave for their party choice in an effort to measure radicalism more directly.

In the 1957 survey, Gallup interviewers asked respondents their "one biggest reason" for supporting the party they did. The way in which these free responses were coded allows for distinguishing persons who justified their choice on ideological grounds from those who gave some other reason, such as family tradition or admiration for the current party standard-bearer. In this way, it seems possible to greatly increase the meaningfulness of party affiliation as a measure of attitudes towards existing social arrangements. By comparing those persons for whom American party politics is primarily seen in ideological (liberal versus conservative) terms, it ought to be possible to maximize differences in church attendance between Republicans and Democrats. This is the case as can be seen in Table 11–8. Among ideological party supporters, the original five percentage- point difference in church attendance among white-collar workers (Table 11–7) increased to 15 percentage points, while

---

18. The original relationship between social class and church attendance was reduced when party affiliation was controlled.

TABLE 11-8

A Comparison of Church Attendance Between Ideological Republicans and Democrats With Occupational Prestige Held Constant (Protestants Only, Study 580-K, 1957)

	Percentage Who Attended in Last Week			
	Ideological Republicans*	Non-Ideological Republicans	Non-Ideological Democrats	Ideological Democrats**
White Collar	48 (69)	47 (64)	44 (16)	33 (40)
Blue Collar	46 (41)	43 (65)	42 (21)	27 (78)

*Those who answered that their "one biggest reason" for registering as Republicans was: "Like the way Republicans handle things in general, like policies better, like platform," "Better for business," "Not so pro-union," or "More conservative," were classified as Ideological affiliates, in contrast with those who responded "Family tradition," "Husband or wife is," "Like Ike," etc., who were classified as non-Ideological.

**Similar to above, Democrats who responded, "Democrats are more for common man, working class, labor," "Times more prosperous when Democrats in office, lower prices," "Like the way Democrats do things in general, like policies better, like platform," or "More interested in minority groups," were classified as Ideological affiliates, while those who responded "Family tradition," or "Keep promises," were classified as non-Ideological.

Persons without a party preference or who "didn't know" why they supported a particular party were omitted.

the original 14 percentage-point difference among blue-collar workers jumped to 19 points. On the other hand, as would be expected, differences between nonideological party supporters are trivial.

So far, we have seen that the mild left-right differences between Democrats and Republicans produce mild differences in church attendance. But are corresponding corrosions of religious belief also associated with mild American radicalism?

We have argued that the greater the degree of a political group's radicalism, the more likely it is to extend an alternative value orientation in competition with the prevailing religious sanctioning system. But it seems less likely that the mild radicalism of the Democratic Party, despite its effect on church attendance, will lead American Protestants to reject the basic Christian value orientation of their society, for the Democratic Party does not explicitly present an ideological alternative to Christianity. Indeed, Democrats are quite as punctilious as Republicans about invoking God in political speeches, and both parties carefully open all sessions of their national conventions with a prayer. Thus, we ought to expect that any differences between the two parties in the proportion holding Christian beliefs will be exceedingly small, if there are any differences at all.

Items on religious belief are not common in American Gallup surveys, but one which was available seems especially relevant for this study: belief in life after death. As pointed out in the previous chapter, belief in an afterlife is particularly crucial for religious solutions to the dissatisfactions with the *status quo*. For the faithful, relief from the deprivations of this life lies beyond the grave and will last for eternity. But if men do not believe in heavenly reward, they are forced to view this life as an all-or-nothing affair. Thus, radical concern for reform here and now goes hand in hand with a rejection of a world to come. Table 11-9 shows, perhaps surprisingly, that among white Protestants, Democrats *are* less likely to believe in life after death than are Republicans. The differences are quite small, but the direction is the same in both samples which contained the question, and the relationship holds for both white-collar and blue-collar workers. Because of the small expected difference, the political variable has been strengthened by combining vote in the 1956 Presidential election with current party preference.

Thus, we must conclude that even in the United States where left-right differences are slight, political affiliation does affect both church attendance and religious belief.

RELIGION AND POLITICS IN COLOMBIA, SOUTH AMERICA

A recent paper by Kenneth Walker on the political behavior of university students in Bogota, Colombia provides data which

TABLE 11-9

Politics and Belief in Life After Death (Protestants Only)

		Percentage Who Believed in Life after Death		
		Republicans for Eisenhower	Democrats for Stevenson	%-point Differences
625-K (1960)	W. Collar	85 (65)	71 (24)	14
	B. Collar	76 (67)	72 (39)	4
	Total	83 (227)	71 (97)	12
580-K (1957)	W. Collar	77 (122)	72 (32)	5
	B. Collar	77 (86)	70 (54)	7
	Total	77 (208)	71 (86)	6

further support our general thesis.[19] Walker's analysis of support for Fidel Castro among college students showed that religious commitment was by far the most powerful factor affecting this form of radicalism. He reported that 21 per cent of the practicing Catholics were pro-Castro, in contrast to 51 per cent of the nonpracticing Catholics and 74 per cent of the agnostics. Furthermore, among practicing Catholics, Castro support ranged from 12 per cent among those who attended church several times a week up to 58 per cent of those who rarely attended. Here again we find religious and radical commitments tending to preclude one another.

SUMMARY AND CONCLUSION

This essay began with the hypothesis that to the degree a man was committed to revisions in the status arrangements in his society, he would be likely to have turned from religious institutions. This led to the prediction that within any given political system persons supporting parties on the left would be less involved in religion than those supporting rightist parties, and that the proportions involved in religion would systematically decrease from the furthest right party to that furthest left.

The data examined bore out this predicted relationship in France, The Netherlands, the United States, and Colombia, while the previous chapter reported similar findings in Great Britain.

A second prediction is also generated by the original hypothesis: that the greater the left-right dispersion within a political system the greater the difference in religious involvement between the most extreme parties. This is simply an application of the prediction about individuals and parties raised to the level of nations. The support for this second hypothesis is plain in Table 11–10. The four nations included in this study have been classified according to the degree of left-right dispersion within their political party system. As the data show, the percentage-point differences in church attendance between the most left and most right parties decrease sharply with the degree of dispersion among the parties. Hence, in The Netherlands and France, these differences were 79 and 60 percentage points respectively;

---

19. Kenneth N. Walker, "Determinants of Castro Support Among Latin American University Students," *Berkeley Journal of Sociology,* IX (1964), 31–55.

TABLE 11-10

The Greater the Left-Right Dispersion of Parties Within A Political System the Greater the Differences in Church Attendance Between the Party Furthest Left and the Party Furthest Right

Degree of Left-Right Dispersion of Parties	Nation	Percentage-point difference in Church Attendance Between Furthest Left and Furthest Right Parties
High	The Netherlands	79
	France	61
Medium	Great Britain	26
Low	United States	11*

*Average Percentage-point Difference from Table 6

in Great Britain's 'medium' dispersed system a difference of 26 percentage points was found, and in America, where the parties cling to the center of the political spectrum, the differences averaged 11 percentage points.

In conclusion, warning must be given against imputing a completely determinate view to the theoretical notions offered here about the functional relationship between radicalism and religious involvement. While it has been argued that religious institutions characteristically support the *status quo* and oppose political revision of a society, they are not to be thought of as the helpless pawns of some blind social forces. Since men record their own history as well as make it, there is no reason to suppose that a religious hierarchy might not give support to a radical movement, if for no other reason than because they suspect it will succeed in any event. One might particularly expect that an international church like Catholicism could apply lessons learned when opposition to radical movements has led to the ultimate harm of the church. But, so far, only Catholicism which has directly experienced such lessons seems inclined to favor such foresight, and exportation of these sentiments to fellow Bishops and pastors in Latin America, or even Spain, seems difficult.

One must not overlook, however, that even the moderate support the Spanish Church recently gave to striking miners is an extraordinary departure from the days of the Civil War, when priests sometimes blessed the rifles of Franco's firing squads. Thus, while there is excellent empirical support for supposing that religious involvement and radicalism tend to be mutually exclusive, widespread study and discussion of such a relationship might lead to changes in the strategy of religious institutions to such an extent that this ceases to be the case. But since far-sighted realism is uncommon in the conduct of human affairs, such a turn of events seems less than probable.

Chapter 12

Church Policy and the Attitudes of Ministers and Parishioners on Social Issues [1]

IT has been postulated in previous chapters that religious institutions are prone to take conservative positions regarding political change. However, the question remains, How does this come to pass? What are the internal processes by which churches, as formal organizations, arrive at, or at least countenance, this conservatism? In this chapter, we shall look at the inner workings of the Protestant Episcopal Church in the United States to observe the dialectical process between clergy and laity out of which church policy on political and social issues is formulated.

Underlying the analysis in the last three chapters is a view of the church as an adaptive institution in society, an institution which is prone to compromise with the dominant secular point of view. The idea that the church seldom acts to foster social

1. The preparation of this chapter was facilitated by a grant from the American Philosophical Society. The Society does not, of course, assume any responsibility for any statement made or any point of view expressed.

The study, upon which much of the chapter is based, was conducted by the Department of Christian Social Relations of the National Council of the Protestant Episcopal Church with the collaboration of the Bureau of Applied Social Research. The authors wish to acknowledge the major contribution of Rev. M. Moran Weston in the initiation, design, and execution of the project. We are also particularly grateful to Rev. Almon R. Pepper for his continuous support and encouragement.

change but rather functions to preserve the *status quo* was the central theme in our discussion of religion and the integration of society, as well as in our discussion of religion and politics.

This perception of the church as a conservative force in society is not, of course, peculiar to this book. It is the prevailing view of most sociologists of religion. Troeltsch, Durkheim, Weber, and Yinger have all noted in one way or another the tendency of the church to become "broadly inclusive and representative, inevitably taking on the character of the community as a whole."[2]

On both theoretical and empirical grounds, considerable support has been provided to document these assertions about the way in which the church interrelates with society. There remains the question, however, whether the assertion is universally true or whether there are conditions under which the church is instrumental in fostering, rather than inhibiting, social change.

One useful way to examine this question is to consider the performance of particular churches in the arena of public affairs. What stance do they adopt on particular issues of social, economic, and political policy? How do their positions relate to prevailing sentiment on these same issues among their members?

The present chapter attempts to answer these questions for one church—the Protestant Episcopal Church in the United States. Specifically, the chapter is concerned with examining the relationship between what the church has adopted as its official policy on a number of social, economic, and political issues and the prevailing climate of opinion on these same issues among the membership of the church. At the same time, we are interested in examining the position of the clergy, particularly on those issues where there is conflict between official church policy and parishioner sentiment.

The inquiry is based, in part, on the secondary analysis of data which were obtained originally to help guide the Protestant Episcopal Church in planning its social relations program. These data are derived from questionnaires which were collected in 1951–52 from a sample of ministers and 1,530 lay persons of the

2. F. Ernest Johnson, "Do Churches Exert Significant Influence on Public Morality?" *The Annals of the American Academy of Political and Social Science,* CCLXXX (March, 1952), 127.

denomination, the latter being randomly selected from the parishes of the ministers included in the study. The sample encompassed two distinct but interrelated data collection operations. First, a national sample of 234 congregations, stratified according to size of parish, was selected. Their ministers were sent a questionnaire which sought information on the characteristics of the local church: its size, wealth, surroundings, etc.; on the nature of its community activities; and on the extent of its participation in the social education program of the church.

Then, a probability sample of lay members from the sample parishes (as well as the ministers of these congregations) was sent a questionnaire designed to measure their attitudes on social problems and on public issues, particularly those upon which the church had taken an official stand, to obtain information about the kind of role they would have the church play in public affairs, and to identify, in the case of parishioners, the nature and kinds of ties they have to the church.

The lay sample was selected from the membership lists of the local parish, and the number of respondents sought in parishes of a given size was based on the percentage of the total church population represented by parishioners in congregations of that size. As a result, the distribution of respondents according to size of parish corresponds closely to the distribution of communicants in these parishes. (See Table 12–1.)

Both men and women were included in the sample, but women comprised the larger number: 60 per cent, women; 40 per cent, men. The age distribution of the sample was: 18 per cent, younger than 30 years of age; 44 per cent, 30 to 49 years of age; and 38 per cent, 50 years of age or older.

TABLE 12-1
Per Cent of Communicants and
Respondents by Size of Parish

Size of Parish (No. of Communicants)	Percentages of Total Communicants in Each Group	Percentage of Respondents in Each Group
1-350	35	37
351-750	31	30
751 and over	34	33
	(N = 1,619,703)	(N = 1,530)

Aside from these data, we examined the pronouncements on social issues adopted by the church at its triennial national meetings, at which all of the dioceses in the United States as well as overseas missions are represented.

We were able to derive from the questionnaire attitudinal data about how parishioners felt on nine public issues. The questionnaire included two to five items on each issue, the average being three items per issue. By combining these items, an index for each issue was constructed. These indices enabled us to identify each respondent's attitudes roughly along a continuum ranging from the most unfavorable to the most favorable position.

The specific issues included and the range of parishioner attitudes which they invoked are reported below:[3]

    1. *War* deals with the acceptability of war as an instrument of international policy. Attitudes range from unqualified acceptance of war as an instrument of policy to rejection of its use under any and all conditions.

    2. *Political role of the church* treats of attitudes toward participation of the clergy in political affairs. Attitudes range from approval of a partisan political role for the clergy to rejection of even the minister's right to encourage his parishioners to vote.

    3. *Government control* deals with attitudes toward government control of business. Attitudes range from approval of increased governmental regulation of private industry to rejection of any form of governmental control, even in wartime.

---

    3. In view of the church sponsorship of the study, the directors of the study were aware of the probable temptation on the part of some respondents to reply to various questions according to what they believed the 'correct' or 'right' answer should be and not according to their private convictions. Accordingly, the directors were careful to emphasize the need for frankness and to point out the existence of varying points of view on each question. They also stressed the confidential nature of the replies and assured respondents of anonymity.

    Despite these assurances, it is probable that some bias may have manifested itself. However, it is the considered opinion of the authors that if it is present, it is not sufficient to affect the results. For, if it were a major factor, then we should have expected a much greater unanimity, a much greater consensus on certain issues, particularly those upon which the church has a clear and identifiable stake and on which, accordingly, we would expect temptation to be greatest for giving an 'expected' or 'correct' answer. Yet, interestingly enough, on two of three such issues—intermarriage with Catholics, and treatment of conscientious objectors—instead of consensus, there is diversity of opinion. Marked differences also exist between the opinions of clergy and parishioners on these two issues.

    This and other inferential evidence suggest that the answers of most clergy and parishioners to the various questions in this study were primarily expressions of their own private feelings rather than of public expectations.

4. *Labor* deals with attitudes toward labor unions. Attitudes range from partisanship toward labor in its relations with management to rejection of labor's right even to organize.

5. *United Nations* bears on the acceptability of the United Nations as an agency of international cooperation. Attitudes range from support of the United Nations to opposition to it.

6. *Immigration* treats of attitudes toward the immigration policy of the United States government. Attitudes range from support for a liberal immigration policy to support for a restrictive one.

7. *Conscientious objectors* bears on the right of conscientious objectors to refuse to bear arms. Attitudes range from complete endorsement of this right to refusal to grant it.

8. *Human rights* deals with treatment of persons belonging to ethnic, racial, or religious minorities. Responses range from acute concern with rights of these persons to indifference toward the problem.

9. *Intermarriage* treats of attitudes toward intermarriage with Roman Catholics and the rearing of children born of such unions as Catholics. Attitudes range from opposition to intermarriage to acceptance of both intermarriage and the rearing of children as Catholics.

CHURCH POLICY

The Episcopal Church has a long tradition of concern with the social and economic problems of society. It expresses this concern officially through passage of resolutions at its triennial denominational meeting, at which both clergy and laity are represented.[4] From the 1901 convention, which, according to one writer, initiated or established a tradition, as it were, of passing resolutions on social relations issues, to the 1949 convention, resolutions on approximately seventy-six different social topics were presented. These resolutions, once adopted, become the official policy of the church. They are reported in the minutes of the meeting and are disseminated to the membership and clergy through a rather elaborate social relations program which the church has established. Acceptance of these resolutions by clergy and membership is, however, purely voluntary.

Of the nine issues with which we are dealing, the church has

---

4. For a resolution to be adopted as the official policy of the church, it must be passed by both the House of Bishops and the House of Delegates. Membership in the former is restricted to Bishops of the church; membership in the latter is divided equally between clergy and laity, four clergymen and four lay members representing each diocese. Wherever church policy is cited hereafter in this paper, it refers to the policy set forth by the national governing body of the church, and not to policies voted upon at either the diocesan or parish level.

passed resolutions which clearly identify its position on seven.

On five of the seven the church has taken a firm and clearly identifiable stand. The resolutions are explicit and signify unqualified endorsement of a given position. For example, the church has taken an extremely strong stand in support of the United Nations:

> *Resolved:* That it should be a fundamental objective of the foreign policy of the United States of America to support and strengthen the United Nations and to seek to develop through the United Nations, or otherwise, a world government open to all peoples with defined and limited powers to preserve peace and to prevent aggression through the enactment and enforcement of world law. . . .

Similarly, it has adopted a clear-cut, firm position on the rights of minorities exemplified by the following resolution adopted at the 1952 meeting:

> *Resolved:* That we consistently oppose and combat discrimination based on color or race in every form, both within the Church and without, in this country and internationally.

In addition, the church has unequivocally endorsed a liberal immigration policy, the rights of conscientious objectors to refuse to bear arms, and it has opposed intermarriage of parishioners with Roman Catholics where children born of such unions would be reared as Catholics.

No such firmness of viewpoint typifies the church's position on the other four issues under study. We were unable to learn of any resolutions bearing directly on the political role of the church and government control. However, the inference can be drawn from examining related issues that the church has avoided serious consideration of these issues, in part, because they bear on matters which are subject to different interpretations in the light of Christian thought and in part because they are considered by some to be outside of the church's authority.

On the two remaining issues, war and labor, resolutions have been passed. Unlike the issues discussed above, the church's position on these is equivocal rather than committed. Reservations and qualifications are clearly introduced. For example, the church condemns war, but the pertinent resolution also provides for conditions under which war is authorized. We quote from the resolution passed at the 1952 meeting:

> *Whereas,* the first Assembly of the World Council of Churches, meeting in Amsterdam in 1948, confessed that although Christians are one in proclaiming to all mankind that "war as a method of settling international disputes is incompatible with the teachings and example of our Lord Jesus Christ," they are nevertheless divided on the question of actual participation in war, and
> *Whereas,* the World Council urged upon all Christians the duty of wrestling continuously with the difficulties raised by these conflicting opinions and of praying humbly for God's guidance; therefore be it
> *Resolved,* that this Convention, acknowledging with penitence the existence of the same unhappy division within our own communion, urge all members of this Church
> 1. To seek through study, conference and prayer a clearer understanding of the will of God with regard to war, and endeavor to come to a common mind in Christ, and
> 2. That it request the National Council of the Protestant Episcopal Church to make available materials for the purpose of such study.

Other resolutions testify to the church's deep-rooted desire for peace and disarmament, and its vigorous disapproval of preventive war. Yet, the church does not accept a pacifist position. It recognizes, but grudgingly, the legitimacy of war under certain conditions.

In its stand on labor, the church is also equivocal. While recognizing the rights of labor vis-à-vis management, it shies away from a position which could be interpreted as partisan. As a church spokesman states:

> (In labor-management relations) the church is not a bystander but it is not partisan either. It is equally responsible for capital and labor and should strive to be an interpreter of one to the other and to serve as a mediator. Both capital and labor have rights which must be respected as well as duties which must be performed.

Thus, the church's position on labor is a relatively moderate, balanced one without any show of partisanship for labor. It is a qualified endorsement of the general rights of labor, but equally, a recognition of the rights of management.

In effect, resolutions passed by the church on the nine issues under study can be distinguished roughly as being partisan or equivocal in the positions they support. On five issues—the United Nations, human rights, conscientious objectors, immigration, and intermarriage—the church has adopted a *partisan* position in favor of a given point of view. On four issues—the political role of the church, government control, war, and labor—the church's ideology is or may be interpreted to be *equivocal*, i.e., balanced, and moderate in tone and form.

As the two types of issues are compared, certain striking differences may be noted. Issues upon which the church has taken a strong position are, with one exception, the United Nations, those dealing with normative responsibilities of parishioners either toward their church or toward individuals and noneconomic groups in the larger community. They may be classified as *ideological* issues reflecting an interpretation of the basic principle, Do unto your neighbor as you would have him do unto you. Issues on which the church has taken an equivocal position, on the other hand, all hold in common a somewhat different attribute. They, along with the United Nations issue, deal with the question of *power*—either that relating to the distribution of power between classes as in labor and government control, between communities as in war, or within the community as with the political role of the church.

CHURCH POLICY AND PARISHIONER SENTIMENT

Based on the theoretical assumptions presented earlier in this chapter, the following propositions about the relationship between parishioner sentiment and national church policy might be expected to apply:

1. That where parishioners hold divergent views on an issue, the church will be equivocal in its position on this issue.

2. That where parishioners are partisan on an issue, the church will be equally committed in its position.

Presumably, the church can most effectively retain the loyalty of its membership by being partisan on certain kinds of issues and equivocal on others. When parishioners are in substantial agreement on an issue, they will feel that their attitude is being reinforced by the church's committed stand, and they will not experience conflict with the church's equivocal position when their attitudes are divergent.

With these expectations in mind, an examination was made

of the data obtained from interviews with parishioners. We first examined those issues on which the church's position had been identified as equivocal. Using a coefficient of relative variation (standard deviation divided by the mean), we were able to classify parishioner sentiment on each of these issues as being convergent or divergent:[5] *convergent* meaning that there was more or less unanimity of opinion among parishioners, *divergent* meaning relative heterogeneity in parishioner opinion. On three of the issues on which church policy is equivocal—war, the political role of the church, and government control—parishioner opinion is relatively uniform. On the fourth issue—labor—parishioner opinion is divergent.

Thus, only on the issue of labor are our expectations clearly confirmed, namely, that the church will adopt an equivocal or conciliatory position where parishioner sentiment is divided. Having a membership which is divided in its attitudes toward labor and existing in a broader community in which this divergency of view is also reflected, the church's equivocal position would seem indeed to represent an attempt to conciliate both sides. It might be noted, paranthetically, that equivocation has not always typified the church's position on this issue. In the late nineteenth century before the rise of the labor movement, church policy was informally committed to a position in support of management's point of view. The fact that the church later adopted an equivocal position in the face of labor's ascendancy would appear to be a further reflection of its adaptive propensities.

On the other three issues on which the church is equivocal—war, government control, and the political role of the church—parishioner sentiment, contrary to our expectations, is convergent; parishioners are more or less agreed on given points of view on these issues. They are agreed that war is justified under many conditions, that governmental control of economic

---

5. The classification of parishioner sentiment as convergent or divergent was accomplished in the following manner. The nine issues were ranked on the basis of the size of their coefficient of relative variation. The four issues with the lowest values were considered as issues upon which parishioner sentiment was relatively *convergent;* the remaining as those upon which parishioner sentiment was relatively *divergent.*

The nine issues ranked by their coefficient of relative variation are reported in footnote 8.

life should be severely limited, and that the church should not engage in partisan politics.[6] The church does not, however, identify with these views in a partisan way, and it would seem that our propositions concerning the relationship between church policy and parishioner sentiment are not confirmed, in these instances, at least. However, while the manifest nature of the relationship is different from that anticipated, the church's position nevertheless reflects a desire to keep from alienating parishioners.[7]

On the issue of war, for example, although religious ideology might very well justify a pacifist opinion, the church, in the face of prevailing parishioner sentiment, would seem to have compromised its position to the secular one. Even though it recognizes the conflict between its religious ideology and prevailing secular attitudes, it has not taken a resolute stand in favor of the former. It seeks to reconcile the two. It neither accepts war as a desirable method for settling international disputes nor rejects

TABLE 12-2
Degree of Member Consensus on Issues

Rank Order	Issue	Coefficient of Relative Variation
1	War	.29
2	Political role of the church	.43
3	United Nations	.46
4	Government control	.49
5	Immigration	.64
6	Intermarriage	.64
7	Labor	.68
8	Human rights	.69
9	Conscientious objector	.77

Men and women exhibit similar tendencies. Despite minor variations in rank order of issues within each of the two classes, the *convergent* and *divergent*, the same issues were found in each class among men and women. The Spearman rank correlation coefficient is .77.

6. This is not to suggest that there is unanimity of opinion among parishioners on these issues but rather that there is relatively more agreement on these issues than on those on which we have identified parishioner opinion as divergent.

7. It should be remembered, however, that the church's position is determined, in part, by lay representation at the triennial national meetings.

its use under present world conditions – a view which is unlikely to antagonize its membership.

On the other two issues – government control and the political role of the church – the church's resistance to speaking out would also seem to reflect a compromise with parishioner attitudes. By adopting an equivocal attitude in the case of war and by remaining silent on the matters of government control and the political role of the church, the church does not, as we had expected, explicitly identify with convergent parishioner attitudes, but implicitly the effect is the same as if it had.

Is this apparent propensity of the church to adapt its position to secular values also in evidence where the church takes a committed position on an issue? Are parishioners equally committed on such issues and in the same direction? Overtly, our data provide more evidence in support of negative than in support of positive answers to these questions. On only one issue – the United Nations – are parishioners in essential agreement with the stand the church has taken. Wherever else the church is committed – on human rights, conscientious objectors, intermarriage, and immigration – there is wide divergency of opinion among parishioners. On these issues, the church has elected to adopt a point of view in the face of considerable diversity of opinion among its parishioners. This is not what we would have expected in the light of our adaptive propositions concerning the relationship between church policy and parishioner sentiment.

Unfortunately, the data do not provide the evidence necessary for an explanation of the interesting relationships they reveal. However, looking at the findings from a historical perspective, we can suggest some of the conditions which may have led the church to adopt its partisan position on these issues.

The church's present position on intermarriage with Roman Catholics was only officially adopted as church policy at the triennial national meeting of 1949. However, this represented no more than formal recognition and reinforcement of a position included in the mores of the church throughout its history. The 1949 resolution was adopted as a reaction to an increasing propensity among Episcopalians to take a lenient view on this question and to regard intermarriage with Catholics as acceptable even where this included raising the children of such marriages as Catholics. In this instance, then, the church is attempting to retain its traditional view despite an increasing shift among parishioners to a more permissive attitude. It can be assumed that if parishioner sentiment becomes even more permissive on this issue, the church will be placed in an increasingly difficult situation in defending its own position. However, since the survival of the church is tied in with this issue, it is unlikely to compromise its position despite opposing parishioner sentiment.

Just as in the case of the intermarriage issue, the church's partisan resolutions on human rights, conscientious objectors and immigration are of relatively recent vintage, all having been passed since the turn of the century. Earlier resolutions on these issues were in each case equivocal. These changes in church policy parallel shifts in parishioner sentiment that occurred over the same time span. Although there are no specific data, it would appear that twenty or more years ago, there was less divergence of opinion and a greater number of parishioners were then agreed on a conservative point of view on these issues. The adoption of a partisan position on the church's part, then, appears as a response to this shift in parishioner sentiment. Only, in this case unlike the intermarriage issue, the church does not seek to support the conservative point of view. It has, instead, joined forces with the advocates of social change.

This is also seen in the church's support of the United Nations. In this case, it will be recalled, parishioner sentiment reflected the church's point of view. Again we must rely on a presumption, but it might be reasonably surmised that the church's advocacy of a positive attitude towards the United Nations may have contributed to the development of a convergence of parishioner opinion on this issue. This interpretation is supported in part by the fact that the church has devoted particular effort to bringing its position on this issue to the attention of its parishioners through its social relations program.

Earlier reference was made to the fact that the church's partisan position with respect to the United Nations represented something of a departure from the character of the stand it has taken with respect to other issues involving questions of power. The explanation for the exception undoubtedly is related to the Episcopal Church's traditional ties with Great Britain and the Church of England. Among all American denominations, the

Episcopal Church has been the most consistently internationalistic and has given strong support to both the League of Nations and World Court, as well as to the United Nations.

These results do not refute the adaptive hypothesis concerning the church's participation in secular affairs, but they do warn of some important qualifications. The church does not merely support the *status quo,* nor merely follow the lead of its parishioners in the formulation of its social and economic policy. Our data show that the church is in fact ahead of (more liberal than) its laity on most issues. It is more receptive to social change than its parishioners.

But in supporting social change, the church must proceed cautiously lest its stand offend the collective sentiments of its parishioners. This danger is most acute on issues which bear directly on the distribution of power in society, such as war, labor, government control and political role of the church. On these issues parishioners have definite convictions and their self-interest is clearly identifiable. As a result, the church seeks to avoid a head-on collision with the collective will of its laity on these issues. It treads softly and resorts to equivocation in its pronouncements. At the same time, it does not identify completely with parishioner sentiment but includes in its pronouncements reference to the normative principles which an issue involves.

However, on issues of an ideological or moral character, the church finds it less necessary to temper its stand in accordance with the will of its parishioners. There is no solidified collective will of parishioners which can serve as a brake on church policy. Parishioner sentiment on these issues is largely unsettled and divergent, suggesting the lesser importance of these issues for the self-interest of parishioners. As a result, the church has a greater opportunity to exercise its leadership. It can express itself through strong and clear-cut pronouncements.

The church's social policy, then, depends on the nature of the issue and the state of sentiment among parishioners. On issues where parishioner sentiment is relatively homogeneous, and self-interest considerable, the church's ability to deviate from the views of its parishioners is severely limited. It must compromise its policy and accommodate itself to the views of its parishioners. But on issues where parishioner sentiment is relatively unsettled and the church has a definite normative interest, the church is better able to step forth in a firm and decisive manner.

CHURCH POLICY, MINISTERS' ATTITUDES AND PARISHIONER SENTIMENT

There is still one major question to be answered with respect to our analysis. What is the position of the Episcopalian minister on the issues under discussion? The minister of the local parish is, of course, the crucial link in communicating church policy to the church's membership. However, at the same time, his position is such that he becomes the individual most subject to cross pressures where conflict arises between church policy on an issue and how his parishioners feel on this issue. Our data do not provide any evidence on the degree to which the minister experiences such cross pressures and how he reacts to them. However, we do know something about how his attitudes on the nine issues we have been discussing are related to those held by his parishioners.

Using a coefficient of disagreement,[8] the nine issues were ordered in terms of the amount of disagreement which exists between the attitudes of ministers and parishioners.

---

8. In order to measure the relative disagreement between parishioner and his minister on each of the nine issues, we constructed a coefficient of disagreement in the following manner: the parishioner's score on a given issue was subtracted from his minister's, the difference was squared and then the squared differences for all parishioners were summed. To standardize the values for purposes of comparing the various issues, the sum of the squared differences was divided by maximum possible disagreement score (squared) multiplied by the total number of parishioners. The range of values this coefficient can take is from 0 to 1. The latter indicates maximum disagreement; the former, minimum disagreement.

A coefficient value for each of the nine issues was obtained, and the issues were ranked according to the size of the value. The rank order is reported below:

Rank Order	Issue	Coefficient of Disagreement
1	Political role of the church	.1124
2	War	.1252
3	United Nations	.1656
4	Government control	.1681
5	Labor	.1948
6	Immigration	.2047
7	Intermarriage	.2433
8	Human rights	.3076
9	Conscientious objector	.3205

The rank order of issues among men and women is quite similar, the Spearman rank correlation coefficient being .89.

With the exception of the United Nations issue, ministers and parishioners differ least in their attitudes on the four issues — war, the political role of the church, government control, and labor — on which church policy is equivocal. They differ most, again except for the United Nations issue, on those issues on which church policy is partisan — immigration, human rights, intermarriage, and conscientious objectors.

Ministers' attitudes clearly tend to reflect church policy. Where the church has elected to compromise on an issue, the minister also has compromised with the views of his parishioners. However, where the church has taken a partisan point of view, the minister generally identifies with this view despite the opposition of a substantial segment of his parishioners.

As might be expected, there is a tendency, although it does not hold true in all cases, for ministers to differ least among themselves on issues on which church policy is partisan and to differ most among themselves on issues on which church policy is equivocal. Where the church has made up its mind, so have the ministers; where the church is equivocal, so are the ministers.

Chapter 13

On the Origin and Evolution of Religious Groups

IN previous chapters, we have examined the affinity of religious institutions for political conservatism and have suggested that much of the discontent that once found expression in new religious movements has more recently been channelled into radical politics. But the fact must not be overlooked that sometimes religion does function effectively to prevent dissidence and unrest, and to compensate persons for many sorts of problems. In this chapter we shall examine this compensating aspect of religion in detail, to see what it may tell us about the origins and development of religious groups.

During the nineteenth century the impact of Darwinian biology on social thought led to a scholarly preoccupation with the origins and evolution of social institutions. Consequently, an enormous amount of work in the sociology of religion sought to establish how it was that religious ideas and traditions sprang up in human societies. But, as social Darwinism passed out of vogue, it was recognized that the question of how men first came to be religious is shrouded in the unknowable past, and is badly put in any event.[1] Nevertheless it has remained relevant and seemingly fruitful to ask about a process of religious innovation

---

1. An excellent critique of this work has been provided by Kingsley Davis, see his *Human Society* (New York: The Macmillan Co., 1949), especially Chapter 19.

and development that is still with us: What accounts for the rise and evolution of new religious groups in society?

This question remains generally unanswered although it has received more attention than any other problem in the sociology of religion. In this chapter we shall review the current state of social science knowledge on the origins of new religious groups, particularly those theories which attribute these innovations to class conflicts. Then we shall propose the outlines for a more general theory which seems to overcome the limitations of existing theories, and suggest how this broader conception can also help account for the directions in which religious groups evolve.

Current thinking about the origin and development of religious groups in Western society has been largely informed by so-called 'sect-church' theory. The distinction between church and sect, as formulated in the work of Max Weber[2] and his contemporary, Ernst Troeltsch,[3] was initially an attempt to distinguish types of religious groups and not an effort to discover the conditions under which religious groups originate. Sects were characterized, for example, as being in tension with the world, as having a converted rather than an inherited membership, and as being highly emotional in character. Churches, in contrast, were seen as compromising with the world, as having a predominantly inherited membership, and as restrained and ritualistic in their services.

The sect-church distinction was later refined by H. Richard Niebuhr who postulated a dynamic interrelationship between the two types and saw in this interrelationship a way to help account for the development of new religious groups.[4] Briefly, the compromising tendencies of the church lead some of its members to feel that the church is no longer faithful to its religious traditions. These dissenting members then break away to form new religious groups. At the outset, these new groups take on a highly sect-like character, eschewing the dominant characteristics of the church they have rejected. They assume an

---

2. Max Weber, "The Social Psychology of the World's Religions," in Gerth and Mills, eds., *From Max Weber: Essays in Sociology* (New York: Oxford University Press, 1940).

3. Ernst Troeltsch, *Social Teachings of the Christian Churches* (New York: The Macmillan Co., 1949), esp. Vol. I, pp. 331–343.

4. H. Richard Niebuhr, *The Social Sources of Denominationalism* (New York: Henry Holt and Co., 1929).

uncompromising posture toward the world, they gainsay a professional clergy, they insist on a conversion experience as a condition for membership, and they adopt a strict and literalistic theology.

Over time, however, the conditions which gave rise to the sect change, and a process begins which leads the sect slowly to take on the church-like qualities which it had originally denied. Once it has made the transition from sect to church, the religious group then becomes the breeding ground for new sects which proceed anew through the same process.

New sects, according to sect-church theory, recruit their membership primarily from the economically deprived, or as Niebuhr calls them, "the disinherited" classes of society. Their emergence, therefore, is to be understood as a result not only of religious dissent but of social unrest as well. The theological dissent masks an underlying social protest. However, the new sect functions to contain the incipient social protest, and later, to help eliminate the conditions which produced it.

The containment is accomplished through a process of derailment. The sects provide a channel through which their members come to transcend their feelings of deprivation by replacing them with feelings of religious privilege. Sect members no longer compare themselves to others in terms of their relatively lower economic position, but in terms of their superior religious status.

Built into the sect ideology, however, is a puritanical ethic which stresses self-discipline. Thrift, frugality, industry are highly valued. Over time, their ideology helps to elevate sect members to middle-class statuses which in turn socialize them to middle-class values. Because the economic deprivation itself has been eliminated, feelings of economic deprivation no longer need to be assuaged. As the sect members become accommodated to the larger society, their religious movement proceeds to accommodate itself too. In so doing, it makes the transition from sect to church.

This is an admittedly brief and simplified account of sect-church theory and omits the many refinements that have been made in it over the last decades.[5] However, for our purposes, it conveys the essential points of traditional theory, namely, that

5. See, for example, J. M. Yinger, *Religion in the Struggle for Power* (Durham, N.C.: Duke University Press, 1946); Bryan Wilson, "An Analysis of Sect Development," *American Sociological Review*, XX (February, 1957); and Leopold Von Wiese and Howard Becker, *Systematic Sociology* (New York: John Wiley and Sons, 1932).

new religious movements begin by being sect-like in character, that they arise by breaking off from church-type bodies, that they are rooted in economic deprivation, and that they gradually transform themselves into churches.

This theory is valid for many cases. Nevertheless, in a number of ways it falls short of being a general theory of the origin and evolution of religious groups. Overlooked is the fact that not all religious groups emerge as sects. Some are churches in their original form. This was true of Reform Judaism in Europe and of Conservative Judaism in America. Most Protestant groups were from their beginnings more like churches than like sects.

Not only may new religious groups emerge in other than sect form, they need not, contrary to the theory, draw their membership primarily from the lower class. The American Ethical Union was clearly a middle-class movement from its inception, as were Unity and, probably, Christian Science.

The theory also does not take account of cults. These are religious movements which draw their inspiration from other than the primary religion of the culture, and which are not schismatic movements in the same sense as sects, whose concern is with preserving a purer form of the traditional faith. Thus, while the theory may be adequate to explain the Pentecostal movement or the evolution of such religious groups as the Disciples of Christ (The Christian Church) and the Church of God in Jesus Christ, it does not provide a way to account for Theosophy, or the I AM movement, or the Black Muslims. Nor does the theory account for religious movements which show no signs of evolving toward the church form. Finally, the theory ignores the question of the conditions which produce a secular rather than a religious response to economic deprivation.

As may be clear, our quarrel with sect-church theory is not over what it does, but what if fails to do—too many innovating religious movements fall beyond the present scope of the theory. Consequently, in attempting to formulate the elements of a more satisfactory theory of religious origins we shall not discard sect-church theory so much as try to generalize and extend it. We shall continue to regard deprivation as a necessary condition for the rise of new religious movements. However, the concept of deprivation seems due for a general extension and restatement.[6]

6. This chapter has also been informed by Robert K. Merton, "Social Structure and Anomie," in *Social Theory and Social Structure* (Glencoe, Ill.: The Free Press, 1957).

Sect-church theory conceives of deprivation almost entirely in economic terms. To be sure, in every society there are individuals and groups which are economically underprivileged relative to others, and some are always at the very bottom of the economic hierarchy. However, there are forms of deprivation other than economic ones, and these too, we suggest, have implications for the development of religious and, as we shall see, secular movements as well.

Deprivation, as we conceive it, refers to *any and all of the ways that an individual or group may be, or feel disadvantaged in comparison either to other individuals or groups or to an internalized set of standards.* The experience of deprivation may be conscious, in which case the individual or group may be aware of its causes. It may also be experienced as something other than deprivation, in which case its causes will be unknown to the individual or the group. But, whether directly or indirectly experienced, whether its causes are known or unknown, deprivation tends to be accompanied by a desire to overcome it.[7] Efforts to deal with deprivation will differ, however, according to the degree to which its nature is correctly perceived and individuals and groups are in a position to eliminate its cause.

TYPES OF DEPRIVATION

There are five kinds of deprivation to which individuals or groups may be subject relative to others in society. We shall call these five: economic, social, organismic, ethical, and psychic. The types are not pure; any one individual or group may experience more than one kind of deprivation. However, we can distinguish among them not only analytically, but empirically, since one type of deprivation is likely to be dominant for particular individuals and groups in particular situations.

Economic deprivation has its source in the differential distribution of income in societies and in the limited access of some individuals to the necessities and luxuries of life. Economic deprivation may be judged on objective or on subjective criteria. The person who appears economically privileged on objective criteria might nevertheless perceive himself as economically deprived. For our purposes the subjective assessment is likely to be the more important.

---

7. This is not the case, however, where the value system of the society warrants deprivation, for example, the Hindu caste system.

Social deprivation, our second type, is based on society's propensity to value some attributes of individuals and groups more highly than others and to distribute such societal rewards as prestige, power, status, and opportunities for social participation accordingly. Social deprivation, then, arises out of the differential distribution of highly regarded attributes. The grounds for such differentiation are virtually endless. In our society, for example, we regard youth more highly than old age, greater rewards tend to go to men rather than to women, and the 'gifted' person is given privileges denied the mediocre.

Social deprivation is additive in the sense that the fewer the number of desirable attributes the individual possesses, the lower his relative status, and the reverse is also true. In our society, it is in general 'better' to be educated than uneducated. But one's status is further enhanced if one is white rather than Negro, Protestant rather than Catholic, youthful rather than old.

The distinction between economic and social deprivation is akin to the distinction sociologists make between social class and social status. Designations of social class tend to be made on economic criteria. Social status distinctions, on the other hand, give greater attention to considerations of prestige and acceptance. While the two tend to go together, the correlation is not perfect. For our present purposes, we will consider social deprivation to be limited to situations in which it exists independently of economic deprivation.

Organismic deprivation comprises ways in which persons are disadvantaged relative to others through physical or mental deformities, ill health, or other such stigmatizing or disabling traits. Within this class of deprivations would be persons suffering from neuroses and psychoses or who are feeble minded. On the physiological side, it would include the blind, the deaf, the dumb, the crippled, the chronically ill, in short all who suffer physical impairment.

Ethical deprivation refers to value conflicts between the ideals of society and those of individuals or groups. Such conflicts seemingly may stem from many sources. They can occur because some persons perceive incompatibilities in the values of the society, or detect negative latent functions of rules and standards, or even because they are struck by discrepancies between ideals and realities. Often such value conflicts occur because of contradictions in social organization. For example, some persons may find themselves embedded in situations conducive to the development and maintainance of values not held by the greater society, and, indeed, that conflict with general societal values. A classic example of ethical deprivation of this sort is provided in Veblen's analysis of the role strain on engineers who are torn between their own attachment to efficiency and excellence as standards for judging their own products, and the value of maximum profits imposed on them by management.[8]

The celebrated conflicts of the intellectuals, induced to 'sell out' their own criteria of excellence in art, journalism, and the like, because their standards are not shared by the public, have been used to explain the propensity of these objectively privileged groups for radical politics.[9] Such conceptions fit well with current theories of revolution which specify that there must be a defection from the ranks of the elite in order that direction and leadership be provided for lower class discontent, if revolution is to occur.

Ethical deprivation, then, is basically philosophical. Many great religious innovators, such as Luther and Wesley, as well as political innovators such as Marx, seem to have been motivated primarily by a sense of deprivation stemming from their ethical conflicts with society—an inability to lead their lives according to their own lights.

Psychic deprivation occurs, not in the face of value conflicts, but when persons find themselves without a meaningful system of values by which to interpret and organize their lives. Such a condition is primarily the result of severe and unresolved social deprivations which, by denying access to rewards, cause men to lose any stake in, and commitment to, existing values.

A likely response to psychic deprivation is the search for new values, a new faith, a quest for meaning and purpose. The vulnerability of the deprived to new ideologies reflects their psychic deprivation. In contrast, the ethically deprived have a firm commitment to values, albeit values that conflict with prevailing conditions. Thus, psychic deprivation can be thought of

---

8. Thorstein Veblen, *The Instincts of Workmanship and the State of Industrial Arts* (New York: The Viking Press, 1943).

9. Seymour Martin Lipset, *Political Man* (Garden City: Doubleday & Co., 1960), pp. 318–319.

primarily as an intervening variable, state of despair, estrangement, or anomie stemming from objective deprivations (social, economic, or organismic) that leads to actions to relieve these deprivations.[10]

We suggest that a necessary precondition for the rise of any organized social movement, whether it be religious or secular, is a situation of felt deprivation. However, while a necessary condition, deprivation is not, in itself, a sufficient condition. Also required are the additional conditions that the deprivation be shared, that no alternative institutional arrangements for its resolution are perceived, and that a leadership emerge with an innovating idea for building a movement out of the existing deprivation.

Where these conditions exist, the organizational effort to overcome deprivation may be religious, or it may be secular. In the case of economic, social, and organismic deprivation—the three characterized by deprivation relative to others—religious resolutions are more likely to occur where the nature of the deprivation is inaccurately perceived or those experiencing the deprivation are not in a position to work directly at eliminating the causes. The resolution is likely to be secular under the opposite conditions—where the nature of the deprivation is correctly assessed by those experiencing it and they have, or feel they have, the power, or feel they can gain the power, to deal with it directly. Religious resolutions, then, are likely to compensate for feelings of deprivation rather than to eliminate its causes. Secular resolutions, where they are successful, are more likely to eliminate the causes, and therefore, also the feelings.

These tendencies do not hold for ethical and psychic deprivation. In the case of ethical and psychic deprivation, as we shall see, a religious resolution may be as efficacious as a secular one in overcoming the deprivation directly. In America, resolutions to psychic deprivation usually tend to be religious, defined in the broad sense of invoking some supernatural authority. However, radical political movements may be the outcome of psychic deprivation combined with economic deprivation.

---

10. Despite the enormous amount of work done on various forms of this concept under a variety of names, it has been primarily treated as an outcome of economic deprivation or as a cause of political extremism, and too few attempts have been made to place it in a context of deprivation plus action.

Both religious and secular resolutions, then, may follow from each kind of deprivation. However, whether religious or secular, the resolution will be different in character according to which type stimulates it.

ORGANIZATIONAL RESOLUTIONS OF DEPRIVATIONS

Economic deprivation, once it becomes intense, has in it the seed of revolution. And indeed, where the movements which it stimulates are secular, they are likely to be revolutionary. However, to be successful, revolutions require a degree of power which the deprived group is unlikely to be able to muster. Consequently, even when it is intense, economic deprivation seldom leads to revolution.

Religious resolutions to economic deprivation, while not literally revolutionary, are symbolically so. The latent resentment against society tends to be expressed in an ideology which rejects and radically devalues the society. Thus, for those in the movement, the society is symbolically transformed while actually, of course, it is left relatively untouched.

This is characteristically what sects do, and it is this form of religious organization which is likely to arise out of economic deprivation. This is in accord with what we have said earlier in our discussion of sect-church theory, and we need not elaborate further on the way in which sect members compensate for economic disadvantage by substituting religious privilege in its place. We would add, however, that the religious movement which grows out of economic deprivation need not have its theological base in the traditional religion of the society. The Black Muslim movement, for example, borrows heavily from an 'alien' religious doctrine. Yet, in its strong tone of social protest and its doctrine of Negro superiority, it exemplifies the kind of religious movement which grows out of economic deprivation (with, of course, its accompanying social deprivation).

Social deprivation, where it exists without a strong economic component, ordinarily does not require a complete transformation of society, either literally or symbolically, to produce relief. What is at fault is not the basic organization of society, but one or several of its parts. Consequently, efforts at resolution are likely to be directed at the parts, without questioning the whole. As with economic deprivation, however, resolutions are not always possible. Once again, responses to the deprivation are most likely to be secular where its cause can be attacked more or less directly.

Many secular movements with roots in one or another kind of social deprivation have arisen in America over the last century. The woman's suffrage movement, the Townsend movement, the NAACP, and various professional organizations such as those for druggists and beauticians, all represent movements whose purpose has been to eliminate the social deprivation of some particular group by raising its status.

Other semi-secular groups have attempted to compensate for lack of status by supplying an alternative status system. In particular, fraternal clubs and lodges have played such a role, especially for disadvantaged racial and ethic groups. A man may amount to little all week long, but on Friday nights he can become the Most Venerated, Consecrated, and All-Powerful Poobah of the Grand Lodge of Water Buffalo, dress in a gaudy costume, and whisper secret rites.

Social deprivations may be directly connected with religious status and hence generate religious innovations. Such groups as the African Methodist Episcopal Church and the ethnic subdenominations of Lutheranism were organized because the existing religious structure was incapable of meeting the status needs of the groups involved. While overtly a means to overcome religious disadvantages, these organizations also served to overcome sources of social deprivation.

Classic instances are provided by the Jewish Reform movement and the founding of Conservative Judaism. Both movements were launched as an effort to provide Jews with a religious connection with their heritage while allowing them to dispense with those aspects of Orthodoxy, particularly customs of dress and food, which interfered with their attaining status in secular society.[11]

The organizational form of religious groups which emerge out of social deprivation tends to be church-like rather than sect-like. This is because the basic interest of the socially deprived is to accommodate themselves to the larger society rather than to escape from it or, alternatively, to completely transform it. Consequently, they also tend to adopt those institutional arrangements with which the larger society is most comfortable.

---

11. Stephen Steinberg, "Reform Judaism: The Origin and Evolution of a 'Church Movement,'" *Journal for the Scientific Study of Religion,* forthcoming.

The psychoanalytic movement, group dynamics, and Alcholics Anonymous are examples of a secular response to organismic deprivation where the mental component of this form of deprivation is dominant. In turn, the Society for the Blind, the Society for Crippled Children, and the myriad formal and informal social groups constructed around an ailment exemplify secular efforts toward resolution where the physiological element is primary. However successful or unsuccessful are these movements, they all represent attempts to deal with a problem directly. They are revolutionary in that they seek to transform the individual either mentally or physiologically. However, they do not question the value system of the society per se.

There have been religious movements—healing cults, for example—which are organized primarily as resolutions to organismic deprivation. More often, however, we find that religious responses to this form of deprivation are not the entire *raison d'être* of a religious movement, but are included as one aspect of it. We may note that a faith healing movement has been organized within the Episcopal Church. Many sects—Father Divine, for example—include a healing element as do cults such as Christian Science and Unity. Thus, religious responses seem not to be identified with any particular organizational form. We suspect, however, that where healing is the exclusive concern of the religious movement, it is more likely to be cult-like in character, such as early Christian Science, than to be a sect or a church.

Responses to ethical deprivations are more typically reformist than revolutionary, and, we suspect, more likely to be religious or secular depending on the prevailing ethos of the time in which they occur. Reformers in medieval times sought to enforce or establish religious values, while since the Enlightenment a great deal of ethical deprivation has been expressed in humanistic terms. In our own time both kinds of response flourish.

Secular movements based on ethical deprivations sometimes lead to revolution, particularly when an ethically deprived elite enlists the support of economically deprived masses. But more often ethical deprivations lead to reform movements aimed at enforcing some neglected value or changing some portion of the prevailing value system without abandoning a commitment to the general outlines of existing social organization. The American Civil Liberties Union illustrates one secular response to ethical deprivation. This group is concerned with enforcing the ideals expressed in the Bill of Rights upon day-to-day realities. Similarly the American Planned Parenthood League derives from ethical deprivation, but is concerned with establishing a general value concerning family planning, and with altering religious prohibitions against birth control. Political reform groups, both of the left and right often are motivated by a sense of ethical deprivation. Indeed, the current right wing activity in American politics seems to stem to a great extent from the perceptions of small town and rural Americans that their traditional values are no longer predominant in American society.

Religious movements growing out of ethical deprivations can lead to religious revolutions, as in the case of the Lutherans, when the movement is both powerful and powerfully opposed. But it must be recalled that Luther did not intend to found a new faith or lead a revolution, rather he hoped to reform the Church to make it more closely correspond to its avowed ideals. More commonly religious movements based on ethical deprivations do not lead to religious revolutions, but to reform movements. The Prohibition movement in the early part of this century is a classic example, while the participation of white religious leaders in the current civil rights movement is another.[12] Other examples are the Ethical Culture Union and Unitarianism, both of which seem to have been produced as a solution to the conflict felt by some persons between traditional religious orthodoxy and scientific discovery. Secular counterparts may be seen in the beatnik and existentialist movements.

Ethical deprivations may well be typically limited to members of society's elites, or at least to the middle classes or above. The notion of value conflicts presupposes a certain intellectualism, such as that required in theological or philosophical disputation, which is commonly regarded as an idiosyncracy of the leisured and learned classes.

---

12. The involvement of Negroes in the Civil Rights movement obviously is based on their economic and social deprivation. However, white clergymen do not share the Negroes' deprived lot, but instead are responding to the discrepancies between Christian and social ideals of equality and the actual denial of equality to Negroes.

Whether the movement is secular or religious, responses to psychic deprivation are generally extreme because it constitutes a rejection of the prevailing value orientation of the society. When persons have become psychically deprived in response to economic deprivations they may adopt a new ideology that embodies a revolutionary political program (whether on the left or the right). When they take up a religious solution it will typically be of the cult variety. Recent research among members of a millenarian religious group showed that all had passed through a period of 'church-hopping,' ultimately rejected all available religious perspectives, and passed through a period of religious despair before being converted to the new movement.[13] The entire occult milieu, referred to in Chapter 1, is made up of persons afflicted with psychic deprivations. Movements born in this setting, such as Theosophy, Vedanta, the I AM, or the various Flying Saucer groups, are essentially religious innovations that reject dominant American religious traditions, and are classified as cults.

Deprivation need not be immediately present to stimulate an organizational response. The prospect of deprivation may produce a similar effect. The White Citizens' Councils in the South, for example, can be conceived of as organizations growing out of anticipated economic and social deprivation. The John Birch Society is a response to anticipated social deprivation. Protestants and Other Americans United is an example of a religious movement organized around anticipated ethical and social deprivation.

In sum, deprivation — present or anticipated — would appear to be a central factor in the rise of new movements. The organizational response to deprivation may be either religious or secular. In the case of economic, social, and organismic deprivation, religious responses tend to function as compensations for the deprivation, secular ones as means to overcome it. The type of deprivation around which a movement arises is influential in shaping its character in all cases except those of organismic and ethical deprivation. Generally speaking, religious movements emerge as sects where they are stimulated by economic deprivation, as churches where the deprivation is social, and as cults where it is psychic.

---

13. See: John Lofland, *The World-Savers*, forthcoming.

DEPRIVATION AND ORGANIZATIONAL EVOLUTION

Deprivation is important not only to the rise of new movements but to the path of their development and their potential for survival. Movements may evolve in a myriad of ways, and we have no intention of trying to cope with all of their variety. We would suggest, however, that movements tend to follow one of three basic patterns. They may flower briefly and then die. They may survive indefinitely in substantially their original form. Or, they may survive but in a form radically different from their original one. How movements develop, and whether or not they survive, is influenced by the type of deprivation which stimulated them, how they deal with this deprivation, and the degree to which the deprivation persists in the society, and therefore, provides a continuing source of new recruits.

Movements arising out of economic deprivation tend to follow a pattern of either disappearing relatively quickly or of having to change their organizational form to survive. They seldom survive indefinitely in their original form. This is because the deprivation they respond to may itself be short-lived or because they themselves help to overcome the deprivation of their adherents.

Few sects survive as sects. They either disappear or evolve from a sect into a church. Where they follow the former course, it is likely that their souce of recruitment suddenly withers because of conditions over which they have no control. Thus, depression-born sects tend to have a low survival rate, lasting only as long as the depression itself. Sects also have the tendency, noted earlier, to socialize their members to higher economic status. In the process, their organizational form is transformed to conform to the changing status of their membership.

Secular responses to economic deprivation follow a similar pattern. Depression-born movements—technocracy, for example—tend to flower briefly and then die. More fundamental movements, such as revolutions, tend, where they are successful, to lose their revolutionary character and to survive as movements functioning to maintain the advantages which have been gained.

Organizational responses to social deprivation may also follow a pattern of disappearing quickly, but where they survive, they are likely to do so without radical alteration of their original form. Which of these paths is followed is largely dependent on the persistence of the deprivation which gave rise to the movement. Successful elimination of the experienced deprivation —for example, the successful attempt to gain women the right to vote—is likely to produce an early end to the movement.

It is characteristic of many kinds of social deprivation to persist over extended periods of time and to continue from generation to generation. This is because the value systems of societies tend to change slowly, and the differential social rewards and punishments of one era are not likely, in the natural course of events, to be radically altered in the next.

The ability of churches to survive in basically unchanged form is, in substantial part, a consequence of the persistence of social deprivation. Participation in a church, we would suggest, functions to provide individuals with a source of gratification which they cannot find in the society-at-large. Since there are always individuals who are socially deprived in this sense, there exists a continuing source of new recruits to the church. Furthermore, church participation only compensates for the deprivation; it does not eliminate it. Thus, in contrast with the sect, the primary reasons for the existence of the church are not likely to be dissipated over time.

The contention that a major function of church participation is to relieve members' feelings of social deprivation is made here primarily on theoretical grounds. What little empirical evidence there is, however, suggests that churches tend to gain their greatest commitment from individuals who are most deprived of the rewards of the larger society. Thus, it is the less gifted intellectually, the aged, women, and those without normal family lives who are most often actively involved in the church.[14]

Organismic deprivation produces movements whose evolution is likely to be influenced by the development of new knowledge about the causes and treatment of mental and physical disorders. Existing movements can expect to thrive only so long as the therapies they provide are subjectively perceived as efficacious and superior to prevailing alternatives. However, the survival of these movements is constantly threatened by innovations in therapy or treatment which eliminate their *raison d'être*. Under such conditions, they may simply disband—like the Sister Kenny Foundation, for example—or they may elect to

---

14. See Chapter 7.

chart their course along a different path, like the National Foundation.

Religious movements or submovements which are sustained by organismic deprivation may, of course, survive for a very long time, and indeed recruit new members from those who cannot find relief through secular sources. However, in the long run they too are likely to fall victim to innovations in medical knowledge. For, as Malinowski reported of the Trobriand Islanders, people do not resort to magic when they have more effective means of control.

Many movements which arise out of ethical deprivation, we suggest, have a propensity to be short-lived. This is not because ethical deprivation is not a persistent element in society; there are always likely to be individuals who feel that some portion of the dominant value system ought to be changed or reapplied. However, the ethically deprived are likely to generate strong opposition to their efforts to reform or change society and, furthermore, resolutions that seem appropriate at one time are not likely to be so at another. Consequently, ethical deprivation tends to be subject to fads, and while responses to ethical deprivations may capture attention for the moment, they tend to be quickly replaced by new solutions. The various beatnik and bohemian movements are cases in point.

The exceptions—the movements of this kind which survive—do so because they provide solutions which have relevance to long-term trends in society. Such trends function to provide these movements with a continuing source of new recruits. For example, the long-term trend toward secularization in American life is, we suspect, a major factor in the survival and recent acceleration in growth of the Unitarian movement. In general, ethical deprivation characterizes only a small minority of a population at a given time and movements which respond to such deprivation are likely—whether they survive or not—always to be minority movements.

Movements based on psychic deprivations typically follow one of two courses. Either they rise to power and transform societies, and are then themselves transformed, or they die out quickly. Since movements stemming from psychic deprivations take on value orientations incompatible with those prevalent in a society, they engender strong opposition and must either succeed or be crushed. When they take a religious form they are usually defined as cults and subject to public definitions of 'evil', 'demented,' 'dangerous,' and 'subversive.' We have elsewhere sketched the degree to which cults are the object of public harassment and even persecution.[15] However, cult movements may also succeed (for example, Christianity was a cult viewed from the standpoint of traditional Roman religions), and by success find themselves faced with problems similar to those of the religion they replaced. That is, once in power a new religion is not in a much better position to resolve the endemic basis for economic, social, organismic, and even ethical deprivation than the religious institution that it replaced. Thus, while new religious movments like I AM, Theosophy, Mankind United, or Understanding, Inc., may initially provide a new meaning system to their converts, they are not able to overcome the social sources of deprivation which initially produced psychic deprivation, or despair. These are left to produce a new clientele for new movements, or to at least form a festering sore in the integration of any society.

Similarly the extremist secular movements that spring up in response to psychic deprivations are faced with massive opposition. If they succeed in overcoming such opposition, they too face the problem of being transformed by their responsibilities so they may no longer provide a suitable outlet for the psychically deprived.

CONCLUSIONS

Our aim in this chapter has been to assess some implications of an extension of the concept of deprivation for the origin and evolution of social movements, particularly religious movements. Our speculations have been informed by the assumption that religion functions to compensate persons for deprivations for which direct means of resolution are not available.

We have tried to show that the original form and subsequent development of religious movements may be largely determined by the variety of deprivation which provided them with an available clientele. A summary of our suggestions appears in Table 13–1.

---

15. Volume on religion and anti-Semitism by the authors, to be published spring 1966 by Harper & Row. Especially the chapter on religious libertarianism.

TABLE 13-1

Origins, Forms, and Development of Religious Groups

Type of Deprivation	Form of Religious Group	Success Expectations
1. Economic	Sect	Extinction or trans-formation
2. Social	Church	Retain original form
3. Organismic	Healing movement	Becomes cultlike or is destroyed by medical discoveries.
4. Ethical	Reform movements	Early extinction due to success, opposition or becoming irrelevant.
5. Psychic	Cult	Total success result-ing in extinction through transforma-tion, or failure due to extreme opposition.

We must, of course, acknowledge the fact that our observations on the relationship between kinds of deprivations and types of religious groups are imprecise and very provisional. This is necessarily the case since these suggested extensions of existing theory have not yet been subjected to empirical testing. Nevertheless, no matter how greatly our notions may be altered by future analysis, it seems likely that some theoretical extension along these lines will be necessary if we are to achieve any precise understanding of the forces which give birth to and shape new religious and secular groups.

PART IV

RELIGIOUS AND HUMANIST PERSPECTIVES

IN Part III attention was given to the basic incompatibility between those value orientations associated with religious institutions of a society and those of groups committed to social change. In recent times radical movements seem prone to adopt humanist, not just heretical, perspectives, and to search in the material world for solutions to questions of ultimate meaning. This has caused the strain between religion and radicalism to be especially acute. In this last section we should like to consider the question of conflicts between religion and humanist perspectives not associated with political radicalism.

Chapter 14

On the Incompatibility of Religion and Science[1]

RELIGION is perhaps the most ubiquitous of social institutions. Whatever other social institutions one is concerned with—the body politic, the economic order, the family—religion's influence on these institutions is always something to be considered. However, the influence of at least traditional religion on the other institutions of our society appears to be declining, and as these institutions generate their own value orientations, the link with traditional religion has become increasingly tenuous and may eventually be broken. A case in point may be the relationship between religion and science. Spawned by what many agree was a religiously inspired ethic, science, over time, has generated an internal and independent value system. Whether this value system is still compatible with the value orientatons of traditional religion has been the subject of much speculative discussion. The present chapter examines the question empirically.

In recent years, a lull has settled over the battle which once raged between science and religion.[2] The militant and crusading

1. We are especially indebted to the National Opinion Research Center for access to these data on American graduate students. The first report from these materials appears in James A. Davis, with David Gottlieb, Jan Hajda, Carolyn Huson, and Joe L. Spaeth, *Stipends and Spouses: The Finances of American Arts and Science Graduate Students* (Chicago: University of Chicago Press, 1962).

2. For a detailed and colorful account see: A. D. White, *A History of the Warfare of Science with Theology in Christendom* (New York: Dover, 1960).

spirit of an earlier era seems to be dissipated, and the public forums no longer ring with cries of "superstition" or "heresy." In these calmer days, a spate of recent apologetics suggests that a major preoccupation of many American theologians is to show either that there never was any basis for conflict between science and religion, or that old differences have been successfully accommodated.[3] Philosophers of science, on the other hand, seem less inclined to agree that any such *rapprochement* has taken place.[4] Clearly, the canons of logical positivism leave little room for religion to constitute anything more than humanistic ethics.[5] Thus, the issue persists. Does the prevailing quiet represent an actual settlement of differences, or have religion and science merely become isolated from one another within a secularized social climate where attacks on either have lost their power to attract attention?[6] For this reason it seems proper to raise the fundamental question once more: Is there a basic incompatibility between scientific and religious outlooks?[7]

The traditional argument that religion and science are incompatible perspectives is based on their contradictory evaluations of the authority of human reason. Religion, because of its ulti-

---

3. For example, see a recent collection: John C. Monsma, ed., *Science and Religion* (New York: G. P. Putman's Sons, 1962).

4. A listing of writers and works on this topic would be lengthy, but would surely need to include Bertrand Russell and Hans Reichenbach.

5. For instance, Herbert Feigl wrote in response to the question of whether science and religion were incompatible, that:

> If by religion one refers to an explanation of the universe and a derivation of moral norms from theological premises, then indeed there is a logical incompatibility with the results, methods, and general outlook of science. But if religion means an attitude of sincere devotion to human values, such as justice, peace, relief from suffering, there is not only no conflict between religion and science but rather a need for mutual supplementation.

"The Scientific Outlook: Naturalism and Humanism," Herbert Feigl and May Brodbeck, eds., *Readings in the Philosophy of Science* (New York: Appleton-Century-Crofts, Inc., 1953), p. 16.

6. If there are no modern counterparts of Bishop Wilberforce and William Jennings Bryan, there are also no heirs to Sir Thomas Henry Huxley or Col. Robert Ingersoll. And though aspirants to these roles have appeared often enough recently, none has ever been able to attract much of an audience, nor touch off any real controversies.

7. By religion, we are referring here to traditional beliefs and institutions of Christendom. Clearly, the more a particular faith has relinquished its orthodoxy to accomodate scientific discovery, the less likely it will conflict with scientific perspectives. Thus we are concerned with those faiths which posit the existence of a relevant supernatural being, world, or force, and generally ignore those which retain only ethical positions.

mate commitment to a non-empirical system, must take the position that man's reason is subordinate to faith as a means to truth. From this view, reason is at best unreliable, and at worst, sinful pride.[8] Science, on the other hand, defines truth as that which may be demonstrated either logically or empirically, and thus opts for the supremacy of reason. A middle-of-the-road attempt to resolve this conflict has been to argue that religious and scientific truths are different in *kind,* and hence accessible to different modes of knowing and subject to different criteria of validity. But many modern philosophers have been loath to grant religion such a special dispensation from the canons of logic and evidence. Indeed, such separation of truth into truths has recently been branded as 'anti-intellectualism' by Morton White.[9] Thus it appears that scientific scholars are as unwilling to admit religious modes of knowing as religionists are to submit their theology to scientific standards, and a crucial basis for conflict seems to remain.

We must point out here, that by scientific scholars we mean more than just those persons engaged in the natural and physical sciences. It seems likely that the qualities of thought associated with science are characteristic of modern scholarship in general, and not limited to the traditional sciences. The criteria by which an historian identified causes and tests hypotheses are not different in kind from those of the physicist.[10] Similarly, the approach to their data taken by philologists, literary historians, and even modern Bible critics, is in this same style, grounded in skepticism and empirical rules of evidence. Hence modern scholarship generally may be considered scientific and stakes its ultimate reliance in human reason, thus directly conflicting with the methodological modes of religious inquiry.

The argument we have sketched concerning the conflict between science and religion is familiar, and we need not pursue it in greater detail. It is clear that what we have considered so far

---

8. For instance, the Missouri Synod Lutherans have held that
> . . . a scientific hypothesis based on evidence accessible to empirical reason, natural reason, will be damned with the presumption that it is of the flesh; coming under the religious category of the ancient sin of *superbia,* it will be relegated to the limbo of man's presumptions.

Quoted in Heinrich H. Maurer, "The Problems of Group-Consensus: Founding the Missouri Synod," *American Journal of Sociology,* XXX (May, 1925), p. 667.

9. Morton White, "Reflections on Anti-Intellectualism," *Daedalus* (Summer, 1962), pp. 457–68.

10. See the discussion by Ernest Nagel, *The Structure of Science* (New York and Burlingame: Harcourt, Brace, and World, Inc., 1961).

are incongruities between value orientations, specifically between religious and humanist perspectives. Implicit in any discussion of value conflicts is the assumption that contradictory values cannot be readily held by single individuals or integrated groups, and hence, that the adoption of one means the nonadoption of the other. This leads our analysis from the realm of ideology to the level of concrete behavior, making it possible to investigate empirically whether scientific and religious outlooks are behaviorally incompatible. The thesis rests on the determinable prediction that men will tend to be *either* scientific *or* religious, and not both.[11] The remainder of this chapter will be devoted to testing this hypothesis.

THE CONCLUSIONS OF PREVIOUS RESEARCH

The work so ambitiously begun by James Leuba,[12] in the early part of this century, on the religiosity of men of science and scholarship has not been pursued much further. Leuba found that the greater proportion of American scientific scholars did not accept traditional religious beliefs. A small study made several years ago by *Fortune* magazine supported Leuba's early findings.[13] Both studies also found that the more eminent the scholar, the less likely he was to be religiously involved. Further confirmation of the irreligiousness of scientists is supplied by Anne Roe.[14] In her impressionistic report of intensive interviews with 64 selected scientists, she found that although all but one came from a background of religious affiliation,

> . . . now only three of these men are seriously active in church. A few others attend upon occasion, or they even give some financial support to a church they do not attend, but they are not personally concerned over religious matters . . . .[15]

We are left to conclude that the majority of scientists she interviewed neither had religious concern nor engaged in religious activity.

---

11. Those who attempt to be both ought to exhibit the classic characteristics of marginality. We shall not attempt to explore this hypothesis in the present chapter, although considerable impressionistic material exists that supports it.

12. James H. Leuba, *The Belief in God and Immortality* (Boston: Sherman French and Co., 1916).

13. Francis Bello, "The Mighty Force of Research," Chapter Two of "The Young Scientists," *Fortune*, XLIX (June, 1954), pp. 142–148.

14. Anne Roe, *The Making of a Scientist* (New York: Dodd, Mead, 1952).

15. *Ibid.,* p. 62.

Looked at from the other direction, scattered data suggest that men with strong religious commitment are seldom scientific and have not often been major contributors to the on-going scientific quest. For example, recent Catholic writers, including John Tracy Ellis,[16] Thomas F. O'Dea,[17] and John J. Kane,[18] present a bleak picture of Catholic intellectualism in America. They note the lack of eminent scholars and departments in Catholic schools, and how seldom Catholic scholars make any significant contributions to their disciplines. This is further corroborated by a report in the *Catholic World*[19] that a bare 2 per cent of the National Science Foundation Fellowship Awards went to students in Catholic colleges in 1956, and again in 1957.

More generally, Knapp and Greenbaum,[20] in tracing the collegiate origins of young American scholars, found denominational schools, both Catholic and Protestant, contribute proportionately far fewer scholars than do secular schools. And Paul F. Lazarsfeld and Wagner Thielens, Jr.,[21] found in their national study of American professors of the social sciences that scholars in Protestant and Catholic schools are much less apt to be productive than their colleagues in public and private schools, not including teachers' colleges.

These data, while suggestive, are too scattered and unsystematic to provide a legitimate test of the hypothesis. However, if the worlds of scientific scholarship and religious faith do tend to be mutually exclusive, then we would expect the process by which men come to inhabit the former to be accompanied by a corrosion of their ties with the latter. The main feature of the process which makes men into scholars is education, culminating in graduate training at a university. Thus, by empirical exploration of variations in religious involvement within the graduate school setting we may be able to see if and how this process is associated with apostasy.

---

16. John Tracy Ellis, "The American Catholic and the Intellectual Life," *Thought,* XXX:118 (Autumn, 1955).

17. Thomas F. O'Dea, *American Catholic Dilemma* (New York: Sheed and Ward, Inc., 1958).

18. John J. Kane, *Catholic-Protestant Conflicts in America* (Chicago: Regnery, 1955).

19. *Catholic World,* January, 1958, p. 251.

20. Robert H. Knapp and Joseph J. Greenbaum, *The Younger American Scholar: His Collegiate Origins* (Chicago: University of Chicago Press, 1953).

21. Paul F. Lazarsfeld and Wagner Thielens, Jr., *The Academic Mind* (Glencoe: The Free Press, 1958), p. 26.

Previous investigations of the relationship between college training and religiosity have been contradictory. Repeated studies of national cross-sections—the most recent being that of Gallup[22] in late 1964 shown in Table 14-1—have found church attendance rises with education and that the college educated group is more likely to attend church frequently than those with less education.

However, to say, on this basis, that college acts to increase religious involvement would be a gross oversimplification. As the data in Table 14-1 show, even though college people are slightly more likely to attend church than the less educated, 50 per cent were not in church during the past week. From the data we have previously considered on the general irreligiosity of men of science, who also come from this college-trained group, it seems likely that college has different effects on different kinds of people under different conditions. This is borne out by the confusion of studies on the religious involvement of college students. Leuba,[23] Katz, *et al.*,[24] and Wickenden,[25] report a fall-off of religous involvement during college, both in terms of church participation and in orthodox beliefs. On the other hand, Thurstone and Chave,[26] and Gilliland,[27] found no significant

TABLE 14-1*
Church Attendance in America Increases With Education*

Education	Percentage attending Church in past week
Grade School	43
High School	44
Some College	50

*Source: American Institute of Public Opinion, national poll, 1964

22. George Gallup, American Institute of Public Opinion, news release, January, 1965.

23. Leuba, *op. cit.*

24. Daniel Katz, F. H. Allport, and Margaret B. Jenness, *Student's Attitudes* (Syracuse: Craftsman Press, 1931).

25. A. C. Wickenden, "The Effect of the College Experience upon Student's Concepts of God," *Journal of Religion,* XII (1932), 242–67.

26. L. L. Thurstone and E. J. Chave, *The Measurement of Attitude* (Chicago: University of Chicago Press, 1929).

27. A. R. Gilliland, "Religious Attitudes of College Students," *The Christian Student,* XXXIX (November, 1938), 21.

change in attitudes toward religion and the church associated with the college experience. And Cavenaugh[28] reported an increase in church attendance and ritual participation during the college years. Clearly the evidence of the effect of college on religious involvement is not of a piece. The present chapter will attempt to isolate different kinds of things which affect student religiosity in an effort to test the relationship between scientific scholarship and religion.

We shall pursue this quest with data collected from a representative national sample of American graduate students by the National Opinion Research Center in 1958. The sampling frame included all universities which granted the Ph.D. in one or more fields in the arts and sciences. Twenty-five universities were selected through stratified random procedures, and a random sample of graduate students was selected from each, yielding a total of 2,842 respondents. Further details of sampling are presented in the volume reporting initial analysis of these data.[29]

A MEASURE OF RELIGIOUS INVOLVEMENT

Our initial task is to build a satisfactory measure of religious involvement, or religiosity. As pointed out in Chapter 2, religiosity is a complex and multidimensional phenomenon. It was suggested that religion may be conceptualized as consisting of five analytically discrete though interrelated dimensions. It was noted that no study has ever examined all of these facets of religious commitment, and rarely have more than one or two been explored. Since these different dimensions of religiosity need not be related, and several may even be negatively correlated, this neglect has been of crucial importance. However, only data concerning religious affiliation and attendance at worship services were available in these studies. Still it seems reasonable to proceed, since in this particular case the crudeness of the indicators should work *against*, rather than for, the hypotheses to be tested. Certainly many corrosions of religiosity may have taken place within a group which still claims affiliation with some faith and still attends church to some extent. We cannot examine such subtle differences, nor use them to support our thesis. Rather, we shall have to find more drastic differences

28. J. J. Cavanaugh, "Survey of Fifteen Survey's," *Bulletin of the University of Notre Dame*, XXXIV (1939), 1 – 128.
29. Davis, *et al., op. cit.*

such as those between claiming a religious affiliation and claiming none, and between claiming to attend church and claiming not to attend. In addition, any normative biases working to inflate estimates of religious involvement will also work counter to our thesis, rather than for it. As a consequence, we may fail to find corrosions in the religious involvement of scientific scholars when, indeed, they are there. But we are unlikely to find spurious apostasy.

Turning to the data, we may ask: In an overall sense, how religious are graduate students in the arts and sciences at American universities? Are they significantly less involved in religion than Americans in general, or are such differences a myth?

The comparisons in Table 14–2 show that indeed graduate students exhibit an unusually large proportion of persons who claim no religious identification as compared with a cross-sectional sample of the United States population collected by the U.S. Census Bureau in 1957.[30] While 3 per cent of Americans in general say they have no religion, 26 per cent of the graduate student sample reported similarly.[31]

TABLE 14-2

A Comparison Between the Religious Affiliations of American Graduate Students in the Arts and Sciences and A Cross-Section of the American Population**

	American Graduate Students	United States Population
Protestant	38%	66%
Catholic	22%	26%
Jewish	9%	3%
Other	5%	1%
None	26%	3%
Not reported	*	1%
Total	100%	100%

* less than one per cent
** Source: United States Bureau of the Census, see fn. 30.

30. U.S. Bureau of the Census, *Current Population Reports,* series P-20, No. 79, February 2, 1958.

31. A similarly large proportion of irreligiousness among British students is suggested by a Reuters dispatch which reported a motion that "this house does not believe in God," was passed by the Oxford University Union Society by a vote of 295 to 259. Reported in the *San Francisco Chronicle,* May 4, 1962, p. 1.

Public opinion polls show that approximately this same proportion of the general population (3 per cent) indicate they do not believe in God.[32] This strongly suggests that when an American says he has no religion he means he not only has no formal church affiliation, but that he also rejects religious faith. Hence, while we have no data on the religious beliefs of these graduate students, there seems some basis for interpreting their reports of no religious preference as implying a rejection of religious beliefs.

We are immediately faced with the question of whether graduate students are selectively recruited from irreligious backgrounds, or whether these percentages represent a change in their religious status roughly coinciding with exposure to the university setting. We may answer these questions only in part. We do not have data on the religious involvement of these students when they entered college. We may, however, examine change against a benchmark provided by the religious context in which they were raised. Thus, while we may not determine exactly when changes took place, in Table 14-3, we may see the turnover pattern by which students came to occupy their present religious status. The major proportion of those who currently report no religious affiliation had one originally, or at least report they were raised in some religious faith. As might be expected, Catholics are the least likely to have relinquished their original affiliation, and Jews are the most likely to have done so. The most significant thing about the pattern of change, however, is that few who relinquished the faith in which they were raised changed to another faith, but nearly always became nonaffiliates. That is, few Protestants, Catholics, or Jews adopted one another's faith, but many from each faith have defected altogether from organized religion.

By substracting the current religious distribution, as reported in Table 14-2, from the distribution of original religious affiliation, which appears across the bottom of Table 14-3, we may arrive at a summary measure of shifting shown in Table 14-4. Here, despite the use of a somewhat crude measure, we may see that a major religious phenomenon associated with being a graduate student is a loss of faith. While each of the three major religious groups[33] have a smaller proportion of the graduate

32. For example, see American Institute of Public Opinion, national poll of December 18, 1954.

33. "Other" category dropped from analysis.

TABLE 14-3
Pattern of Turnover In Religious Affiliations

Current Religious Affiliation	Percentage of Original Religious Affiliation				
	Protestant	Catholic	Jewish	Other	None
Protestant	71%	3%	1%	3%	20%
Catholic	2	85	0	2	6
Jewish	0	0	65	0	1
Other	2	0	1	71	2
None	25	12	33	24	71
N =	100% (1438)	100% (673)	100% (371)	100% (146)	100% (195)
Distribution of Original Religious Affiliation	51	24	13	5	7
	Total = 100				

The percentages in bold type along the diagonal of the table represent the proportion of each original affiliate group who have retained their affiliation unchanged.

TABLE 14-4
Net Change in Graduate Student Religious affiliation

Religious Group	Percentage-point difference between original religious distribution and current religious distribution
Protestant	−13
Catholic	− 2
Jewish	− 4
None	+19

student population than they did originally, the None group has made a marked gain in size.

But previous studies have repeatedly shown that mere religious affiliation grossly *overestimates* religious involvement as compared with involvement measured by church attendance. The same overestimate functions among this sample. Of those who say they are currently members of one of the three faiths, 56 per cent report they attend worship services regularly or frequently, while 44 per cent say they attend only occasionally, seldom, or never.

By combining these data on attendance with those on religious affiliation, we may construct a three-point index of religious involvement. The first category (None), consists of those who report no religious affiliation. The second (Low), contains those who claim affiliation, but attend only occasionally, seldom, or never. The third (High), is that group who claim affiliation and attend regularly or frequently.

Using this index as a dependent variable, we may now attempt to see if the process of creating scientific scholars is associated with religious apostasy; on the behavioral level, are science and religion mutually exclusive domains?

EXPOSURE TO SCIENTIFIC SCHOLARLY PERSPECTIVES

If our hypothesis is valid, then we would expect to find that religious involvement is affected by the degree to which students are exposed to scientific scholarship. Certainly all graduate students in the arts and sciences are exposed to some extent, but it seems likely that the degree of exposure may vary in at least three ways: (1) the kind of school they are enrolled in; (2)

the quality of this school; and (3) the quality of the school in which they received their undergraduate training. These three conditions are clearly somewhat interrelated, but each should have an independent effect on religious involvement.

The Kind of School

Basically, American graduate schools are of two kinds, secular and parochial. Of the secular schools, many are public institutions and, as such, religiously neutral, if not indifferent. Many of the rest have emerged from a denominational past, probably partly to escape conflicts between religious doctrines and scientific inquiry, and are today effectively without religious commitments. The rest are private schools which began as secular schools by maintaining extensive controls and restraints over the theological implications of their curricula. As contrasted with the spirit of free inquiry at secular schools, parochial schools often explicitly require their students and faculties to limit the kinds of study and theoretical approaches they may take to scientific and scholarly pursuits. Sensitive and controversial issues tend to be excluded. For example, Lazarsfeld and Thielens[34] report that professors at parochial schools were much less likely to be permissive towards the expression of radical dissent on their campuses than were professors at secular schools. Analysis of these same data by Jerry Mandel[35] revealed that, as a group, professors in parochial schools (both Protestant and Catholic) were much less favorable towards free speech and civil liberties in general, as well as more opposed to several varieties of dissent, than were their colleagues in secular schools. We need not elaborate such practices as restricted access to books and journals, revisionist textbooks, and doctrinal bans against a variety of scientific theories, to make the point that parochial schools are relatively intellectually restrictive.

Secular schools, on the other hand, may not always enjoy complete academic freedom, but are by comparison intellectual cafeterias. Seldom do professors concern themselves with how this or that notion may square with a student's religious ideology, especially since his classes are likely to contain students from an extensive array of different faiths. In short, students

---

34. Lazarsfeld and Thielens, *op. cit.,* p. 128.
35. Jerry Mandel, "Religion and McCarthyism in Academia," unpublished paper on file in the Department of Sociology, University of California, Berkeley.

do not receive similar instruction at secular and parochial schools—the latter providing students with less exposure to scientific scholarly perspectives than the former.

If this is so, and if exposure to such perspectives is related to corrosions of religious involvement, then we would expect to find very different patterns of religious change among students in secular and parochial schools. As may be seen in Table 14–5, this is clearly the case. Both Catholics and Protestants are more likely to be highly involved in religion and less likely to have shifted to None in the parochial school setting, although all of the schools so classified are Catholic institutions. These data seem to support strikingly Catholic beliefs about the relative danger of secular education to 'the faith.' However, a disclaimer must be made here. While these effects may be in large measure a function of differences in context between the two graduate school settings, it is probable that some of this effect, and perhaps much of it, is produced by recruitment. That is, even though both groups share a religious background, persons with a less religious orientation gravitate to secular schools, while their more committed counterparts enter parochial schools. This does not seriously affect our general argument about the mutually exclusive tendency of scientific and religious perspectives, however, for we are predicting only that a man will likely be either one or the other, and we can see that students in secular schools, who are more likely to become first-rate scientific scholars than their parochial school colleagues, are less likely to be involved in religion. The lack of data assuring equal religious commitment of these groups when they entered their respective settings does, on the other hand, make it impossible to conclude that secular schools destroy faith. We may only say that graduate training, probably at a secular school, is a usual part of the *process* by which men come to be scientific scholars and it appears that during that *process* religion is falling away.

This relationship, and all others reported in this chapter, proved to be independent of sex, class origin, marital status, and major. The latter could be expected to have an effect on the degree to which a student is exposed to scientific scholarship, but since the sample contains only arts and science majors it was not possible to compare them with less scholarly fields.

TABLE 14-5

Religious Involvement is Higher, and Apostasy Lower, In Parochial Schools

Type of School	Original Religion							
	Protestant		Catholic		Jewish		None	
Current Religious Involvement	Secular	Parochial	Secular	Parochial	Secular	Parochial	Secular	Parochial
High	38%	55%	69%	97%	6%	—	10%	—
Low	36	37	13	2	60	—	16	—
None	26	8	18	1	34	—	74	—
N =	100% (1349)	100% (52)	100% (427)	100% (244)	100% (360)	(8)	100% (185)	(6)

—Too few cases for stable percentages.

The Quality of the Graduate School

Regardless of the kind of school, the degree to which a student is exposed to scientific scholarly perspectives is partly a function of the quality of the institutions he attends. The better the school, the more likely it is that professors will be competent in their disciplines and able to impart these perspectives fully to their students. In Table 14–6, we may see that religious involvement is markedly affected by the quality of the graduate school. The quality index was developed by Davis, *et al.*[36] No matter what a student's religious background, he is considerably more likely to have given up his religious ties the higher the quality of the school he is attending. And, of course, the higher the quality school in which a student is trained, the greater the chance he will emerge as a practicing, scientific scholar.

Quality of Undergraduate Training

An excellent predictor of success in graduate school, and hence of eventual participation in scholarly and scientific disciplines, is the calibre of training the student receives in his undergraduate days. In this regard we may note the exceptional records of graduates from such famous small colleges as Oberlin, Swarthmore, Reed, and Antioch, and the similar proficiency of students trained at the high-quality universities. As graduate students are more exposed to scientific scholarship at higher-quality graduate schools, they were similarly more exposed at high-quality undergraduate schools. Thus we may expect religious involvement to be highly related to the quality of the undergraduate school attended. This is obviously the case, as may be seen in Table 14–7. Among both students from universities and those from colleges, the quality of school has a marked effect on religious involvement. The quality criteria used for universities are the same used to rate the graduate schools. Since colleges could not be rated in this same way, they were considered to be of high quality if they appeared among the top 50 schools in Knapp and Greenbaum's overall ratings,[37] or if they appeared in the top 20 in two of the three special areas rated by the same authors.

---

36. Davis, *et al., op. cit.* In addition they found quality and size to be so highly correlated that it is impossible to consider them separately. For that reason, size of school does not enter into our analysis.
37. Knapp and Greenbaum, *op. cit.*

TABLE 14-6

Religious Involvement Declines as Quality of School Rises

Quality of School	Original Religion											
	Protestant			Catholic			Jewish			None		
Current Religious Involvement	High	Medium	Low	High	Medium	Low	High	Medium	Low	High	Medium	Low
High	30%	41%	44%	63%	78%	89%	6%	5%	15%	8%	13%	18%
Low	38	35	36	14	9	6	59	61	62	10	16	20
None	32	24	20	23	13	5	35	34	23	82	71	62
	100%	100%	100%	100%	100%	100%	100%	100%	100%	100%	100%	100%
N =	(393)	(635)	(373)	(139)	(293)	(239)	(139)	(190)	(39)	(67)	(79)	(45)

TABLE 14-7

Religious Involvement Increases as Quality of
Undergraduate Training Decreases

		Universities			Colleges	
Quality:		High	Medium	Low	High	Low
Religious	High	20%	37%	48%	26%	53%
Involvement	Low	39	33	27	44	27
	None	41	30	25	30	20
		100%	100%	100%	100%	100%
	N =	(372)	(450)	(445)	(211)	(1155)

The effects of undergraduate school quality were, of course, highly related to the kind and quality of graduate school, and those two variables were also highly interrelated. However, each of the three variables had an effect on religious involvement independent of the others.

AN INDEX OF EXPOSURE
TO SCIENTIFIC-SCHOLARLY PERSPECTIVES

To examine the combined impact of these three variables on religious involvement without creating a table too complex to be easily read, and to minimize the attrition of the sample size to allow further analysis of these findings, an index of exposure to scientific scholarly perspectives was constructed. The index has a possible range of from zero (lowest exposure) through six.[38] If exposure is the factor which underlies the relation of all three variables to religious involvement, then their effect ought to be cumulative and strongly influence the degree of religious involvement.

Table 14-8 markedly supports this interpretation. The relationship between the exposure index and religious involvement is consistent and ranges from 89 per cent highly involved to 17 per cent. Clearly, this relationship between the degree to which students are exposed to scientific scholarship and their religious involvement supports the original hypothesis that

---

38. The scoring was as follows:
a. graduate school quality: high = 2; medium = 1; low = 0.
b. undergraduate school quality: universities: high = 2; medium = 1; low = 0. colleges: high = 1; low = 0.
c. kind of school: secular = 2; parochial = 0.

religion and science tend to be mutually exclusive perspectives. Still, there is variation in religious involvement unaccounted for. Not all of those in the least exposed setting are religiously involved, and some who have been most exposed are still highly involved. Unfortunately, we cannot examine the quality of religious involvement in these two polar settings, which would probably reveal impressive differences. Still, we can pursue our analysis a good deal further in an attempt to account for additional variation.

THE SCHOLARLY ETHOS

So far we have been examining the effect of contextual, or objective, factors on the religious involvement of graduate students. Implicit in any such argument is, of course, a theory that these external factors have subjective consequences for individuals which are then translated into behavior. To refine further our analysis we must turn to an examination of the subjective component of exposure to scientific scholarly perspectives, specifically, the kinds of self-image and values associated with such perspectives.

Certainly one such subjective component is the actor's reference group—the audience before whom he is playing. A person entering on an academic career may generally choose between two reference groups, each with different consequences for his self-image. Robert K. Merton,[39] and Alvin W. Gouldner[40] have

TABLE 14-8
Religious Involvement Increases Sharply as Exposure to Scientific Scholarship Decreases

| | | Index of Exposure to Scientific-Scholarly Perspectives Low - High | | | | | | |
		0.	1.	2.	3.	4.	5.	6.
Religious	High	88%	89%	50%	44%	35%	24%	17%
Involvement	Low	10	8	29	32	35	37	39
	None	2	3	21	24	30	39	44
		100%	100%	100%	100%	100%	100%	100%
	N =	(85)	(201)	(431)	(661)	(750)	(272)	(231)

39. Robert K. Merton, *Social Theory and Social Structure* (Glencoe: The Free Press, 1957), Chapter X.

40. Alvin W. Gouldner, "Cosmopolitans and Locals: Towards an Analysis of Latent Social Roles—I," *Administrative Science Quarterly,* II (1957), 281– 306.

described these two reference groups as Cosmopolitans and Locals. Graduate students with a *Cosmopolitan* reference group make their claims to identity and status on an audience made up of members of their particular discipline or specialty. This audience is spread through many different institutions. *Locals* choose to play to an audience made up of the personnel of the institution in which they work (or study), thus seeking recognition from persons close at hand, but who perform in a variety of disciplines and specialties. Gouldner showed that one of the important differences between cosmopolitan and local academicians was the quality and quantity of their scholarship. Thus, taking a cosmopolitan reference group is probably one consequence of exposure to scientific scholarly perspectives, and, indeed, indicates successful socialization into such a perspective. Hence, we would expect cosmopolitans to be less religiously involved than locals. This is clearly confirmed by Table 14–9. Students were asked whether they would rather be "known and respected throughout the institution where you work or among specialists in your field at different institutions." Depending on their choice, respondents were classified as having cosmopolitan or local reference groups (or aspirations to such reference groups). The data show, as expected, that cosmopolitans are considerably less likely to be highly involved in religion than are locals.

A second component of the scientific scholarly perspective involves accepting the identity of an 'intellectual.' The word intellectual is subject to a double standard in American culture. Among many Americans, the term bears negative connotations associated with what is sometimes called the anti-egghead syndrome. Yet scholars use the word to indicate themselves and

TABLE 14-9
Cosmopolitans are Much Less Likely to be Highly Involved in Religion Than Are Locals

		Cosmopolitans	Locals
Religious	High	35%	54%
Involvement	Low	35	25
	None	30	21
		100%	100%
	N =	(1553)	(1034)

their peers, and to be an intellectual is thus an important part of one's self-image. Graduate students who see themselves as intellectuals have taken on a portion of the scientific scholarly self-image, and, if our proposition holds, should be less involved in religion than their colleagues who reject this identity. Table 14–10 is consistent with this prediction. The less willing the student is to claim to be an intellectual the more likely he is to be highly involved in religion.

The nature of the scholarly and scientific quest requires originality, creativity, and freedom from pressures to conform; thus it is not surprising that scholars and scientists have long placed a premium on self-expressiveness and fought for academic freedom. Indeed, this is reputed to be the very nub of the friction between science and religion. Thus, the degree to which one comes to hold scholarly and scientific points of view should be highly related to putting value on these freedoms.

Joe L. Spaeth[41] has constructed a scale of self-expressiveness based on these data which consists of questions on whether or not it was very important to the respondent that his future job have opportunities for creativity and originality, freedom from pressures to conform, and freedom from extensive supervision. The resulting scale ranges from one (high self-expressiveness) through four. As may be seen in Table 14–11, strongly holding values of self-expression is negatively related to religious involvement—only 27 per cent of those who highly valued self-expression were highly involved in religion as compared with 60 per cent of those who least valued self-expression.

Each of these three subjective variables has told us something about religious involvement. If each is actually tapping an underlying dimension of the self-image of the scientific scholarly perspective, then they should be highly related and their joint effect on religious involvement should be extensive. To allow efficient use of the data, these three variables were combined into an index of the scientific-scholarly ethos[42] which ranged from zero (low scholarly ethos) through nine. Table 14–12 reveals that indeed these subjective elements of scientific

---

41. Joe L. Spaeth, *Value Orientations and Academic Career Plans,* unpublished doctoral dissertation, Department of Sociology, University of Chicago, 1961.

42. The scoring was as follows:
a. Self-expressiveness scale, from high to low = 3, 2, 1, 0.
b. Intellectualism, from definitely through definitely not = 3, 2, 1, 0.
c. Reference group: Cosmopolitan = 3; Local = 0.

TABLE 14-10

The Less a Student Thinks of Himself as an Intellectual, the More Likely He will be Highly Involved in Religion

		"Do you think of yourself as an 'intellectual'?"			
		"Definitely"	"In many Ways"	"In Some Ways"	"Definitely Not"
Religious Involvement	High	26%	38%	49%	55%
	Low	28	32	31	31
	None	46	30	20	14
		100%	100%	100%	100%
	N =	(358)	(877)	(1154)	(220)

ON THE INCOMPATIBILITY OF RELIGION AND SCIENCE   283

TABLE 14-11

The Higher Value He Places on Self-Expression, the Less Likely a Student is to be Involved in Religion

| | | Self-Expressiveness Scale | | | |
| | | High - Low | | | |
		1.	2.	3.	4.
Religious	High	27%	31%	48%	60%
Involvement	Low	32	34	30	27
	None	41	35	22	13
		100%	100%	100%	100%
	N =	(362)	(724)	(1015)	(500)

scholarship have a marked joint effect on religious involvement, with a 61 percentage point difference obtaining between the high and low points on the index. But again, as in the case of the exposure index, some variation is left unexplained.

Since we have argued that the subjective factors – the scholarly ethos – are, in part, a consequence of the objective – exposure – it seems logical to next consider their joint effect on religious involvement. Cross-tabulating the exposure and ethos indices in Table 14–13, we may see the full power of these related elements. *One hundred per cent* of the respondents who fall into the upper left hand corner of the table (low exposure, low ethos) are highly involved in religion. *Only six per cent* of those in the lower right hand corner (high exposure, high ethos) are highly involved in religion. Religious involvement decreases across the rows of the table from left to right, down the columns, and along the diagonal from upper left to lower right. (The several small reversals are not important to the marked overall effect). These findings give convincing confirmation to the original hypothesis of this paper – religion and scientific scholarship tend to be mutually exclusive perspectives.

In summary we may consider three ideal types of graduate students with differing religious involvement and scholarly identities:

The Uninvolved: this student is doing his graduate work at a high-quality state or private university. He did his undergraduate work at a high-quality university or an elite small college. He thinks of himself as an intellectual and feels strongly about being allowed self-expression in his future career. He is more con-

TABLE 14-12
Scholarly Ethos is Negatively Related to Religious Involvement

| | | Low | | | | | Index of Scholarly Ethos | | | High | |
		0.	1.	2.	3.	4.	5.	6.	7.	8.	9.
Religious	High	72%	70%	59%	44%	50%	46%	32%	30%	21%	9%
Involvement	Low	26	17	26	32	42	44	46	31	30	32
	None	2	13	15	24	18	20	22	39	49	59
		100%	100%	100%	100%	100%	100%	100%	100%	100%	100%
	N =	(32)	(194)	(294)	(349)	(285)	(398)	(398)	(337)	(187)	(67)

TABLE 14-13

Per Cent Highly Involved in Religion Under Conditions of Both Exposure and Ethos Indices

| | | Per Cent Highly Involved in Religion Index of Scholarly Ethos | | | | | | | | |
	Low 0.	1.	2.	3.	4.	5.	6.	7.	8.	High 9.
Index of Exposure to Scientific-Scholarly Perspectives										
Low 0.	— (1)	— (10)	95% (19)	— (8)	— (10)	88% (16)	— (8)	— (5)	— (1)	— (1)
1.	— (14)	100% (36)	97% (29)	84% (23)	82% (28)	79% (24)	81% (21)	— (14)	— (2)	— (0)
2.	— (1)	65% (40)	62% (60)	51% (57)	54% (65)	49% (72)	37% (62)	42% (38)	27% (22)	— (6)
3.	— (8)	62% (34)	62% (85)	42% (106)	51% (61)	51% (98)	32% (97)	32% (82)	32% (56)	— (12)
4.	— (7)	61% (57)	40% (68)	38% (92)	37% (71)	42% (113)	29% (138)	26% (104)	23% (53)	11% (19)
5.	— (1)	— (10)	28% (21)	37% (35)	26% (31)	21% (47)	25% (36)	21% (37)	12% (26)	— (12)
High 6.	— (0)	— (7)	— (12)	11% (28)	47% (19)	32% (28)	11% (36)	11% (47)	4% (28)	6% (17)

cerned about his reputation among scholars in his field than he is in being a big man on his local campus. He is from a Protestant or Jewish background, but no longer claims affiliation with any faith.

The Lowly Involved: is a milder version of the uninvolved. He too is likely to be at a public or private university, but of only middle quality. He thinks of himself somewhat as an intellectual and did his undergraduate work at a medium-quality university or lower-quality college. He is mildly concerned about self-expression in his work and tends to be slightly more concerned about success in his field than in a reputation at his local institution. He is from a Protestant, or possibly Jewish background and continues to claim affiliation with this faith. But he seldom or never attends worship services.

The Highly Involved: is likely to be either at a parochial school or a low-quality secular school. He did his undergraduate work at a low-quality university or college and thinks he is definitely not an intellectual, or only in some ways. He is unconcerned about self-expression in his future career and is more concerned with being known and respected in the institution where he works than among specialists in his field at different institutions. He is most likely from a Catholic, or possibly Protestant background and still claims this faith. He regularly or frequently attends worship services.

In short, these types reveal that religious involvement varies with the degree to which a person has become a scientific scholar.[43] At the level of human behavior, religion and scientific scholarship are infrequently found together.

---

43. A recent paper by Jan Hajda, based on these same data, provides further insight into these findings. See his "Alienation and Integration of Student Intellectuals," *American Sociological Review*, XXVI (October 1961), pp. 758–777. Hajda separated these students into four types: alienated intellectuals, integrated intellectuals, alienated nonintellectuals, and integrated nonintellectuals. A comparison of his two polar types shows that the alienated intellectual expected to hold academic jobs after graduation, preferred academic research as a future occupation, and desired to emulate one or more faculty members in his department. The integrated nonintellectuals, on the other hand, expected to hold nonacademic jobs and had no model among faculty members. He reported that the alienated intellectuals (the neophyte scientific scholars) reported infrequent church attendance and tended to have no religious affiliation, while the integrated nonintellectuals (those least apt to become participating scientific scholars) reported frequent church attendance and adhered to the religion in which they had been raised.

CONCLUSION

In conclusion, we may speculate briefly on what these findings may mean, and what they definitely do not mean. While these data seem to demonstrate conclusively that neophyte scientific scholars are likely to be irreligious, this is not to say that religion and science are necessarily or eternally at loggerheads. The data simply show that there is a behavioral basis for the polemic literature concerning a dichotomy between science and religion. And if there were no value conflicts between science and religion, we would have no reason to expect these differences in behavior. On the other hand, if such conflicts (should they exist) were resolved, we would expect these relationships to disappear.

Assuming, for heuristic purposes, that there actually are value conflicts between science and religion, certain trends seem to indicate the basis required for any eventual *rapprochement*. For the sake of simplicity and brevity, we have so far largely ignored the content of various theologies and spoken of religion in general terms. But it seems certain that the potential for conflict with scientific points-of-view is greater for some Christian theologies than for others. Indeed, a fair portion of the differences among Christian theologies can be traced to the degree they have been influenced by science. Clearly, the less a particular faith emphasizes an active, intervening supernatural, the less it ought to conflict with the empiricism of science. Had we data available on the theological content of the religion adhered to by these graduate students, there should certainly be marked differences between the religiously involved student in the most scientific setting and the involved student in the least scientific setting. Furthermore, data on the scientific orientation of various religious groups, and the proportion of their members who engage in scientific pursuits, should show that the less traditional and less supernatural faiths are more science-oriented and have more scientist members than the conservative bodies.[44] This would suggest that any eventual value consensus

44. Data from a pre-test sample of Protestant congregations collected recently by the Survey Research Center, University of California, Berkeley, show that attitudes toward various scientific activities and perceptions of the conflict between science and religion are highly related to the degree of supernaturalism in the prevailing theology. The least fundamentalist congregations saw little conflict between religion and science and were favorable towards science. The conservative congregations saw much conflict and were quite unfavorable towards science.

between scientific scholars and theologians could include little or no supernaturalism, and indeed might have to resemble the humanistic ethics described by Herbert Feigl.[45]

A present trend in American society is making the scientific scholar into a cultural hero—the presiding genius of progress. If this results in men of science having greater influence on our culture and value system, as surely it must, and if by becoming a scientist a man is likely to be detached from traditional religious orientations, then we must suspect that future American society will either become increasingly irreligious, or that religion will be extensively modified. In either case, the historic conflict between religion and science may finally be resolved.

---

45. Feigl, *op. cit.*

Chapter 15

Religion and the Social Sciences: Images of Man in Conflict

THE existence of tensions between religion and other social institutions, as well as between religion and certain apects of the social structure, has been documented directly and indirectly throughout the previous chapters. The sources and nature of these tensions have also been examined, but primarily from a sociological point of view. However, the philosophical aspects of these issues are also the source of some tensions. These philosophical issues are the subject of this final chapter.

The claim advanced and partially documented in the previous chapter, that men act as if religious and scientific perspectives are incompatible, is in contradiction to a prevailing body of contrary opinion. In the eyes of many, the war between religion and science that was waged so fiercely during the period since the Enlightenment is now over.[1] No side is the clear victor; both have had to compromise positions to the other, but neither side has been forced to capitulate entirely.

The claimed accommodation of the two perspectives to each other is not viewed as complete. But there is a high degree of consensus that a new era has begun. Science no longer claims, even implicitly, a capacity to deal with all that religion encom-

---

1. A number of writers holding these views have been collected in John C. Monsma, ed., *Science and Religion* (New York: G. P. Putman's Sons, 1962).

passes; there is a vital area in religious perspectives that science leaves untouched. In turn, religion is no longer adamant that all of its doctrines and dogma are immutable. There is a growing willingness to acknowledge that divine revelation is dynamic rather than static and that science may be the source of new revelations of divine purpose.[2]

We would suggest that there is a degree of wishful thinking in such views. At the same time, we are mindful that the evidence presented in the last chapter does not specifically deal with them. The analysis pursued there was necessarily limited by the character of the data, and it was not possible with such data to encompass all that a scientific perspective might signify, and even less so to cover the entire possible range of religious perspectives. Moreover, the issue with which we were concerned was not the philosophical and intellectual compatibility of religion and science, but the empirical question of whether the two tend to be joined or separated in the value orientations of individuals. We left relatively untouched any interpretation of the reasons for the apparent incompatibility — why do people deeply committed to a scientific perspective typically find it difficult to also entertain a religious perspective and vice versa? It is this latter question which the present chapter considers in the context of a more general examination of the interplay between science and religion.

In most, if not all, discussion about science and religion, science has meant the natural sciences. In turn, religion has most often meant the Christian religion, or at least religion which postulates a being imbued with divine power and purpose. In the present discussion, we propose to retain this definition of religion. However, our definition of science is expanded to include the social sciences; indeed, the focus of much of our discussion will be on the interplay between religion and the social sciences. The themes that we wish to develop are: (1) The seeming *rapprochement* between the natural sciences and religion has tended to obscure a growing tension between religion and the social sciences, and (2) This tension explains, in part,

---

2. An excellent example of the use of scientific discovery as a basis for expanding religious conceptions is provided by the work of the late Pierre Teilhard de Chardin. See his *The Phenomenon of Man* (New York: Harpers, 1959).

the incompatibilities between religious and scientific perspectives revealed in Chapter 14.

Social scientists, when they include religion in their subject matter for study, are prone to adopt a quite different posture than the one we shall assume in this chapter. Commonly, social scientists are not disposed to conceive of their investigations of religion as a threat to religion *per se*. Religion is characterized as being concerned with a different realm of being about which the social sciences have nothing to say. There are no grounds in the social sciences for establishing that there is or is not a supernatural world, a divine being, or a hereafter. These are questions which social scientific inquiry into religion must leave untouched. At most, what the social sciences can do is to assess how the religious institutions of societies and the religious behavior of individuals may be shaped and influenced by cultural, social, economic, and psychological factors and events. The knowledge thus gained, supposedly leaves untouched the supernatural realm of being which religion postulates.

A central point in our own argument is that this assumption is not warranted. We would agree that the social sciences cannot in any ultimate sense prove or disprove the existence of God or of a supernatural realm. However, no religion limits its conception of God to the simple belief that he exists. The conceptions are always more particular than this and include a set of beliefs bearing on God's intentions for man, on man's responsibilities and accountability to God, and on God's capability to enter into human events. It is these more particular beliefs about God or the supernatural that the social sciences are capable of calling into question. The effect may not be to threaten religion's commitment to God's existence. However, we would assert that to conclude as well that the supernatural realm is left completely untouched is incorrect. The results of social science research, as we shall shortly seek to document, are putting religion on the defensive about some of its traditional beliefs and the effect, in the long run, is likely to produce a process of accommodation parallel to that which religion experienced in its earlier confrontation with the natural sciences.

To set a suitable context for a more explicit discussion of the relationship between the social sciences and religion, it is necessary to consider briefly the more abiding controversy between the natural sciences and religion. The primary element in this controversy has been an essentially contradictory image of the forces operating in nature. Every theological system, Christian or otherwise, postulates a divine or supernatural force as operating in and upon nature. This force is responsible for creation and for establishing what appear to be the laws of nature. But it is also a force which is capable of contravening these laws through its own will—for example, the Biblical accounts of the burning bush, of the parting of the Red Sea, of Christ's walking on water and turning water into wine.

Science takes a different posture in its approach to nature. The basic assumptions which inform science are that every event in nature is determined by prior natural events and that the character of this determinism can be discerned through scientific investigation.[3] Individual scientists *as persons* will disagree about the adequacy of this deterministic assumption. *As scientists,* however, they are inextricably bound to it both in the way that they formulate their hypotheses and the way that inquiry is pursued.

Scientists as persons may base a case for God as a causal agent on the existence of phenomena which they have been unable to explain from a naturalistic perspective. However, there is no way for them to account scientifically for divine intervention.[4] They may choose to adopt a different perspective —a religious one, for example, to explain it.[5] If they do so, however, they are no longer functioning as scientists. Confronted

3. Actually, of course, unless one has found causes for all events, it is not logically tenable to assume that causes will always be found. Thus, it is not necessary for scientists to assume that a cause can be discovered for any given event, whether or not there is one can be left an open question, but at least it is necessary to assume that it is not *a priori* true that there is no cause for an event. Methodologically, however, scientists actually do act as if they believed that causes can eventually be uncovered for any recurrent event.

4. Heisenberg's principle of indeterminacy in subatomic physics has been badly distorted and misapplied by many attempting to establish a basis for free will doctrines within the scientific perspective. For a clear explication of the fallacies in such applications see: Hans Reichenbach, *The Rise of Scientific Philosophy* (Berkeley and Los Angeles: University of California Press, 1959).

5. Some scientists may disagree that a religious perspective is appropriate on the grounds that indeterminacy essentially means that a phenomenon occurs randomly. A religious perspective would undoubtedly avow that God acts purposefully, not randomly. In either case, however, what is being asserted is that the phenomenon in question cannot be understood at our current state of knowledge within a deterministic model.

with inexplicability, the scientist as scientist has no recourse but to assume that his knowledge is incomplete and to look further for variables which will explain the phenomena in naturalistic terms.

There is an element of faith in both religion and science; both are committed to a set of propositions which cannot be entirely proved or denied within our present capacities. There is, however, this important difference between the two commitments. Religious commitments are wholly based on faith; scientific ones only partially so. Religious commitments are not capable of being warranted except under the extraordinary condition of divine revelation about which there is consensus. It is debatable, indeed highly unlikely, that the informing assumptions of science can ever be wholly warranted. However, unlike the assumptions of religion, they are and have been subject to partial proof. That is to say, there exists irrefutable scientific evidence that the naturalistic assumption is in part, at least, correct.

In the conflict between religion and science, science has had the best of it so far because its assumptions are subject to some degree of empirical proof. Theoretically, the balance could tip the other way if it were possible within the canons of science to warrant the existence of a supernatural agency. This is not possible, however. Science is in a position to understand only that part of reality which fits its naturalistic model. Phenomena which do not fit the model remain a residual category to which religion may refer as support for its assumptions. Science, however, is not likely to be persuaded so long as the possibilities for natural explanation have not been exhausted.

Viewed in these lights, the seeming *rapprochement* between religion and science is illusory. The grounds for conflict have not been settled; and without the innovation of a wholly new perspective which would resolve the determinacy issue, there is little prospect for a genuine *rapprochement*. At the same time, it does not appear likely that the foreseeable future will find religion and science engaged in the same kind of open conflict that characterized the past. In part, this is because of the accommodations which religion has already made in its positions. There is simply less of a concrete nature about which to argue. Moreover, on science's side, current doubts about the adequacy of its assumptions constitute, in effect, a compromise on its part with religion. Until such doubts are clarified, consequently, the principle issues which have divided religion and science are likely to be latent.

However, religion is not likely to be in a position to relax during this period of quiescence in its relations with the natural sciences. While this conflict has abated for the time being, the grounds for a new controversy have arisen with the emergence and growth of the social sciences. The issue revolves once again around a conflicting set of basic assumptions. Now, however, the assumptions concern not the order of nature but the nature of man.

The idea that man's behavior, like behavior in nature, might be not only naturally explicable, but also wholly determined was not entirely alien to the historical controversy between religion and science. It was almost inevitable that the determinism issue as it arose with regard to nature would also be raised with regard to the image of man. However, the issue never became dominant. The natural sciences have only a limited interest in the study of man's behavior, and natural science findings were not of a kind to make the determinism issue vis-à-vis man highly visible.

With the emergence of the social sciences, however, man becomes the focus of study—and with theory and methods borrowed very heavily from the natural sciences. The borrowing became so complete, in fact, that the social sciences adopted a position with respect to man which is virtually identical with the natural science's position on nature. That is to say, the basic methodological assumption which has come to inform the social sciences is that man's behavior is determined in the same way that other natural phenomena are determined; that potentially every human act can be understood as a result of antecedent factors which operate to make that act inevitable.

Once again, it is important to recognize that this is the informing ideology of the social sciences and not the personal ideology of social scientists. As persons, social scientists, by and large, are likely to reject the idea that man is wholly determined. Certainly, as they pursue their daily lives, they act, for the most part, as if this were not true. But, when they conduct scientific research, they have no alternative but to adopt the deterministic assumption. Hypotheses, whether simple or complex, are invariably stated in a deterministic mode—e.g., for y to occur, x must be antecedent. The major methods of the social sciences — the experiment, survey research, econometrics — are each oriented primarily to testing such hypotheses. And new advances in methodology — new statistical procedures, longitudinal (panel) studies — are designed in an effort to be more rigorous about testing such hypotheses.

This is not to say that all work which is assigned the label social science research is undertaken from this perspective. It does not inform, for example, purely descriptive research where the aim is to describe systematically a personal or social situation. Nor does it inform that part of the research process commonly called conceptualization and index formation. To suggest that the populations of societies can be ordered into social classes or to postulate the idea of an authoritarian personality is to say nothing about the way social classes arise or the conditions under which authoritarian personalities occur. Finding answers to such questions may have motivated conceptualization; however, the concepts themselves do not necessarily involve a deterministic posture. Nor is such a posture necessary to all examinations of the relationship between variables. In the construction of an intelligence test, for example, the psychologist may discover that certain mental abilities are highly associated with one another without drawing any inference that one ability is the cause of another.

There is likely to be disagreement as to whether or not such work is scientific. If it were assigned this designation, it would represent an exception to the proposition we are advancing. We would not assert that descriptive research in the social sciences needs to be informed by a deterministic image of man. We are asserting, however, that whenever the goal of social science research is explanation, the model which the researcher adopts is a deterministic one. In fact, there is no alternative assumption which allows causal hypotheses to be stated, much less tested.

The basic impulse behind explanatory research in the social sciences, then, is to test the deterministic assumption and to discover just how it operates. But, as in the natural sciences, the assumption has not been wholly validated. We can state the causes for only a small part of human behavior; and even the most carefully worked out models of certain limited aspects of behavior fail to account for all of the cases. In smaller and, more often, larger proportion, there are always deviant cases which do not fit a given explanatory model.[6]

The existence of such cases leaves the possibility that the deterministic assumption is not wholly correct; that there is a range of behavior which cannot be accounted for within this assumption. Faced with such evidence, the social scientist may, as a person, agree that his perspective is an incomplete one. Functioning as a social scientist, however, he has no other alternative but to search for factors overlooked in his research which in subsequent efforts might explain the deviant cases.

Theological images of man differ, of course, in different religions and, over time, may differ in the same religion. In the midst of differences in detail, two central ideas about the functioning of man are curiously combined in virtually all religions. The one idea sees man as created by God and subject to God's will. The other accepts God as creator but conceives of man as essentially in control of his own destiny. The idea that man is controlled by God seems, at first glance, in contradiction to the idea that man controls himself. However, the two ideas are so juxtaposed that they complement more than conflict with one another.

The idea that God is in control is conveyed by such general themes as 'We are all created in God's image,' 'We are all children of God,' or 'We exist to reflect God's glory.' More explicitly, it is conveyed in Hinduism in the divine law of Karma, in Islam in the idea that man's position in life has been fated by Allah, in the Calvinistic conception of predestination, and more generally in Christianity, in the notion that whatever happens to us is God's will. What God determines, however, is never complete. In all religions, man is left with considerable control of his own destiny. The law of Karma established the 'rules of the game' to be sure, but within these rules, man is left with considerable authority to decide his own fate, if not in his present incarnation, at least in his next. The fatalism of Islam asks man to resign himself to his station in life. At the same time, whatever his station, man is called upon to work for Allah's glory. Similarly, Calvinism conceives of man as having considerable free-

---

6. At issue here, of course, is the question of what explanation means. For our present purposes, a quite minimum definition will suffice. Simply to find, as we do in Chapter 8, that religious experience is influenced in large part by the individual's social context would meet our minimum criteria of explanation.

dom of action even though he comes to this life with his eternal fate predestined.

Both the belief that God possesses the power to intervene in human events and the belief that man is largely in control of his own destiny are crucial to religion. In combination, they form the bases for religious commitment. The one warrants commitment by establishing the ultimacy of divine authority. The other makes reasonable the reward and punishment system through which that authority is exercised. To assert God's power as absolute without a free-will image of man would leave man's fate entirely in God's hands. What man is and how he acts would be altogether God's will. Thus, there would be no grounds for distinguishing good from evil or for asserting that good is preferable to evil. Because God would be in complete control, man's actions would be God's not man's responsibility.

The belief that man is possessed of extensive free will shifts the burden of responsibility and accountability to man. It makes meaningful both the establishment of standards of right and wrong and the universal religious injunction against sin. Together with the belief in God's ultimacy, it also gives meaning to religion's systems of eternal rewards and punishments and to the commitment which these systems generate. Only within a free-will image of man can man be held accountable for his actions, and only if man is accountable can religion command his allegiance and commitment.

It is true that there is an element in some religions, including some versions of Christianity, that man's fate cannot be influenced by his actions, i.e., by 'works.' This motif has never been a dominant one, however, at least for any period of time. Invariably, to generate commitment, religions have had to include in their theologies some version of the idea that through his actions, man indeed contributes to his destiny.

Religion and the social sciences could be expected to live comfortably together if the only issues to be decided were the existence of God and the question of whether or not man is possessed of free will. No social scientist would make the claim that we have the knowledge and understanding to decide either issue. Few, indeed, would claim that the answers can ever be known through human effort, and most perhaps would relegate the subjects as fit only for philosophical, not scientific, debate.

On both issues, then, the social sciences would neither confirm nor deny religion's claims, nor would they question religion's right to assert them.

The claims of religion, however, are not simply that God and free will exist. Religion professes that not only does God exist but that he is able to, and indeed does, intervene in human affairs. In turn, not only does free will exist, but it is held to be *relatively unrestricted*. Man enjoys wide latitude in the range of choices which he can make and for which he can be held responsible and accountable. It is with these claims and particularly their use as explanations for human behavior that the social scientist is likely to take exception. And it is because the social sciences (sometimes with the aid of other sciences) are increasingly capable of producing evidence to challenge these claims that the conflict between the social sciences and religion arises. Thus, increasingly, human behavior which would be explained from a religious perspective as God's will or as a result of man making a conscious and responsible choice to accept or reject God's will, is questioned by the results of social science research. Not only is the intervention of God rejected as a causal factor, but the idea that man's freedom is as extensive as religion allows is rejected as well.

We must digress here to clarify a number of ambiguities in the terms 'free will' and 'determinism' lest our main point be obscured by essentially irrelevant objections. Most simply put, a *deterministic* model regards human behavior as the invariant (though perhaps stated in probabilities) outcome of prior conditions. *Free-will* doctrines assert that a knowledge of prior conditions does not facilitate predictions of subsequent behavior because at some moment in the shaping of an act men enjoy a moment of individual choice, a momentary liberation from all causation during which they may assert control over their future action independent of all prior conditions. As is apparent, the free-will doctrine is extremely difficult to express in any meaningful way because we have no appropriate language for describing or explaining the chaos of noncausality.

A major issue in all discussions of free will and determinism concerns the matter of *choice,* a term that has been misconstrued to distort the implications of a causal approach to the study of man. A number of writers have used the word choice to mean a subjective state of assent, or a psychological process of formulating intentions and selecting a course of action, and by establishing the existence of such traits in human behavior have thereby sought to salvage a metaphysical commitment to notions of free will.[7] But it is obvious to any serious social scientist that such states will of necessity play an important role in the formulation of deterministic propositions about human behavior. Surely if we take psychology seriously as a science, whatever its current state of unpreparedness, we mean to presume that these subjective states of the human psyche are themselves lawful, that is, subject to prediction on the basis of prior factors, of both psychic and external origins. Thus, equating choice with subjective mental states in no way eludes the implications of determinism in social science.

The motive for this kind of attempt to salvage a theological concept of free will often seems to derive from a misunderstanding of the implications of deterministic thought for man's conception of himself as a dignified and self-aware creature. It seems that the notion of determinism, at first glance, constitutes a savage assault upon our sense of control over our own acts. This is largely because it seems to be assumed that to posit lawfulness in human behavior is to imply that men are the hapless creatures of great, skulking, blind forces; that human behavior, when viewed as determined, becomes puppetlike, and rationality and self-awareness are but mere illusions. This is an absurd reification of causality.

To say that particular features of human behavior are the probabalistic and even invariant outcomes of certain specifiable prior conditions in no way asserts that men will be unaware of any or all of these conditions, that acts thus caused are irrational, or that such acts occur contrary to human volition.

Consider this greatly simplified example. A social scientist approaches men mounted on the barricades and informs them that they have joined the revolution because of a number of prior conditions: social and economic deprivation under the prevailing stratification arrangements; their recognition of this deprivation; a rejection of, or failure to be adequately compensated by, available rationales such as religion, so that their sense of deprivation was not accommodated; the appearance of a

---

7. For example, Warner Wilson, "A Brief Resolution of the Issue of Free-Will versus Determinism," *Journal for the Scientific Study of Religion,* IV: 1 (Fall, 1964), 101.

leader with a new ideology for reformulating society to relieve their deprivations, etc. If told these things, the revolutionaries are not likely to be surprised (provided they could penetrate the social scientific jargon). Yet, while this may fall well short of a fully adequate account of the prior conditions which invariably resulted in men taking up arms in the revolution, to the degree that this is the case, their behavior may be seen as determined, i.e., predictable and, in that sense, necessary. But this does not mean that it is unreasonable or unconscious; nor does it necessarily mean that they were *compelled* to become revolutionaries. If 'compelled' means actions taken contrary to one's volition, then the notion of causation does not necessarily imply it. Russell put the matter succinctly decades ago:

> This belief [that causes compel effects] seems largely operative in the dislike of determinism; but, as a matter of fact, it is . . . [incorrect.] We may define "compulsion" as follows: "Any set of circumstances is said to compel A when A desires to do something which the circumstances prevent, or to abstain from something which the circumstances cause." . . . What I want to make clear at present is that compulsion is a very complex notion, involving thwarted desire. *So long as a person does what he wishes to do, there is no compulsion, however much his wishes may be calculable by help of earlier events.* And where desire does not come in, there can be no question of compulsion.[8]

> . . . We have in deliberation, a subjective sense of freedom, which is sometimes alleged against the view that volitions have causes. This sense of freedom, however, is only a sense that we can choose which we please of a number of alternatives: *it does not show us that there is no causal connection between what we please to choose and our previous history.*[9]

It is possible that sometimes behavior is compelled, that is, taken against one's volition. At least we speak of compulsive drinking and the like. In such instances, uncovering the causes for such compulsion, if such it be, provides a means for liberating men from compulsions.

To the degree that human behavior is reasonable and conscious, surely deterministic approaches to explaining it are no threat to man's sense of identity. Where behavior is irrational,

---

8. Bertrand Russell, "On the Notion of Cause, with Applications to the Free-Will Problem," in Herbert Feigl and May Brodbeck, eds., *Readings in the Philosophy of Science* (New York: Appleton-Century-Crofts, Inc., 1953), p. 393. (Italics added.)

9. *Ibid.*, p. 405. (Italics added.)

and the reasons for which men think they are acting are not the
actual ones producing their acts, determinism may imply an
attack upon the human sense of freedom. But such an uncovering of hidden causes may also be seen as liberating the human
spirit. Merely to unveil and admit that such unperceived forces
are shaping one's life is to provide some opportunity to suspend
their operation.

Lastly, the implications of a deterministic model of human
behavior for man's sense of identity greatly depend on what one
assumes the identity of a man to be. If, in order to predict a
man's behavior, it is necessary to include in the model all the
salient details of his past experience, his conceptions of himself,
his social situation, his physiological and psychological capacities and propensities, it may be that many would feel that the
essense of this man's identity was built into the explanatory
model. If this is the case, then such a model would seem virtually tautological to the man in question: Because the essential
me is built into the model, the prediction is no more than saying
that I will do what I will do. Such a model is unlikely to be
undertaken, except in extraordinary circumstances, of course,
and we shall never likely give much attention to predicting much
of the concrete behavior of given individuals. It would simply be
too expensive and relatively uninteresting. Rather, we shall likely
limit our actual application of determinism to groups of men,
where the outcomes are of considerably greater interest and
utility and where the predictions are never likely to be invariants, but rather probablilities which still leave room for men to
be exceptions to any rule.[10]

Relative to the natural sciences, the social sciences are in
their infancy and there are still few assertions that they can make
with authority concerning the ways in which man's behavior is
determined. Nevertheless, enough work has been done to challenge seriously the assumptions that man is endowed with
unlimited or even extensive free will. Not only is there evidence
to make and support this general point increasingly, but the
social sciences have also been able to document their contention
in concrete ways. In only a few cases has this involved the

---

10. Statistical laws, however, enjoy the same causal legitimacy in all
sciences as do laws stating invariants. Indeed, probabilities are the form given to
predictions of occurrences in other than ideal (isolated) circumstances in all
sciences, and for virtually all practical purposes, ideal circumstances never do
exist. See: Reichenbach, *op. cit.*

social sciences in direct confrontation with religion. Indirectly, however, religion is being profoundly affected by what the social sciences are learning about human behavior.

Religion is confronted directly with the results of social science research when these bear explicitly on religious phenomena. To some extent, the impact of such research is benign, or nearly so, because it is done in a descriptive mode. Religion, or more appropriately the church, is likely to feel itself informed by descriptive findings. On occasion, descriptive research may arouse apprehensions—as when it reveals gaps between what the church preaches and what its followers practice. It is unlikely, however, to threaten the church's more basic commitments, and specifically its commitments to view man as free and as responsible.[11]

These commitments are challenged, however, by social science theory and research which purports to explain religious phenomena in social and psychological terms. At the theoretical level, the challenge has existed, of course, for a considerable period of time. By the early part of the present century, Marx, Freud, Durkheim, and Weber, among others, had suggested that religion could be understood within naturalistic categories. In 1897, in fact, M. Guyau in his *The Non-Religion of the Future* was already postulating what society would be like when man came to recognize the illusory quality of his religious commitments.[12]

These early writings were not, in their time, without effect. And, since they were written, they have undoubtedly influenced many who have been exposed to them to question their own religious convictions. Marxist ideas, of course, have influenced the course of religion in entire societies.

---

11. It is of more than passing interest to the present discussion that the major thrust of research on religion conducted by Roman Catholic scholars is descriptive. In Europe, for example, Roman Catholic sociology of religion has been dominated by the work of Gabriel Le Bras and his followers. This work is highly empirical involving studies of the ritual practices and social characteristics of parishioners. The data collected are highly suitable for explanatory analysis. Yet, it is invariably treated in descriptive ways. In America, the work of Fathers Joseph Fichter and Joseph Schuyler can be characterized in much the same way. Fichter, for example, in his study, *Social Relations in the Urban Parish*, (Chicago: University of Chicago Press, 1954) describes his now almost classic types of parishioners—nuclear, modal, marginal, and dormant—in great detail. It would have been an easy matter for his to turn his data around and to analyze them following the by then well-known deterministic models developed by Paul F. Lazarsfeld. His book, however, is virtually devoid of explanatory propositions, much less explanatory analysis.

12. (New York: Schocken Books, 1962.)

Despite these signs of erosion, there is no evidence as yet that religion stands ready to capitulate to these conceptions. Certainly, in the West and particularly in America, there is little respect for Marxist ideas about religion. Freud's conception of religion as an illusion is not paid much heed—even by those who are committed to Freudian thought in other respects. On the other hand, the views of Durkheim and Weber are highly respected by professional sociologists. Few religionists, however, are aware of them and among those who are, there is little disposition to accept them as valid alternatives to their own religiously informed postures.

The burden of our case, however, does not rest on these macroscopic theories of religion. They are early straws in the wind of the emerging conflict between the social sciences and religion. The theories do question God's existence. In and of themselves, however, they do not directly confront religion's view of man as free and responsible. In part, this is because the conceptions remain theoretical. There is little empirical evidence in their support. Moreover, none of them deals explicitly with the question of free will. Basically, religion's validity is questioned on other grounds.

More recent social science research on religion does confront the free-will question more directly. In fact, some of the earlier empirical chapters of this book do so. In Chapter 5, for example, it is inferred that the religious beliefs man holds are in large measure a result of the social context in which he operates. Similarly, in Chapter 8, the burden of the argument is that religious experience can be accounted for to a considerable extent in sociological terms. And (in Chapter 14), the equivalent inference is drawn concerning the conditions giving rise to contrasting commitments of religion and science.

On these matters, the traditional Christian view has been that it is man who is making the decisions. He, appraised of the alternatives, decides whether to believe and what. He decides whether or not to worship, to participate in the sacraments, to pray, to study the scriptures, etc. God's collaboration is necessary for man to have a religious experience but the experience is not likely to come if man elects against it.

Our own studies and other recent studies of religious phenomena do not deny that man enjoys some freedom in making these choices. They do, however, suggest that the freedom is much narrower than religious perspectives can presently accommodate. Hence, they also question the correctness of the religious view that man can be held entirely accountable for his actions. It is here perhaps that religion may be most vulnerable to the findings of the social sciences. By making ambiguous just what it is for which man can justifiably be held to be freely accountable, the social sciences make ambiguous as well what it is that religion can justfiably ask man to be.

It is to be recognized that there have been very few studies of religion done in the explantory mode employed in the studies in this book. Were it necessary to base our case on these studies alone, we would be much more cautious in asserting that the social sciences make ambiguous some of the fundamental claims of traditional religion. The fact of the matter is, of course, that the central thrust of all explanatory research in the social sciences is to document that the deterministic assumption is, at least in part, a valid one. Religious commitments to accept God as a causal factor in some known events and to view man as free and responsible, consequently, are called into question not only by research on religious behavior *per se* but by explanatory research on all other aspects of man's behavior as well.

This more general point is best exemplified perhaps by social science research on so-called 'deviant behavior' in society. Here, the social sciences have made considerable progress in showing how cultural factors, the nature of the individual's social environment, and his personality influence both the incidence and character of deviant behavior. Again, the results do not explain all the variance. They do, however, raise serious doubts that man can be held entirely responsible for his actions and make ambiguous how the deviant is to be treated. Thus, it is no longer clear that the poor are poor because they fail to exercise their free will in a responsible fashion, or that the delinquent ought to be punished for his delinquency, or even that the murderer can be held entirely responsible for his act.[13] That

---

13. The fact that social science findings militate against judging a criminal as having freely chosen to violate the law, does not mean, of course, that we must relinquish our objections to law violation. Simply because we change our evaluation of the actor does not require that we change our evaluation of the act. Because we no longer feel justified in punishing a man for his actions does not mean we cannot protect ourselves from repetitions of the act by locking the transgressor away, either to protect society against him or with the hopes of changing the forces acting upon him in such a way as to change his future behavior. This seems to characterize the modern philosophy of penology, but is far from universally accepted by the general public.

these have become contemporary issues is a sign of the still subtle but nevertheless profound influence which the social sciences are having on current mores.

It is difficult to assess just how much effect the results of social science research have already had on traditional religion. Judging from the evidence presented in Chapter 5, the members of some religious groups have been relatively untouched by what the social sciences are learning about human behavior. Their belief in divinity remains inviolate and they continue to be committed to the idea that man will be held accountable for his actions in a day of final judgment. In other religious groups, there is greater hesitancy to acknowledge such beliefs unequivocally. The evidence in Chapter 5 does not justify a conclusion that the revealed erosion in belief is a direct consequence of the intrusion of a scientific perspective into the public consciousness. In that chapter, the causal chain was simply not investigated. However, it was examined in Chapter 14 and, it will be recalled, there was relatively clear evidence both of the saliency of a scientific perspective for large numbers of students and of a strong propensity for the acceptance of such a perspective to be accompanied by a denial of a religious perspective.

Looking to other evidence than our own, there are a number of signs which point to efforts on religion's part to accommodate traditional belief to the findings of social science research: Bishop Robinson's book, *Honest to God*,[14] current efforts on the part of theologians to demythologize the scriptures, the intrusion of psychiatry into pastoral counseling, the increasing introduction of social science courses into the curricula of theological seminaries, can all be interpreted as having been influenced, at least in part, by the new perspectives on man which the social sciences are providing.

How far these perspectives will eventually add to our understanding of man and what will be their ultimate impact on religion as we have traditionally known it are questions about which it is possible only to speculate. It seems highly unlikely that the determinism hypothesis which informs science can ever be wholly confirmed. And, whatever the degree of confirmation, the effect is not likely to be the elimination of the religious component from human society. In the end, the existence of the uni-

---

14. (Philadelphia: The Westminister Press, 1963.)

verse, of nature, and of mankind will remain unexplained—man can only investigate the causal chain so far. Thus, there will always be a warrant for a supernatural realm and for God's existence.

The more fundamental question posed by the prospect of additional scientific knowledge about nature and about man is what its effect will be on the saliency of religion. If there is truth to the general theme we have been pursuing, there is the possibility that no one will care whether God exists or not because he will become irrelevant to everyday existence. If what can be attributed to God's will is made narrower and narrower, and if man's accountability for his actions is found to be more and more circumscribed, religion seems destined to lose much of its power to inform and guide the human condition.

The dilemma will thus be created as to how the need for a system of ultimate meaning is to be satisfied. Science itself cannot fill the gap. It cannot supply the glue—the values and norms—which hold societies together and which makes existence meaningful. Perhaps Guyau's prediction will come true and humanistic perspectives will come to supplant religious ones. Some, undoubtedly, would argue that the transition has already occurred for a large part of the world.

Such a view, however, overlooks the capacity of institutions to survive and indeed, through threats to their survival, to be renewed and to enhance their authority and power. That religious institutions will change, there can be no doubt, and that they must find ways other than their traditional reliance on eternal reward and punishment systems to generate commitment seems also clear. That they will be weakened permanently by their confrontation with the social sciences is not, however, inevitable. Knowledge of how man is determined can have the consequence of enhancing rather than reducing man's freedom. Knowing how determinism operates may enable man to transcend it and indeed exercise greater control over his destiny. If the bounds of free will were clearer, the realm for which a religious perspective is truly relevant would also be clearer, and the validity of that perspective might be greater. The prospect of this happening is made ambiguous by our inability to conceive a final resolution of the determinism—free will issue. Thus, while we can safely predict that religion's role in society will change, only the future can decide its ultimate fate.

Index

Printed in U.S.A.

F